Gustave Weigel, S.J.
A Pioneer of Reform

Patrick W. Collins

Foreword by
Walter J. Burghardt, S.J.

A Michael Glazier Book
THE LITURGICAL PRESS
Collegeville, Minnesota

In memory of my parents
Eugene Stowell Collins (1905–1979)
and
Juanita Winchester Collins (1906–1984)

and

In gratitude to
Most Reverend John B. Franz, D.D.,
Bishop of Peoria (1959–1971)
who permitted me to pursue
this doctoral research

and

Rev. Francis J. Alagna, Ph.D.,
whose friendship and humor
enlightened the dark days of scholarship

A Michael Glazier Book published by The Liturgical Press

Cover design by David Manahan, O.S.B.

1   2   3   4   5   6   7   8   9

Library of Congress Cataloging-in-Publication Data

Collins, Patrick W.
   Gustave Weigel : a pioneer of reform / Patrick W. Collins.
     p.　cm.
   "A Michael Glazier Book."
   Includes bibliographical references.
   ISBN 0-8146-5004-X
   1. Weigel, Gustave, 1906–1964.　2. Catholic Church—United States-
-Clergy—Biography.　3. Jesuits—United States—Biography.
4. Ecumenists—United States—Biography.　I. Title.
BX4705.W415C64　1991
230′.2′092—dc20
                                                91-7113
                                                CIP

Contents

Foreword

Two remarkable personalities dominate my memories of fellow Jesuits. Gustave Weigel and John Courtney Murray were my dearest friends in the Company of Jesus—John for twenty-one years, Gus for fifteen, sharing the same third-floor corridor at old Woodstock College in Maryland, sharing minds and hearts.

Similar they were, but hardly the same. Kindred spirits indeed: fascinated by life and in love with ideas; at home in an impressive number of intellectual disciplines and at ease with non-Romans and unbelievers; powerful rhetoricians and profound but witty conversationalists. Still, quite different: Gus of the peasant frame, John of the distinguished gait; Gus the "quick read" and intuitor, John the tireless scholar; Gus the descendant of Plato and fascinated by Paul Tillich, John the heir of Aquinas and captivated by Bernard Lonergan; Gus the more earthy, John the eagle soaring. Gus dead in a bathtub, John in a taxicab!

Together with colleagues like ecclesiologist Avery Dulles and biblicist Joseph Fitzmyer, they lent Woodstock an intellectual prestige unmatched among Catholic seminaries and schools of thelogy. Besides, Murray and Weigel played prominent parts at Vatican II and infused unaccustomed vitality into a hesitant, suspicious, suspected Catholic ecumenism.

Murray's influence is not likely to be lost. The drawing power of his church-state and religious-liberty ideas promises to keep him in the public eye. It is frightening to think that, but for Patrick Collins' tenacity over two decades, Weigel might have disappeared

5

into history, with only forty-eight lines in the *New Catholic Encyclopedia* to remember him by.

Hardly a trail blazer theologically, the pioneer whom Collins here rescues from oblivion should revivify our slackening efforts toward unity. We desperately need his realistic stress on convergence rather than conversion (unlikely) or compromise (unacceptable); his utter trust in God as ultimately the architect of unity; his total gift of self to the other whoever he or she might be; his humble acceptance of human limitation, of deep frustration, of temporary defeat.

Walter J. Burghardt, S.J.

Preface

This study of the life and work of Gustave A. Weigel, S.J., is based upon my doctoral dissertation in theology at Fordham University.

"Gustave Weigel, who is he?" This was the response when, in the fall of 1971, I told my theology students at Maryknoll Seminary the subject of my dissertation. They were honestly unaware of the existence of this man whose efforts between 1950 and 1964 were largely responsible for the first stirrings of the ecumenical movement in the Catholic Church in America.

Weigel himself was aware that his work was transitional, that others would come after him to carry the movement on to more advanced stages, and that his own part in the work would be simply taken for granted. Though ecumenism continues, especially among theologians in dialogue, the spirit of newness and hope that accompanied the rise of the movement in this country has for the most part faded. It is, then, not surprising that few young people remember the one whose deep, lovable humanity and profound Christian faith were largely responsible for first bridging the gaps between Protestants and Catholics in this country. No doubt Weigel, because of his pervasive realism, would not be terribly surprised that his widely publicized contribution is today largely unknown among many American Christians.

This does not make it any less unfortunate that the ecumenical work of Gustave Weigel is not remembered in our day. Though the ecclesiology which he taught was quite conservative and traditional, his approach to non-Catholic Christians was largely liberal

7

and completely human. It is for his warm, generous humanity, placed so completely at the service of the Church he loved, that he deserves to be remembered and honored. It is for his total dedication to Truth that he stands as an inspiration to those who knew him. His difficult yet willing submission to that Truth can still move and encourage those who have taken up the banner of Christian unity which he so nobly bore in those days when an ecumenist in this country was suspected by most as a borderline heretic.

This study of Gustave Weigel's life, his ecclesiology, and ecumenical thought and work is dedicated to all those who follow Weigel in what appears to be now a long twilight struggle against the divisions persons have caused in the community of Christian faith. May these insights into his life and times serve to kindle anew the unquenchable, yet often dimmed, flame of hope for Christian unity.

This study was made possible by the cooperation of many people. It was most impressive and heartening to the author to see the obvious enthusiastic interest of those asked to help. These were people who loved Gustave Weigel and who consequently willingly gave of their time to preserve his memory in this study.

First, gratitude is due to the director, Gerald Fogarty, S.J., for his patient and painstaking guidance. His personal insights into the life of a Jesuit were most helpful in interpreting Weigel's life and thought. To Robert McNally, S.J., who was a close friend of the subject and shared his personal recollections with love for his friend; and to Sabbas Killian, O.F.M., who was especially helpful in the study of Weigel's ecclesiology, I owe thanks.

Walter J. Burghardt, S.J., was the third member of the Woodstock College triumvirate, whose other members were John Courtney Murray and Gustave Weigel. It was Burghardt who gave me the idea of writing on his friend. I am indebted to him for this original inspiration and for countless other conversations in which he shared his experiences with Weigel.

One of the things which made this study so delightful is the master's thesis done by Sr. Olga Neft which compiled the entire bibliography of Gustave Weigel, together with an extensive list of references to him in publications other than his own. It was done at The Catholic University of America in 1968 and is entitled, "A Bio-Bibliography of Gustave Weigel, 1906–1964." Sister Neft allowed me to use the fruit of her personal research. Interviews conducted by her are so specified. I am very much indebted to her splendid work and for her personal kindnesses to me.

The Weigel Papers are catalogued and filed in the Archives of the Woodstock College Library. The warm reception and assistance offered by the librarians there was deeply appreciated: Henry Bertels, S.J.; Edward Dunn, S.J.; and Robert Richards, S.J.

Archives in other lands were checked for me very graciously by Jesuits who were interested in Gustave Weigel. To J. Edward Coffey, S.J., who checked the records of Father Weigel at The Gregorian University in Rome; to Vincent O'Keefe, S.J., who checked the archives of the superior general of the Society of Jesus in Rome; to Edward Rooney, S.J., who researched the archives of the Society of Jesus in Santiago, Chile, and also The Catholic University archives there—to them, a sincere thank you.

Gratitude to the many persons who consented to be interviewed or who wrote and taped their personal reminiscences of Gustave Weigel can only be expressed by listing them in the footnotes. However, to Father Weigel's sister, Louise Daigler, and to his niece, Sr. Jeremy Daigler, R.S.M., I am most grateful for the visits and letters which enabled me to penetrate Weigel's personality. Special gratitude goes to the late Dr. Francis J. Otenasek, who allowed me to copy nearly one hundred letters which Father Weigel had written to him between 1930 and 1937. Letters exchanged during Weigel's years in Chile, between 1937 and 1948, were temporarily misplaced by Otenasek. To David J. Bowman, S.J., I am indebted for his collections of letters and newspaper and magazine clippings regarding the ban on the four theologians at The Catholic University of America. To Vincent Arthur Yzermans I owe thanks for sharing his tapes of conversations with Weigel concerning the Second Vatican Council.

I owe a very personal debt of gratitude to James Hennesey, S.J., who served as my counselor during two years at Fordham University. Father Hennesey introduced me to the historico-theological method employed in this study.

Finally, my gratitude is extended to my dear and long-time friend Walter J. Burghardt, S.J. In my dark doctoral days between completing comprehensives and writing the dissertation, I was floundering for a dissertation topic. At dinner one evening with Father Burghardt at Woodstock College in New York City, he suggested, "Have you ever thought about my dear friend Gus Weigel as a subject for your dissertation?" He it was who prodded me again and again over the years to revise the manuscript for publication. He it was who introduced me to publisher Michael Glazier and who, with his accustomed editor's eagle eye, painstakingly proofread the book's galley text. Like his friend Weigel, Walter Burghardt is truly "One of a Kind."

Beginnings in Buffalo: 1906–1922

Theological thought is situated not only in the mind of the thinker but also within the milieu which conditions the theologizing process. Extra-theological factors such as time, place, events of the day, errors condemned and enemies fought—all of these and many other human and historical factors enter into the shaping of theological thought.

Edward Gibbon, in *The Decline and Fall of the Roman Empire,* points poignantly to this truth.

> The theologian may indulge the pleasing task of describing religion as she descended from heaven, arrayed in her native purity. A more melancholy duty is imposed on the historian. He must discover the inevitable mixture of error and corruption which she contracted in a long residence upon earth, among a weak and degenerate race of beings.[1]

Gustave Weigel, the North American Jesuit, also knew well that theologians are conditioned by their times. Acknowledging that the prime data of revelation must be carefully guarded, Weigel wrote that "in theology the prime data are necessarily fused with some contingent formulation so that it is not an easy thing to separate the ephemeral from the abiding core."[2]

The study of Weigel's thought, therefore, is not confined merely to his writings and speeches. Where and when he lived, where and with whom he studied and taught, who his friends and enemies

11

were, what issues he confronted in his public and private life, the type of personality he developed—all of these factors, and others, yield deeper insight into his theologizing. Because history, that is, life as lived, is so deeply involved in shaping a person's thought, this study of the ecclesiology and ecumenism of Gustave Weigel will begin with an examination of his own personal background. For Weigel, like all people, was a product of his past but, unlike many, was not largely imprisoned by that past. His life reflected both consistency and change: consistent development.

Gustave Weigel's parents were Alsatians who emigrated to the United States shortly after the turn of this century. Their Alsatian roots were very much a part of the formative years of Weigel.

Alsace-Lorraine, or Elsass-Lothringen in German, is a territory of 5,607 square miles between France and Germany. In May, 1871, as a result of the Franco-Prussian War, the territory was ceded by the defeated French to the new German empire. It was constituted as a Reichsland, that is, it belonged to the empire rather than to any of the individual states of the empire.

The people of Alsace-Lorraine were not pleased with their new political ties. They were more interested in their former relationship with France and in the new French republic than in Otto von Bismarck's new Germany. Until 1890, practically every delegation from the area to the German parliament was opposed to the German regime. During this period, many residents of the area left, unable to reconcile themselves to German rule, even though the majority of the population was German-speaking.

It was during this complex political period in Alsatian history that August Weigel and Leontine Kieffer, the parents of Gustave Weigel, were born and grew to maturity. August Weigel was born in Werenzhausen, Alsace, on June 20, 1869. He was one of the six blond and blue-eyed children of Martin and Marie Haamann Weigel. The family lived frugally as it was never endowed with much money. Marie died when August was two years old. He received only a few years of education before going to work as a laborer.

12

One of the places where August and two of his brothers worked was the "fair sized farm" of Count Philemon Kieffer of Seenheim, who also owned a restaurant-hotel. Philemon and Mathilde Cueni Kieffer had six children, like the Weigels. But, unlike the Weigels, the Kieffers were prosperous. They owned certain uncommon possessions such as a sewing machine. Leontine, Gustave Weigel's mother, was born on January 25, 1869. The count, according to his daughter, Leontine, though exceptionally handsome, was an arrogant, miserable man who thought more of his horses and dogs than of his children. In contrast to the "light" complexioned Weigels, the Kieffers were dark, swarthy people, sometimes referred to as "The Black Ones."

The two families responded quite differently to the edict from the German government that French was no longer to be spoken in Alsace-Lorraine. Martin Weigel complied but the more independent Philemon Kieffer, refusing to be dictated to by any German, continued to speak French in his home. Consequently Leontine Kieffer spoke both French and German whereas August Weigel spoke only an Alsatian dialect of German.

These two sharply contrasting families were triply joined when the three Weigel brothers who worked for Philemon Kieffer married three of their employer's daughters. August married Leontine on April 1, 1899. They lived the first years of their marriage in their homeland. Then, in 1902, they emigrated to the United States.

The Weigels settled in Buffalo, New York, a center of industry, marketing and transportation. Around the turn of the century, the development of hydroelectric power from nearby Niagara Falls had furnished further impetus to Buffalo industry. The population was largely immigrant: Polish, German, Irish, Canadian and Italian.

August and Leontine Weigel settled on Mortimer Street in the German section of the city. August held many jobs during his working years. At first he worked in a soap factory and in an iron works. Then he was hired as a janitor at a pharmaceutical company. He was also a truck driver for a time. Though he never earned much money, the family never knew poverty but his son, Gustave, was always saddened by how hard his father had to work for such small recompense. Later, as an adult, he would say he felt the greatest sin was defrauding the working man.

After the death of their first-born, John, who lived only a short time, Leontine Weigel gave birth to a second child on January 15, 1906. He was described as a "big, fat cry baby." According to a family legend, the doctor jiggled the infant and said: "feels like the ten pound ham we had last week."[3] The child was baptized in St. Gerard's Church, receiving the name, Gustave.[4]

Four years later, May 17, 1910, much to Gus' annoyance, another child was born and named Louise. At that time the baby was looked upon by the older brother as "an unnecessary aggravation." Life in the Weigel home was simple and warm. The neighborhood could be described as respectable, frugal and placid. Alsatian was the language spoken in the home, a strange patois mixture of French and German. Gus and Louise disliked this Alsatian dialect very much[5] and Gus was rather embarrassed by it later in his school years.[6]

Louise described life in their home:

> Our parents were completely un-Americanized. My mother dressed as a European—long, ankle length dress, hair with a bird's nest on top, etc. When the two . . . parents wanted to disparage or ridicule something or someone, they referred to them or it as "Americanish." This made us uncomfortable but never rebellious.[7]

John Courtney Murray, who became Weigel's intimate friend in later years, knew August and Leontine Weigel slightly. He remarked "that to have known the father and mother . . . was to understand the son. The father was a grave gentleman of great dignity; the mother was a pleasant woman full of warmth and kindness. Often I teased Gus about the peasant quality in him. He always gloried in it."[8]

14

In 1912, Gustave Weigel began his formal education at St. Mary of Sorrows parish school. He was an excellent student from the beginning. He skipped the third, fifth and seventh grades. While in the sixth grade, the family moved to 123 Peckham Street in the Jesuit St. Ann's parish where he was put in the eighth grade due to his excellent record at St. Mary's. Although Weigel later claimed he had to work very hard to be a top student, his sister judged that studies were always easy for him. He graduated from the eighth grade in 1918 at the age of twelve. Louise related that he was liked by everybody, including older people.

> He was short for his age and of course always younger than the rest of his classmates. Yet he was always a leader, always included. He was a very polite, likeable boy . . . Never a "pious" youngster. My mother hated attending Church with him and would complain of his inattention.

He did not attend daily Mass with any regularity nor was there much external show of religiosity in his young life.

The Weigel family could not afford to send Gustave to a Catholic high school. But through the kindness of their pastor, Father Herman Edleman, S.J., who had a fund for deserving boys, their son was able to enroll in 1918 at Canisius High School run by the Society of Jesus. There he continued his good scholastic record.

At Canisius, Weigel developed his public speaking ability under the guidance of Father James McDermott, S.J. He joined the debating team and was a huge success. Taking up declamation, this chubby little fellow, with a voice so soft you had to strain to hear it, won contest after contest.[9] One newspaper, describing one of these declamation contests, referred to young Weigel as a boy "with a silver tongue" when he won the fifth annual contest for the Canisius Cup for elocution. The Canisius school publication commented: "The Elocution Cup is now a permanent resident due to the splendid efforts of Gus Weigel. We are proud of that Cup, but much prouder of Gus."[10]

15

Weigel's efforts to be a clear speaker during his Canisius years were matched by his desire to be a persuasive writer. In his third year English composition book, he wrote: "I write to make another understand. My writing to accomplish this purpose must have certain qualities." He listed these qualities as clearness, vividness and fullness.

The skills of intelligible and intelligent speaking and writing would characterize his entire life as a teacher, author, lecturer and ecumenist. He was always eminently understandable.

Socially, Weigel was not very active at Canisius. Although he mixed well with his classmates, he had no apparent desire to date girls and never did so. His sister later said he had neither the time nor the money for dating while at Canisius.

Gus was a delight to his parents and Louise worshipped him. There was no jealousy between them. Weigel often said: "She got the looks—I got the brains." When Weigel was in high school, his little sister came down with the mumps. Everyday while Louise was ill he saved his lunch money to buy her a small gift. He was equally sensitive toward his mother. When she was sick, he would buy her flowers. His generosity prompted him to save every nickel he could lay his hands on in order to buy Christmas presents for his family. Although Gus and Louise would have the usual brother-sister spats, unavoidable in close families, Gus was a non-fighter in his youth. Actually he would turn the other cheek.

Young Weigel was an avid reader. Once, when he was about eleven years old, he was browsing over the book counter in the neighborhood Woolworth store. He picked up a book, started to read it, and was startled when another book fell to the floor. "He could lose himself to the point of complete oblivion when he read," recalled his sister. A floor-walker came over to him, accused him of trying to steal the book and yanked him into the store's office. Young Weigel came home in tears and the family was shocked and saddened that anyone would think this of their son and brother.

During his last years in Buffalo, Gustave Weigel used to play the clown and ham it up before his friends. One of his acts was "The Magician." Louise told about these "shows."

> They were clever. He had a wonderful flair, I was the stooge—with whom he had very little patience. If I failed in my conduct I was threatened with dire consequences like not being allowed to go to the library Saturday morning with him. And that was a dire consequence.

Weigel loved card games for money and would have a circle of friends at his home on Sunday and they would play for money. Today's mothers would be justly shocked, reflected Louise, but it didn't faze their mother. "Her Gustave could do no wrong. She worshipped him as did we all. He left mornings whistling—he came home whistling. He was a rough, teasing, loveable torment."

Weigel's closest friend was a Lutheran boy who lived in his neighborhood. Their religious differences intrigued Weigel.[11] Years later, as a popular ecumenist, Weigel told of his relationship with this boy.

> Our preadolescent group was made up of Catholics and Protestants, roughly half and half. We went to different schools but after school hours we were together. My closest friend, to whom I was closely attached, was a Lutheran boy.
>
> As a group we rarely talked about religion or church. It is hard today to explain this reticence, but I suspect that boys do not discuss religion much, and besides we were unconsciously shrewd enough not to raise questions which would divide us; for our union was strong and happy. Yet I remember talking once about religions with my Lutheran friend, and he mentioned that in his church the minister wore vestments like our Catholic priests . . . There was a fundamental similarity in the two religions. He and I were both taught the Apostles' Creed, whose articles with the exception of the one on the Catholic Church we understood in much the same way. We were both taught by our respective churches that there was a transcendent God. We believed in the divinity of Jesus of Nazareth, Christ, our Lord. We believed in His Virgin Birth. We believed that Easter Sunday was

17

the memorial of his rising from the tomb in the flesh, after His saving death for us. We were taught that there was a Holy Spirit, and the Father, Son, and Spirit were three distinct persons in one Godhead. We were prepared to look for the final judgment when we should rise bodily from the dead to enter into life everlasting.

Our morality was substantially the same. We were not supposed to lie; we had to respect our elders; it was wrong to steal or destroy other people's property; we were not to do "dirty things," concerning which our notions were disturbingly vague and hidden in silence. It was a matter of course that we should go to church on Sunday in our best clothes, which more than the holiness of the day prevented us from practicing the sports and games of weekdays. There was at that time a conscious and willed Catholic-Protestant division; but actually we were less divided in belief and conduct than today, when such divisions are strongly deprecated.[12]

Another close friend in his Buffalo years was a Jewish boy who used to tell him about the "Jewish Persuasion." Gus was interested in these other boys' religions and never tried to criticize or convert them to his way of thinking.

Another sign of his early interest in religions other than his own was his enthusiastic attendance at the revivals of Billy Sunday. When the evangelist would come to Buffalo, Weigel and his friends would never miss his "show." The other boys went for carnival, said his sister, but for Weigel, Billy Sunday was a challenge which intrigued him.

One thing Gustave Weigel could never tolerate was a fake. Years later Louise identified Gus with Holden Caulfield, the youth in J.D. Salinger's novel, *Catcher in the Rye*. Holden, too, had one younger sister, Phoebe, whom he loved very much. For Holden and for Weigel, the phoney was unbearable.[13] "If you were crude, uneducated, dull, stupid—anything—he suffered you—not gladly—but he suffered you—but a FAKE—he could be very haughty and cold. Likewise, 'gush' irked him to an out of proportion degree."[14]

In 1922, Gustave Weigel graduated from Canisius High School. *The Arena,* the school yearbook, printed beneath his graduation picture a quotation from Henry Clay, meant to typify him. It read: "Sir, I would rather be right than President." This motto was prophetic of his entire life: a search for "the Truth," "the Real."

After graduation, Weigel entered the novitiate of the Society of Jesus. His sister reflected on the days prior to his departure from Buffalo.

> Never was there any "formal" announcement that he was going to be a priest. He used to "play" priest when he was about 7—and I would be altar boy for him. There was never any talk about it. It was an accepted fact. . . . He said that if ever anyone "influenced" him—it was a young Fr. McDermott who taught him in his public speaking ventures. This was a quiet, gentle young priest. As Gus attracted attention in high school, people began to say, "What a lawyer he'd make! Corner bum—saw him on the corner with a bunch of boys pitching pennies and nickels last Sunday afternoon."

And so, in July of 1922, the first phase of Gustave Weigel's life came to an end. Shaped by his Alsatian homelife, strengthened by the warm love of his mother, the quiet, kind, serious presence of his father, and the adoring love of his sister; a young man of many friends, academically successful and a rather skilled debater and public speaker, Gustave Weigel left Buffalo, not to return for seven years. Louise poignantly recalled: "We were never the same without him."[15]

Endnotes

1. Edward Gibbon, *The Decline and Fall of the Roman Empire* (New York: Modern Library, n.d.), vol. I., pp. 382–385.

2. Gustave Weigel, "The Historical Background of the Encyclical Humani Generis," *Theological Studies,* v. 12, 1951, p. 209.

3. Reflections of Louise Weigel Daigler, February 8, 1967 (Neft). (Hereafter referred to as Daigler reflections.) Year laters, Gustave Weigel visited the farm. In describing the visit to his sister, Weigel snorted, "Y'know that 'big tobacco plantation' Ma used to tell us about? Haw! It was nothing more than a little farm. And that 'Hotel'—that wasn't even a good sized saloon."

4. Louise Daigler to Patrick W. Collins, Buffalo, N.Y., November 14, 1971.

5. Daigler reflections.

6. Interview with Edwin Quain, S.J., Daigler reflections.

7. Daigler reflections.

8. *One of a Kind: Essays in Tribute to Gustave Weigel* (Wilkes-Barre, Pa.: Dimension Books, 1967), p. 16. Hereafter referred to as *One of a Kind*.

9. Daigler reflections.

10. Weigel Papers, Woodstock College Archives (Hereafter referred to as WCA), II F. 303.22a.

11. Daigler reflections.

12. Gustave Weigel, S.J., *Faith and Understanding in America* (New York: Macmillan, 1959), pp. 131–132.

13. Interview with Edwin Quain, S.J.

14. Daigler reflections.

15. Daigler reflections.

The Formation of a Jesuit: 1922–1930

On July 30, 1922, at the age of sixteen, Gustave Weigel began his two-year novitiate at St. Andrew-on-Hudson, north of Poughkeepsie, New York, together with twenty-nine other young men. By September, seventy-six novices were in residence.[1] There in this large, beautiful, red-brick Georgian building which housed 224 Jesuits, including the novices, the boy from Buffalo began to become a priest of Jesus Christ. St. Andrew's was perched on a hill overlooking the expansive Hudson River Valley.

Strict rules and discipline were the order of the day in the House of Probation. It was a test of will-breaking and obedience to authority. Though there were tight restrictions on letter writing, Gustave Weigel was encouraged to and did write to his parents faithfully once each week and continued this practice conscientiously until they died.[2]

The short, chubby, rosy-faced "Dutch boy"[3] from Buffalo was not immediately accepted by his peers in the novitiate. He was sometimes teased as a "kid."[4] His combination of Buffalo and "Heinie" accent together with his boyish appearance made him the butt of many jokes at first. Perhaps it was as a result of this teasing that Weigel began to learn a new way of speaking, a way that would hide his Buffalo-Alsatian background of which he was never very proud. His speech became "veddy Oxford," sounding quite affected. His sister once asked him if this was truly affected.

21

"Of course," he replied. He spoke this way in public and private for the rest of his life. He rejected much of his Buffalo past which was justified by "smugness,"[5] as he told his sister. A close friend remarked:

> He had nothing but contempt for Buffalo and all that it stood for. He wanted no part of it whatsoever. . . . Part of Gus' desire to accomplish things was, I'd say, a reaction against what he felt Buffalo and his family background was. He felt he did not belong in that kind of milieu and it was almost as if he were going to become such a person that nobody would ever associate him with being a little Dutch boy from Buffalo.[6]

Some in the novitiate with Weigel described him as generally younger than the others, yet mature in his ideas. He struck them as very friendly, easy-going, prone to hearty laughter, "a happy kid transplanted from a Germanic Buffalo background to a wider range of outlook."[7] In classes he was a great interrogator and, since he had a retentive memory, could discourse on everything he read. His piety was solid. He was not remembered as ever "kicking over the traces" or being uncertain in his vocation. In general he appeared to be a conformist with the *modus vivendi* of the novitiate.[8]

In 1924, after the two years of novitiate and first vows on July 31, Weigel began his juniorate or humanistic studies at St. Andrew's. He was taller, thinner and wiser.[9] These two years saw him chiefly engaged in the study of English and Latin. Many of his Latin exercises were marked "Bene" and "Optime" in the instructor's red pencil. He also developed his flair for writing. Several essays survive.[10]

The essay on the Church bears quotation in the light of Weigel's future work in ecclesiology. It rests upon the moral miracle argument, which would become his favorite apologetic as Woodstock College's ecclesiologist.

> Any religion that insists on self-conquest and yet is spread over the earth in spite of hostility and survives for twenty centuries

22

must be of divine origin. But the Catholic Church insists on self-conquest, is spread over a hostile world and survives for twenty centuries. Therefore, the Catholic Church must be of divine origin.[11]

The strength of Weigel's commitment to the life of the priest shines through in another of his compositions, "A Missioner's Address to the Students of Campion College." Purporting to be a Christian priest-missioner in India, he "addresses" his young audience, asking not for their "silver and gold" but for them.

Perhaps reflecting some of his own thoughts and feelings about the sacrifices made to follow his own Jesuit vocation, Weigel wrote:

What I do appeal to is your heroism. Unless your souls are warmed by that coelestial fire, India does not need you. You must rend all the strings that tie your heart to home. Brother must be a memory, sister a dream. The gleaming tears on a mother's cheek must only spur you on to make her sacrifice enduring. The silent beauty of the northern sky must be changed into the fury of the tropic sun. Friends and comrades whom you loved must give way to a dirty self or half-civilized illiterates. Your mother-tongue must be forgotten and you must master a difficult tongue. All, all you have, you must throw aside, and come, "Come follow Me." Follow Christ to Poona or the Bombay. Be lonely there with your divine Master, be friendless with the crucified Christ, be toiling with the Carpenter of Nazareth. I ask no more.[12]

According to his sister, Gus Weigel was very happy in the novitiate and juniorate. He saw his family seldom and never went to Buffalo during those years. His father made the trip to visit his son three years after Gus had entered the society. His often ill mother, ailing from diabetes, gall stones and migraine headaches, was not able to join August Weigel on that trip. Five years after her brother entered the Jesuits, Louise herself went to Woodstock to visit him. She was only twelve when she had last seen her brother. Both had changed so much that Louise confessed that she didn't recognize him when they first met.

The chubby boy was a six foot painfully thin young man. And his nose had grown along with the rest of him. His new voice, new mannerisms and new personality made him a stranger to Louise. Nevertheless she spent three "heavenly days" with him. "No brother and sister were closer than we two," Louise declared years later. "We didn't see each other for years but we were 'closer' than people who see each other daily."[13] Edwin Quain recalled Louise's visit. To her, he said, Gus was "the next thing to God."

Weigel's days at St. Andrew's came to an end in the early summer of 1926. This lithe, strong young man, patient with traditional curriculum and Jesuit life and with his full innovative powers still latent[14] moved to Woodstock College in Maryland.

Woodstock College is an immense, rambling, stone building, situated about fifteen miles from Baltimore, Maryland. It had been the home of the Jesuits since 1869. In the quiet, rolling, tree-covered Maryland countryside, through which flowed the Patapsco River, the minds of men were molded in the academic and spiritual traditions of the Roman Catholic Church and the Society of Jesus.

For several years past, no philosophy had been taught at Woodstock. It had been taught in Weston, Massachusetts, to students from the Maryland-New York Province. In the fall of 1926 philosophy classes were resumed at Woodstock due to the fact that New England had become an independent province in that year. Weigel was among the fifteen students from the Maryland-New York Province to begin the re-established philosophy curriculum.[15]

The final two years of college studies were quite traditional with the philosophy courses taught in Latin. One of Weigel's classmates, Laurence J. McGinley, S.J., said those years were

> the end of an era. The new approaches to philosophy were not discernible yet to most of us and probably not trusted by most of our teachers. All courses except philosophy were "sidelines."

Throughout his years of school, from Buffalo to Woodstock, Gustave Weigel was acknowledged to have an unusually gifted intellect[16] by both teachers and students. In his quest to develop his mind, he became intensely interested in understanding the process of human cognition. For him, it would seem, the crucial philosophical question was one of epistemology. Metaphysics or ontology was not his prime interest. In later years, he would say that metaphysics is not an absolute view of reality which you must justify rationally. It is simply a way of putting things, a relative way of systematizing thought.[17]

Gustave Weigel studied the epistemology of Immanuel Kant (1724–1804) and the twentieth century theologian, Joseph Maréchal. He took ninety pages of detailed notes as he read Kant's *Critique of Pure Reason*. He also read Maréchal's study, *Le point de départ de la métaphysique. Leçons sur le développement historique et théorique du problème de la connaissance*,[18] published 1923–1926. This compared Kant and St. Thomas epistemologically. According to John Courtney Murray[19] and James Rohan, S.J., one of Weigel's fellow students, this intense study of Kant and Maréchal determined Weigel's later metaphysical and epistemological positions.

During his first year of philosophy, Weigel wrote an essay entitled, "Kant's Theory of Knowledge," which compared Kant in the intellectual world to Luther in the religious: a major reformer. Weigel saw Kant's work as an answer to the question, "What can I know?" He disagreed with Kantian commentators who depicted Kant as a skeptic asking the question, "Can I know?" As Weigel claimed, "Kant's position was to be the golden mean between Skepticism and the old Rationalism, both of which he condemned as Dogmatistical." This middle position was the subject of *The Critique of Pure Reason*.

For the young Jesuit scholastic, the German idealist's epistemology was rather attractive yet he feared "dim visions of innate ideas" in Kant's a priori knowledge which is independent of all senses. Weigel preferred to explain man's universal ideas by the scholastic doctrine of universality by abstraction. In later life, Weigel became more sympathetic to intuition and innate ideas.

He claimed to be suspicious because Kant examined knowledge before being; epistemology before metaphysics. This approach, however, touched a sympathetic chord in Weigel. The examination of the process of cognition as a propaedeutic to metaphysics, which was characteristic of Plato, Kant and Maréchal, affected Weigel's thought for the reminder of his life. Epistemology preceded metaphysics for him. It is through epistemology that being is grounded.[20]

The following year Weigel discussed Kant and universals in an academy paper. He compared Kant's notion of innate ideas with Thomas' universals and judged them to be reconcilable. In line with Maréchal, Weigel said Kant's forms are simply the abstractive power of the mind in Thomism. "If this is so," he concluded, "then to be a Thomist and a Kantian is no longer impossible but a necessity. It certainly is a lovely thought to picture St. Thomas and Immanuel Kant promenading, arm-in-arm through the Heavenly groves of Academe, discussing Universals in celestial harmony and absolute concord."

During his third and final year in philosophical studies at Woodstock, Weigel prepared his master's thesis on Kant. It was entitled: "Kantian and Scholastic Epistemologies—Contrasts or Complements?"[21] Weigel saw that Kant and Thomas were complements. Kant's a priori knowledge is basically the same as Thomas' abstract universals. Kantian epistemology as interpreted by Maréchal was significant throughout Weigel's life. In his paper, "Kant and the Universals," Weigel uttered his profound suspicion of metaphysics: "Hence our own metaphysical structure of Psychology, Cosmology and Theodicy is a house of cards, empty thought, possible idealism but in reality?"

The emphasis on innate ideas, the primary concern with epistemology rather than metaphysics, the tendency toward subjectivism and relativism, the distrust of metaphysics in itself[22]—these philosophical traits would gain strength within him in the years ahead.

Gustave Weigel completed his philosophical studies in the spring of 1929. His friend, Quain, judged that "what Gus got out of philosophy would have been primarily what his own ingenuity and energy of mind would have gotten." In Quain's opinion, the philosophy faculty was quite mediocre and traditionalist.

Another of Weigel's classmates, Laurence McGinley, recalled that, at the end of the philosophical studies, Weigel's great potential as a scholar was slowly developing. As a person, he seemed still to be seeking his identity, with flights of both daring and moodiness. His sense of religious life seemed to be deepening in maturity, but mostly from within. External piety was never strongly evident in him. His capacity for friendship had grown during these early formative years and he seemed to be growing kinder and more tolerant. "A very strong trait in his character from his very earliest days was a sense of competitiveness . . . Combined with this strongly competitive spirit was a wonderful and equally strong generosity and I mention this because it was at least as important as his competitive spirit in developing his character."

During the summer of 1929, Weigel studied the pedagogy of Latin and English at Holy Cross College in Worcester, Massachusetts, to prepare him for his period of regency at Loyola College in Baltimore where he was supposed to serve his three-year regency, teaching Latin, English and German beginning that fall. He also served as moderator for *The Greyhound,* the bi-monthly school newspaper, and as assistant prefect of discipline for the forty freshmen.

Loyola, a day school offering no boarding facilities, was a charter college of arts and sciences. The courses there led to either a bachelor's or master's degree in the arts, sciences, or philosophy. In addition to the regular sessions, an Extension school was conducted, enrolling mainly female religious. In 1929, there were 158 day students and 79 in the Extension school. The system of education at Loyola was typical of all other colleges of the Society of Jesus at that time. It had a general liberal arts curriculum based on the Jesuit *Ratio Studiorum*. It was aimed at forming culture and mental and moral discipline in the students.

The first semester, Weigel taught an "Introduction to Literature" and, the second semester, the "Principles of Poetry."[23] Though his students had had no previous experience of poetry, he made it a living experience for them. With the beautiful rapport he was able to establish between himself and his students, Weigel stimulated their interest, letting them see the beauty and power of words. Seeing no absolute necessity for rhyme and rhythm in poetry, he was an advocate of free verse.[24] This seems to be in character with his entire life which was independent and free—unfettered by absolute conventions, yet disciplined.

After the last hour of the class day at Loyola, about fifteen or twenty boys would stay around just to talk to "Mister Weigel": the scholastics were commonly addressed as "Mister." The discussions ranged far and wide and covered any conceivable topic. He was the sort of man—young and vibrant—that young men loved to be with. The difference in their ages seemed slight and became less and less as the years went by.[25] The young scholastic was six feet, one inch tall and weighed 170 pounds. He was an immediate success with his freshmen students who were only about six years his juniors. Because of his large nose, they nicknamed him Cyrano de Bergerac and he loved it. His classes were tremendously stimulating, given his flair for the dramatic. He loved to challenge his students to make them think for themselves. For his "boys," Weigel started the Vergil Academy. The initiative taken by Weigel in establishing the Academy, the enthusiasm of the students for their teacher's project, and the willingness of outsiders to help in Weigel's undertaking are all foreshadowings of his later career.

Another of Weigel's life-long characteristics began to manifest itself clearly during his regency. With an ingenious talent for friendship, he was a magnetic personality who drew people to him, especially those with brains and wit. He would seek out those who were especially gifted, encouraging them to grow and mature.

28

Weigel's deepest friendship that year was formed with Francis J. Otenasek, an extemely intelligent and ambitious freshman from a Czech family in Baltimore, whom Weigel often referred to as his "first-born."[26] They spent long hours together talking and supplying a stimulus for each other. Weigel felt Frank had great potential. In fact, he encouraged him to become a Jesuit but Frank never judged that he had that vocation. Once Weigel saw that Frank's life would not be in the priesthood, he opposed his marriage, saying that Frank could do more and get farther in life without the responsibilities of marriage. When Otenasek insisted that marriage was his vocation, Weigel prayed that there would be no children to interfere with Frank's career. There were no children.

Weigel and Frank Otenasek became regular correspondents in those years following his regency at Loyola. This was very unusual since Weigel seldom wrote letters to anyone except his parents. After leaving Loyola, he sent his picture to Otenasek, inscribing it: "To Frank, Quo acutior non alter."[27] (To Frank, than whom there is no one sharper.) This strikingly handsome photograph hung in a prominent place in Otenasek's home until Frank died.

After one year of regency at Loyola, Weigel displayed these traits of character that he would develop throughout his life: a talent for friendship that was deep and lasting, a rapid rapport in the classroom, an ability to stimulate students to individual and creative thought, a magnetic and dynamic personality, a generous giver of himself.

When Gustave Weigel went to Loyola College, he fully expected to stay for the three years of regency required of Jesuits at the time. However, the president of Woodstock College, Father Vincent A. McCormick, S.J., who had noted Weigel's ability during his years in philosophy, did not want to have him spend any more time than absolutely necessary in the regency. Therefore McCormick succeeded in having Weigel returned to Woodstock after one year of regency so that he could begin his theological studies. McCormick planned at that time to send him for graduate studies in philosophy, so impressed had he been with the young scholastic's prowess in that discipline during his three years at Woodstock.[28] McCormick's special interest in Weigel continued throughout his life.[29] "Father McCormick was greatly admired and held in much affection. He related to each of us on our own wavelength—and that would be quite special in Father Weigel's regard," said Laurence McGinley.[30]

The students at Loyola, however, were not pleased with Weigel's unexpected departure. They drew up a petition to have their mentor returned to them for another year, failing to understand the enormous compliment paid to him by this shift in plans.[31]

Mister Weigel left Loyola to return to Woodstock in the early summer of 1930. At first, the idea of "improving his opportunities" by this advancement was alluring to Weigel. But then his "silent troubles" began, as he put it. He missed his students terribly. Persons were always more important in Weigel's life than pure scholarship. In a "pedagogic reminiscence" describing an unnamed, yet obvious neophyte teacher, he wrote:

> A dynamising force had suddenly dropped out of his life and he stood inert and stiff. The psychic forces that used to flow out into receptive channels, now welled up within him, and grew stagnant and oppressive. Nothing but an irritating restlessness resulted. He was too proud to admit his dependence on his pupils and forebade any one of them to see him on his last return.

He tried unsuccessfully to accept the fact that his ten months at Loyola must become simply a memory. He had not so much worked *for* his students but *with* them and they were still with him. With typical Weigelian pessimistic realism he tried to cope with his loss:

> Memory is a deceitful mirror. It is highly idealistic—it heightens and selects its details. In consequence, reality seen face to face can frequently produce unwelcome shocks. Our doubtful hero found reason to return to the old camping ground. To his

chagrin and amazement, he found himself an unwelcome ghost! The dead may be mourned—but they are expected to stay dead.

The ex-teacher returned to his books gladly and swore a mightly oath never to be seen in the old haunts and by the old faces. He might as well have sworn to breathe no air. His fond memories were shaken but not shattered . . . For in all truth the class missed the former teacher and still held him in esteem. But a teacher is only one small element in a student's life. He has home, the girl across the street, local interests, athletics, a hobby, and frequently after-school employment. In comparison with some of these the teacher is insignificant. The teacher rarely thinks of this. He—especially if he be single—has only one preoccupation—his class . . . The teacher is fundamentally a useful thing. Hence any union formed with teachers is chiefly selfish in its aims. Affection is not absent but it is an affection that never wholly rises above the egocentric plane. Between the instructor and the student there is an impassable wall of position and age. You can talk through it; you can act as if it were not there, but it stands adamant forever. If the teacher's voice does not carry, the student soon forgets that he exists.

Weigel's disillusionment was long drawn out and it hurt but, in the end, he said he had learned humility and truth. The experience did not discourage Weigel from the teacher's profession. It merely forced him to orientate himself aright.

He now knows that in the pupil's life he is *an* influence but not *the* influence. He now knows that he must pass out of the student's life as inevitably as death. Therefore while he has the student, while his power on him is strong, he must drop into the pupil's life a seed that will grow in the future without personal attention. That seed is the love of the right, the love of beauty, the love of God.[32]

31

Endnotes

1. *Catalogues Provinciae Marylandiae-NeoEboracensis Societas Jesu,* 1923, pp. 47, 130. (Hereafter referred to as Md-NY Province Catalogue.) Weigel was listed as "Gustavus A. Weigel." He assumed the middle initial, probably for "Austin." He had no middle name. (Daigler reflections).

2. Daigler reflections.

3. Interview with Edwin Quain, S.J.

4. Interview with Laurence Atherton, S.J.

5. Gustave Weigel to Mary Louise Daigler, Woodstock, March 25, 1955. WCA II F 303.34cc (2).

6. Interview with Edwin Quain, S.J.

7. John Clancy, S.J., to Patrick Collins, Portland, Maine, November 17, 1971.

8. J.A. Hughes, S.J., to Patrick Collins, Manhasset, New York, November, 1971.

9. *Ibid.*

10. WCA II F 303.22c. One of these essays is a strong defense of oral examinations. He may have formed ideas in this work which served him later in life when, as a professor at Woodstock College, he was reputed to be one of the toughest oral examiners. (Interview with James Hennesey, S.J.)

11. WCA F II 303.22c.

12. *Ibid.*

13. Daigler reflections.

14. Laurence J. McGinley, S.J., to Patrick Collins, Jersey City, November 30, 1971.

15. Interview with Edwin Quain, S.J.; Md-NY Province Catalogue, 1927, p. 66. Other members of that class were George Bahlman, Stanley Curtin, Franklin Ewing, Joseph Gallen, Harold Gardiner, John Gilson, William Griffith, Anthony Keane, Leo Kinn, Laurence McGinley, William Mulcahey, Thomas Murray, Wallace Pangborn and Stephan Toranich.

After the first two years of philosophical studies at Woodstock, students were awarded a bachelor of arts degree by Georgetown University and, after a third year of graduate studies, they received a master of arts degree. Weigel received these degrees in 1928 and 1929 respectively.

16. The Archives of Woodstock College contain his transcripts from 1926–1929. the grades in philosophy were "A" but in mathematics and the sciences, often "C-" and "C." This continued to reflect his high school lack of special interest and skill in these disciplines.

17. Interview with Erwin Geismann.

18. WCA II F 303.22d.

19. *One of a Kind,* p. 12.

20. Gustave Weigel, "Kant's Theory of Knowledge," WCA II F 303.22d.

21. WCA II F 303.23d. This thesis is not available in the Weigel Papers.

22. WCA II F 303.22d.

23. WCA II F 303.23a, b, c.

24. Interview with Francis J. Otenasek.

25. Interview with Francis J. Otenasek, (Neft).

26. Interview with Raymond A. Kirby, David McManus and Walter Burghardt, S.J.

27. Interview with Francis J. Otenasek.

28. Interview with John Courtney Murray, S.J.

29. Interview with Edwin Quain, S.J.

30. Laurence J. McGinley, S.J., to Patrick Collins, Jersey City, November 30, 1971.

31. Daigler reflections.

32. WCA II F 303.23g.

The Formation of a Theologian: 1930–1934

Gustave Weigel arrived at Woodstock College on July 20, 1930, to begin four years of theological studies. The twenty-four-year-old Jesuit found himself back in his beloved Maryland countryside with twenty-two new classmates. Once again, Weigel was the youngest member of his class. Two hundred fifty-eight Jesuits lived at Woodstock at the time.

Mister Weigel was assigned to teach a German class during the summer. By comparison with his Loyola class, Weigel found his new situation "gloomy." Teaching became drudgery and he wrote: "Impersonality on the one side induced impersonality on the other—and the final grades submitted to the Dean were inhuman."

As summer closed and fall came, theology classes began. New professors, new ideas, novel aspects and untried methods were presented. But to no avail for Gustave Weigel. The lecturers seemed to drone on in staccato rhythms and Weigel wondered, "Who cares?" Life for him was still in his memories of Loyola. Months would pass before he found himself completely at home back at Woodstock.[1]

One of Weigel's new classmates was John Courtney Murray. Years later, Murray would describe his new friend as a "tall, very thin, awkward, angular young man from Buffalo, with the sloping shoulders, then erect, which were to bow with the years. It was an unlikely friendship, between two men who were in almost every respect quite different; but it grew over the years to extraordinary depths of understanding and loyalty."

In those early years, Weigel did not have that wry, ironic sense of humor that so characterized him later. Instead, Murray recalled, he was "serious to the point of intensity, a completely dedicated student, averse to all athletics as he always remained, not inclined, as I was, to run with the 'cowboy set,' as it was called in the slow old days."[2] He appeared to be quite didactic, very precise in his speech, and very much the professor, even in his young manhood.[3] According to Murray,

> The strength and the independence and the confidence of his intelligence were early apparent, and these traits grew more marked with the years. His ideas were wrought out by himself, never in argument with others. In fact, in the beginning as at the end, it was almost impossible to argue with him. Even if there were agreement, he would normally state it by saying, "Let's put the matter in these terms"—his terms. If there were disagreement, that was the end. Except once. I recall that in our student days we clashed on some issue or other (I have forgotten what it was). It was one of many clashes, but this time the outcome was unique. He had argued for position A, and I for position B, far into the night. The next morning he came to my room just before I went to his. "John," he said, with wonted directness, "I've been thinking. You were right and I was wrong." It was the very thing I was about to say to him. We then began the whole argument all over again, having changed sides—and this time with the usual outcome.[4]

James Rohan, who was one year ahead of him at Woodstock, recalled that Gus merited extra respect from his fellow students because of his mind but did not stand out in the crowd as anyone terribly unusual. Like most students in those days, Rohan commented, Weigel was "just a number" and "earned his ordination" by going through the paces like everyone else.

Other classmates remember Weigel as always charitable, likeable, unassuming, friendly, a diligent and methodical worker who took copious notes in class, an observant but not pietistic religious. He was clear-thinking and articulate in the use of the Latin language.

It was taken for granted that he would eventually be sent on for further studies and join either the philosophy or theology faculties at Woodstock. A classmate, Edward Reiser, said that Weigel easily mastered the textbook. He stated:

> I have no doubt that most of his time was devoted to his own theological explorations. I sensed in him great confidence in his abilities and in his opinions, a certain lighthearted attitude towards the class courses, a kind of "tolerance" of the way theology was pursued at Woodstock.[5]

The theological curriculum at Woodstock between 1930 and 1934 was very traditional. Most of those in Weigel's class felt that, though quite boring, the training was orthodox and they were prepared. As Reiser put it:

> We had many "answers," we considered ourselves quite well grounded in the faith, we had few doubts that the "adversaries" were wrong. At the same time, we were conscious of a certain inadequacy in our training. Rome or the General of the Society, the story went, never had to admonish Woodstock of "novelty" because Woodstock always trod the beaten path.[6]

There was an injection of new life into their theology through some new faculty members. One, Father Denis J. Comey, was among the younger group of teachers that began to put new life and new content into the curriculum. Comey recalled that in the spring of 1932 Rome issued a new constitution on studies in seminaries, *Deus Scientiarum Dominus,* which encouraged a strong emphasis on positive theology. When Comey attempted to emphasize this at Woodstock, he was considered an innovator due to the rather rigid tradition of scholasticism, especially Suarezianism. Comey attempted to stress historical background in theology, without totally abandoning the more traditional philosophical argumentation. He remembered that this new approach to positive theology intrigued Weigel, "sparked his interest, attracted his flair for inventiveness and resourcefulness, prompted exploration and evaluation. With characteristic balance he accommodated himself to Woodstock's tradition, yet welcomed complement and supplement."

Father Comey also encouraged his students to read books beyond the theology manuals. "Gus Weigel relished the challenge, endorsed the pattern, applied himself enthusiastically to the chore of searching and researching sources." As a professor at Woodstock years later, Weigel encouraged the same kind of creative scholarship.

Under Comey, Weigel studied the tract, *De Gratia*. The professor had done special studies in this area and had had to read the works of Augustine, Prosper of Aquitaine, Fulgentius, John Cassian and Faustus of Riez. Through Comey, Weigel began to read about Faustus whom he would later study in his doctoral dissertation at the Gregorian.[7]

Gustave Weigel's own reaction to his theological training was jotted down during the tertianship retreat in 1934. His disgust with much of it and his rebellious spirit against outdated thought are clearly seen. He refused to conform to what he considered a narrow orthodoxy that would make him an "organization man."

> The common view is only the view of a very few usually old men, out of sympathy with the present where truth is as much as in the past. Hence a priori it has no claim on truth per se. A posteriori we find it wrong so often. . . .
>
> I am willing to follow them but not merely to follow them. I refuse to be extra poundage to make this machine go. I'll give my poundage to the truth. I obey all commands—but my intellection and vision are subject to vision and not decree.

This independent spirit, dedicating itself to the pursuit of truth, no matter what others may think or say, expressed itself again on the next day in reaction to four Woodstock professors. What is the vow of obedience?

> If that means the Callahan-Kearney-Brosnan-Barrett mentality, then I am caught in a trap. I do not want to be like that. Nor can I see my religious motive to urge me to such an odious mentality. I had better not say any more. My resentment against the class those four names typify is too strong for comfort.

37

Later in the retreat, Father Weigel again poured out his deep disagreement and irritation with his traditionalist professors. His words reveal his quest for "The Real."

> What do the traditionalists stand for? From Donnelly to Keelan to Herzog to Lutz, what is there that gives them inspiration? They are wedded hopelessly to an uncritical epistemology which gives them the world of seeming. Hence free-will, individuation and "common sense" are absolutes for them. Thought-forms, vision, imminent urges and values are to them delusions, dangerous because traitorous to their "real" world. There is the trouble—we are all loyal to the *real*. The difficulty arises on the question—what is the real and how does one reach it?[8]

As the years of theological training went by, Gus Weigel continued to develop one of the hallmarks of his life: "a passionate devotion to truth."[9] But, he believed, one must do this for himself and then fit all his acquired knowledge into a synthesis.

> Each bit of knowledge gives rise to some other bit and so the mind grows and grows because it has ordered its forces into phalanxes:
>
> Never be afraid of the difficult . . . I have found out that a modicum of talent plus an energetic and constant attack at the problem is of more avail than self-satisfied, undisciplined "genius" . . . Genius is the infinite capacity to take pains. This resolves itself into another pet doctrine—for the capacity to take pains rests in the will. If I really will to gain an object, I deliberately take the pains entailed to achieve my end.[10]

One reaches truth and reality, according to Weigel, through an open mind. This does not mean that a person must reject authority and the past. They must be respected but they must be flexible. Past norms "must be reshaped by an honest and informed mind to fit the contingencies that environment and present time occasions." Think for yourself, Weigel counseled Otenasek, using data both from the past and the present. All truth is relative except for the Church's. "Accept facts and always make all truth hang together in one great synthesis which is your mind in its approach

38

to reality.''[11] In another place he wrote: "Preach with me the glory of the open mind constantly developing itself in the assimilation of more and more truth to reach ultimately—through union in the Mystical Christ—Truth Infinite.''[12]

Gustave Weigel's approach to truth, to philosophy, reflected Platonic influences. Truth, as he understood it, can never be legislated from on high. "It must be taught. Teaching is expressed by the Latin word—doceo—and that derives from the Greek—DOKEO—and that means that a thing is *seen*. What men have not seen, they cannot teach.''[13] By the summer of 1932, he claimed that his vision, his *Weltanschauung,* had been rather completely formed. For him, philosophy was "An informal circle!"

> The young men should sit about the mentor beneath a tree in the grove of Academe and ply the wise man with questions and thus build in the real—a Platonic dialogue. Kant says somewhere or other that one cannot learn philosophy for what is it?—but one can learn to philosophize and that is wisdom. However, to philosophize indicates more then mere receptivity—and yet more than the cold formalism of many circles. However I am talking in the ideal order where such things are possible. For hard concrete reality I suppose the lecture system is unavoidable.[14]

Gus Weigel seldom wrote letters. But to his dear friend, Frank Otenasek, he sent many letters, all of which the young Baltimorean saved. When Weigel discovered his epistles were being preserved, he wrote that they would only be good for two things: shaving paper or kindling.

> I doubt if you could use them for blackmail. They are not definite enough. You might be able to write my obituary when I am dead—at least phase of it that dealt with my career at Woodstock. This is true, in those letters you will find me. I often wrote when in a very characteristic mood. When you are a psychoanalyst, read those letters again. We then shall be able to discuss. I wonder if I gave myself away utterly. These psycho fellows see so much where the layman sees too little.[15]

Weigel once urged his protege to be frank with him, brutally frank. He felt that Otenasek tended to be shy and urged him to overcome this tendency. His advice seems to be a good self-description of Weigel himself who was basically shy, yet was always frank and honest with all. Some say he was brusque.

When one is at once naturally frank and also somewhat shy, the two cover each other up and the resultant is—brusqueness. In a young man brusqueness is frequently interpreted as impudence. In an older man it is considered often as cantankerous opposition. You are a young, old man. Draw your own conclusions! I tell you this that you may be forewarned and forearmed. Well what to do? Let me suggest this—get over the shyness with strangers by perfect suavity of manner—that is more than gentility and politeness, you have both. It implies *mental* grace and flexibility—a readiness to accept another's point of view graciously and spontaneously. It also implies what is most abhorrent to you—a readiness to see truth and convictions mutilated without rushing to their defense. Understand I am not advocating the betrayal of principle even negatively but rather a gentle superiority to ignorance and prejudice. It is a species of reserve—but reserve worn like a dinner-jacket, not like a strait jacket.[16]

At another time, Weigel wrote about being "glib." Otenasek had asked how to become so. Weigel's answer reflects the approach he would take in later years as an ecumenist.

First of all, glibness certainly is no end to be sought for itself. Merely to be glib is no virtue—usually it is a nuisance. Therefore it implies a higher end. Now what precisely do you want for which you desiderate volubility? A lion with the ladies? God forbid. I am convinced this isn't the end. Then is it popularity? I doubt it. For popularity depends not on the tongue but on the heart. Besides you are popular enough . . . Perhaps it's the authority and dogmatic preponderance that the easy speaker with a confident air and a ready flow of language can acquire. I believe the aim is there. Well if so 'tis vanity . . . For them you wish to seem rather than to be, to shine rather than to warm. Such a man has only the position of the talker—the politician, the demagogue. These men are weavers of words,—an ephemeral and windy tapestry. The power of speech is the power of communication. This implies three things—something to communicate, someone with whom you wish to communicate (be *one with*), a medium by which the communication is achieved. Consequently he who is interested in letting another know something he knows, and has the adequate command of the medium, he will be glib—i.e., convincing, persuasive, facile. Hence what such a one needs is (a) knowledge, (b) which he considers necessary for the other, (c) whom he loves well enough that he will take pains to impart it (d) and he knows how to get the idea into the other fellow.[17]

Another facet of Weigel's developing personality that revealed itself in his letters to Otenasek was his ambivalent attitude toward institutions. He personally needed them and knew they were important. Obedience to the Society was basic to his posture to life.[18] Yet he valued his freedom above all and always felt the need to transcend institution's limitations. He once told his niece, Sister Jeremy Daigler, that, to be happy in religion, she should stay away from superiors. To Otenasek he wrote shortly before his ordination about outdated institutions that can become a force that oppress rather than liberate people.

Only a strong personality can get the better of the organization that has been imposed in the living present by the dead hand of the past.[19]

Weigel was such a strong personality. He also came to consider himself in the small elite body of men who would rule. In the words of a friend from later years, David McManus, he was an unashamed "snob."

The years of theological training passed. In 1931, Weigel was granted the degree of doctor of philosophy from the Universitas Gregoriana in Rome. Since Woostock was coordinated with the Roman university, it recognized Weigel's philosophical studies at Woodstock and granted him the degree. Later he received a licentiate in Sacred Theology from Woodstock.

Ordination to the priesthood came for Gustave Weigel on June 25, 1933, at the end of his third year of theological studies. Twenty-three Jesuits received the imposition of hands from the Most Reverend Michael J. Curley, Archbishop of Baltimore, in the chapel at Woodstock College. John Murray was also ordained the same day. During his pre-ordination retreat Weigel wrote to Frank Otenasek:

> I am trying to work up some piety so that the Catholic Church will not be ashamed at her latest servant. One thing I can tell you, and that is that she is not getting much this time. Perhaps I, the whetstone, may get her a true son and a true worker. Please pray for me, Frank, that I may be a worthy servant at the beck of God who has been so good to me and whom I have requited rather shabbily.[20]

The chapel was too small to invite many to the ceremony. August Weigel and his daughter, Louise, came with her future husband, Franklin Daigler. Leontine Weigel was unable to come due to chronic illness. Sister M. Claudia, who had taught Weigel in fourth grade, came with a companion from Scranton, Pennsylvania. Also in attendance was a grade school friend, Otto Zimmerman, and his wife.

The next morning, at 9:15, Father Weigel celebrated his first Mass in the small village church at Woodstock. Two of the Loyola class of 1933 drove from Baltimore to serve the Mass: Frank Otenasek and John Bauernschub.

St. Ann's parish in Buffalo tendered their native son a gala celebration at his first solemn Mass on July 9. The preacher was the Jesuit who had encouraged Weigel's vocation to the priesthood at Canisius High School, James McDermott.

Weigel's sister remembered the occasion vividly. She recalled being surprised that a new priest would say Mass so fast. "St. Ann's makes a big thing of ordination—in fact the men at Woodstock had been kidding Gus for some time—about the band—the 'parade' in the street. The 'parade' was a procession of children, societies, and clergy. They marched in the street from the school to the church. A noon meal was held at the rectory. The rector, Father Bernhard Coluhaz, S.J., made it a gala affair for all the visiting clergy.'' His sister recalled that in the afternoon there was a reception at the LaFayette Hotel. In the evening there was a dinner at the same hotel. Gus was delighted. Very thin—gaunt. He had worked hard. He was exhausted with all the to-do and glad to go back to Woodstock. Glad, too, that he had received much money. He was always concerned about the welfare of the Society financially as well as otherwise and he had hoped to take a respectable sum back to defray the ordination expense for Woodstock. He was very appreciative of all that was done for him at this time.[21]

Throughout his years in theological training, Gustave Weigel continued his contacts with some of his favorite Loyola students. Now and then several of them would come to Woodstock to picnic with him along the banks of the Patapsco River and to swim both there and in the quarry-pool in the woods behind the college.[22]

His favorite in the class of 1933, Frank Otenasek, and Weigel continued to develop their deep friendship, something for which both men were mutually grateful. At times the relationship bordered on the paternal but more often it was clearly fraternal.[23] But the Jesuit wished his advice to the young disciples had more grounding in reality. According to his sister, "Weigel, during his days of teaching at Loyola, regretted that he had had no personal dating experience as a young man before entering the Society of Jesus. The boys came to him for advice and he could only advise theoretically. He felt he would have been of much more value if he could have advised from experience."[23a] Gus claimed that he thought of Frank Otenasek as a younger brother.[24]

As classes began for Weigel in his first year back at Woodstock, he feared that his relationship with his "brother" would be forced to change, like one stretching a hand across the past.

In November, 1931, Weigel felt that, indeed, his ways and his friend's ways were parting. He continued to write but to a boy of his imagining, an individual he could not meet anymore.[25] He could no longer talk *ex cathedra* because Otenasek had become wiser.[26] Yet their friendship continued to deepen.

In 1933, Frank Otenasek graduated from Loyola and entered Johns Hopkins University to study medicine. For Weigel, this occasioned a "wrenching with the past." Yet, despite the different directions taken, their paths did not part.

Gustave Weigel's friendship with his former students at Loyola was scarcely confined to that of Frank Otenasek. The affection and loyalty of his former students lasted throughout their college years, and afterwards. And Weigel's affection for and devotion to his first class lived on as well. In their midst, he claimed, could be found a part of himself.[27]

At their graduation, the class of 1933 invited Weigel to speak. In his address the budding theologian expressed his understanding of St. Thomas and Scholasticism. His penchant for systematic thought in the scholastic form was obvious.

Scholasticism, he stated, teaches that all the knowledge that man can achieve can be coordinated into one living system. "Such a system swells in a living mind. In a dead book no living system can survive."

> The Scholastic, in search of "The Real," . . . was never the mere parrot of the theses of the past. His feet rested not on a solemn folio but on the real as science and experience presented it. His point of departure was not a philosophic decree but the fact. To this fact the eternal laws of metaphysics were applied and thus one by one facts were coordinated into a complex but ordered body of knowledge, where every truth had its place and function, and through which the world became a unified and intelligible whole . . .
>
> Through it he is guided by the past but not crushed by any denomination. He has been taught to base weight not on a dead verbal formula but to derive from it the inspirational truth that lies beneath. Critically, he seeks for new facts and correlates them. He makes his own the Scholastic synthesis of the perfect intel-

ligibility of all things. The content of this synthesis is the fact given by the world. Its architectonic is the law of metaphysics imposed by objective nature on the thinker.

Scholasticism, for Weigel, penetrates into all philosophies but is never bounded by them. "Whatever is good—and who will deny that there may be much?—in the different systems belongs to Scholasticism by its sovereign claim." Gustave Weigel himself came to develop, in later years, his own eclectic philosophy.

Scholastic education produces "the complete man." He is not formed pragmatically to do a certain task in society. He is formed to live as a full human being. "There is a glory in simply being human . . . Nothing human is foreign to him. He must try to know everything and have sympathies coextensive with his knowledge. . . . This implies stupendous work. However, the work is pleasant for it is human life and life is pleasant." This quotation could well serve as an epitaph for Gustave Weigel since it describes so well the attitude toward life which characterized his days. He gloried in being human; he took pleasure in knowing life.

In his concluding remarks, Mister Weigel spoke about Truth, ". . . reality in its fullness . . ." For Catholics, this Truth includes the supernatural order whose existence is denied by some non-Catholics, a contrast which his later ecumenical work would come to contradict or modify.

> Unlike our non-Catholic brethren, we are not limited to a knowledge of an external universe, barely intelligible in the wavering light that natural science and mere philosophy reflect. We see in the world the great plan of God working out.

In discussing this plan, Weigel described the Catholic Church as the mystical body of Christ, a biblical image he would later develop as Woodstock's ecclesiologist:

> You and Christ are one—as the members of a body are one with its head. You are all one among yourselves—as the members of a body are one with another. You have in you the mind that is in your Head—a mind that infallibly knows all truth.[28]

45

His enthusiasm for Thomism had grown throughout his years of theological study. During his first year of theological studies, he participated in a Thomistic "Academy" with John Courtney Murray and James Rohan.[29]

Weigel's paper had presented the existential Thomistic positions held by Joseph Maréchal. Such Thomism was not altogether pleasing to several of the faculty members who were more Suarezian in approach. The dean of the theologate and professor of New Testament, Father Edwin Sanders, in particular, brought his objections to the rector, Father McCormick. Sanders felt that Weigel's paper represented the positions of the Modernists which had been condemned by the Holy See at the turn of the century. McCormick disagreed, supported Weigel, and the paper was delivered unchanged.

Weigel later told his friend, Laurence Atherton, who had organized the "Academy" that day, that he could prove all that was written in his paper. He said that he couldn't prove it all when he wrote it but "I can now." According to Atherton, the things stated by Weigel, although quite new at Woodstock at that time, were already common in the theologates of Europe, except perhaps in Spain. Both agreed that Woodstock, not being updated in its approach to theology, was actually "in Spain," i.e., Suarezian.

The conclusion of theological studies at Woodstock left Gus Weigel somewhat disappointed and depressed.[30] As Quain observed, "By and large the faculty was not terribly impressive." It was during his last years of theological study that Weigel penned the poem, "The Arm and the Hammer," in which his feelings of rebellion against an inadequate Jesuit theological system surfaced. It reflected the stirrings of the restless spirit that would refuse to accept things as they were.

> To Wait or to strike;
> That is the riddle.
> To wait is man's duty
> So often.

The Prisoner
And the Victim of a System
Must wait
And too long.
Waiting is in place
Often when striking is luring.
But waiting too long
Or too often
Kills in Man
The soul to strike.
A System Piles
Waiting on men
To kill the soul to strike.
For the striking urge
Is dangerous to Systems.
A System works only
By directing
Mass inertias.
Self-movements
Cannot be controlled
And a heap of self-movements
Soon refuses to be a heap.
No man knows the value
Of his stroke.
Many a man can lose it
To humanity's gain.
But he who links himself
To System
Must know
That his striking arm
Will wither or be broken.
The System can only use
His Mass
Not his thrust.
Sad is he
Who has not lost his striking arm
Nor the heart to use it

And yet is System-bound.
Sometimes he strikes
And crushes himself
Under the weight
Of the System
Which his movement
Started down
Upon him.
Sometimes he strikes
And laughs to see
The Sparks
His stroke brought forth.
And he is not crushed.
For he is but loosely linked
To the System.
He lives parasitically
On the whole
And the whole
Leaves him alone
For he is in it
But not of it.
He has grown big
By it.
But he never grew
Into it.[31]

Endnotes

1. Weigel to Otenasek, July 24, 1930, WCA II F 303.23g.
2. *One of a Kind,* pp. 11–12.
3. Interview with John Courtney Murray, S.J. (Neft).
4. *One of a Kind,* pp. 13–14; Interview with John Courtney Murray, S.J., June 15 and 17, 1967 (Neft).
5. Letter to author from Edward Reiser, S.J., November 11, 1971. Other letters confirm this: William Schlaerth, S.J., October 30, 1971; Raymond Kennedy, S.J., November 9, 1971; Joseph Duhamel, S.J., November 16, 1971; John Bellwoar, S.J., November 22, 1971; Thomas Reilly, S.J., November 12, 1971; Anthony De Maria, S.J., December 7, 1971; Francis Donelan, S.J., December 2, 1971; J.A. Priestner, S.J., November 26, 1971; Joseph d'Invilliers, S.J., November 10, 1971.

6. Letter to author from Edward Reiser, S.J., November 11, 1971.

7. Letter to author from Denis J. Comey, S.J., November 16, 1971. Weigel's S.T.L. dissertation was entitled, "Faustus of Riez: A Reconsideration," WCA II F 303.13b.

8. The professors mentioned in Weigel's diary were: Timothy B. Barrett, S.J., professor emeritus of moral theology, who was the spiritual director when Weigel arrived at Woodstock for the theological studies; James H. Kearney, S.J., had been Weigel's professor of ethics during his third year of philosophy and had also taught him moral theology. Weigel had assisted Kearney, just back from a biennium in Rome, to prepare his notes for ethics class (Interview with Edwin Quain, S.J., October 4, 1971); William J. Brosnan, S.J., had taught Weigel Natural Theology in third philosophy; Daniel J. Callahan, S.J., had taught *De Verbo Incarnato* and a course in the sacraments to Weigel; Francis P. Donnelly, S.J., who taught rhetoric during Weigel's years of college; Vincent L. Keelan, S.J., who taught Weigel in philosophy, logic and metaphysics; Charles Herzog, S.J., who was the lecturer in fundamental theology and taught the tract *De Ecclesia* to Weigel. (Md-NY Province Catalogue, 1923, p. 41; 1924, p. 44; 1925, p. 45; 1926, p. 46; 1927, p. 58; 1928, p. 61; 1929, p. 62; 1931, p. 66).

9. Weigel to Otenasek, June 10, 1931.

10. Weigel to Otenasek, January 5, 1931.

11. Weigel to Otenasek, October 12, 1932.

12. Weigel to Otenasek, November 29, 1932.

13. Weigel to Otenasek, November 18, 1933.

14. Weigel to Otenasek, March 1, 1932.

15. Weigel to Otenasek, May 9, 1933.

16. Weigel to Otenasek, January 5, 1931. In later years Weigel seldom responded to public criticism of his ideas.

17. Weigel to Otenasek, September 13, 1931.

18. Donald Hinfey, S.J., to Patrick W. Collins, Syracuse, N.Y., January 8, 1972.

19. Weigel to Otenasek, May 9, 1933.

20. Weigel to Otenasek, June 16, 1933.

21. Daigler reflections.

22. Weigel to Otenasek, April 17, 1932.

23. Otenasek to Weigel, June 2, 1931, and June 17, 1931.

23a. Daigler reflections.

24. Weigel to Otenasek, Cf. also Otenasek to Weigel, August 30, 1932.

25. Weigel to Otenasek, November 13, 1931.

26. Weigel to Otenasek, January 5, 1932. Weigel had decided that "In your honor and that God may give you strenth, I have relinquished again the smokes I so lately began. Still there is no great struggle in my abstinence. I doubt if a physical habit had set it." In later years, Weigel became a chain smoker.

27. Weigel to Otenasek, September 23, 1930.

28. Gustave Weigel, "Finale," *Green and Gray,* 1933. pp. 44–46. Weigel's statement that "you have in you the mind that is in your Head" is extemely significant in the light of his future teaching that the Christian is carnally incorporated into Christ. (Cf. chap. 8).

29. WCA II F 303.22f; Interview with James Rohan, S.J., September 20, 1971.

30. Interviews with James Rohan, S.J., and Dr. Erwin Geismann.

31. *Woodstock Letters,* vol. 97, no. 4, Fall, 1968, pp. 430, 435–436.

Tertianship—The Final Test: 1934–1935

St. Ignatius of Loyola was an astute observer of the human condition. He was well aware that many years of intellectual pursuits could dry and wither men's hearts. Their initial motivation and fervor could be sapped after years of study, interrupted only by the regency. He feared that they might lose the sense of the forest in their intense scrutiny of the trees. Hence Ignatius wrote in the *Constitutiones* of the Society of Jesus:

> Wait a bit before you get under way with your busy life! Let's return to the Sources of your first love. Let's renew that deep self-examination that moved you so effectively in your far-off noviceship days. You will spend one more year, in still more complete retirement, at a School of the Heart (Schola Affectus), as these long years have been a School of the Intellect.[1]

Joseph de Guibert, S.J., suggests that the idea of this "tertianship" may have come from the "desert idyll" of Ignatius and his companions. These were weeks of retreat "during which the future apostolic workers steeped themselves in the life of solitude, prayer, penance, and poverty, with the purpose of obtaining from this life the realization of the graces of the priesthood which they had just then received."[2]

According to the *Constitutiones* and the *Examen Generale,* this third year of probation has a dual purpose. Primarily, it is a final test of the young priest's suitability for Jesuit life. Secondarily, it is a turning toward the spiritual and corporal works of mercy in order better to prepare a man for the apostolate.[3]

On the first of September, 1934, Gustave Weigel and thirty other Jesuits began their tertianship at the *Domus Probationis* of St. Andrew-on-Hudson. For many of them, including Weigel, it was a return to their Jesuit beginnings, the site of their first two years of probation in the Society.

Father Weigel had hoped to make his tertian year in Europe but he supposed "that the troubled conditions there made it unfeasible to send anyone there." In August, he wrote that he dreaded his coming year of introspection. He feared a return of scrupulosity in the lengthy self-examinations.[4]

He was relieved to be finished with his classics course, taught during the summer at St. Peter's College in Jersey City. Comparing those students with Loyola class of '33 made Weigel dissatisfied both with students and himself. Contact between teacher and pupils was difficult and response was slow.

This unsatisfying experience made Weigel long again for Baltimore. But it was not to Baltimore that he was headed. Instead he had to settle into the quite tertian year at St. Andrew-on-Hudson. He was impressed by the silence at St. Andrew's. His room overlooked the Hudson River, "an honest-to-goodness river," he told Otenasek, giving him an "exquisite view" of the river which compared favorably to the Rhine.

One of the major undertakings during the third year of probation is a repetition of the thirty-day retreat based upon *The Spiritual Exercises,* which had first been made during the novitiate. Weigel's class that October was under the direction of Father Peter A. Lutz, S.J., who had been the Woodstock rector during Weigel's first year there.

Gus voluntarily kept a retreat diary. He inscribed the opening lines: "In this book which is so far the story of sad failure and hopeless lack of proper idealization and motives, I shall write my retreat experiences . . ."

In typically independent fashion, he reacted immediately to *The Spiritual Exercises* which were the basis of the retreat.

> I am making the Exercises on the basis that they leave the soul in freedom . . . I use my own ideas in these meditations . . . I know that the ways taught me years ago are impossible. I shall trust the Spirit.

The second day of retreat found Weigel again critical of Ignatius, this time for a weak theology of grace and free will. Weigel wrote that free will by itself has no power to choose salvation. He felt Ignatius "is either semi-Pelagian or merely idealistic, presupposing grace, which is presupposing everything . . ." Weigel was always sensitive in questions regarding grace and free will. For him, salvation was a free gift of God, not earned by heroic acts of will. This put him at odds often with one of the Ignatian themes which stresses will power. This concern for unmerited salvation would show up later in his doctoral studies of the semi-Pelagian, Faustus of Riez.

A thirty-day retreat, during which silence is required, with the exception of three break days, is a gruelling ordeal, as most Jesuits will testify. For Weigel, it was more so now than in the novitiate, "with its lack of candor and incapacity . . . to do the thing." The first days showed a spiritual enthusiasm, however, as well as his penchant for the psychological.

> For me to meditate on God and myself is easy. I like it. The majesty of God and the yearning that the Supernatural makes possible are all very dear. As I conceived the soul enveloped and absorbed in the great warm darkness that is God, I was frightened at the thought that this was the "back-to-the-womb" urge of psychology . . . What of it? Has not the "back-to-the-womb" urge its fulfillment in the Supernatural? Is not supernaturalized man's subconscious crying for what the psychiatrist thinks is interior but really much deeper, fuller and fullest being? . . .

By mid-month, the self-scrutinizing experience grated on Weigel and he indicated some regrets regarding his personal progress during the retreat. Prayer and liturgy were barren and sterile "as ever." "If only faith were a little stronger. I have not yet met Christ intimately . . . Christ is no nearer though he dwells within me." For the next week, Father Weigel dug in and his boredom seemed to subside. But the doldrums returned again later.

"The Meditations were 00. I feel no warmth—I am more interested in historic accuracy—which I do not really pursue." The retreat was getting long and he was counting the days. "I see more clearly my original vision but it imparts no warmth," he wrote. He closed the third week with his mind "restless, sad, weepy . . ."5

The beginning of the fourth week found him uninterested in the "points" until there "came the voice from heaven." It was a letter from Father Vincent A. McCormick who had been his rector and mentor at Woodstock. McCormick had been transferred to Rome on December 27, 1933, to become the rector of the Pontifical Gregorian University. Of the letter, Weigel commented: "It was so full of spiritual warmth that I felt sorry for my waning enthusiasm and promised once more to go on." The letter revealed the close spiritual and friendly relationship that must have existed between the two men.

> I have often hoped to be able to make another thirty day retreat. So I hope you, too, have just been smothered with the graces God has been wanting to give you. They are certainly calculated to stifle the life of self-seeking. You have now so many new thoughts we could discuss were we tramping through the woods to the upper farm. Keep them against the day next year, God willing, when we shall thrash them out under the shadow of the Palatine . . . Remember, you will never have another year when you can study God and all He means to us cherished mortals so deeply and quietly as now. Make the most of it. The future years will be crowded with the work that God has appointed for you.6

Retreats occasion spiritual struggles and insights. Weigel's diary indicates his share of each. It is the custom during a tertianship retreat to make a general confession, one which covers the entire period of one's life or from the last general confession. Weigel, thorough as was his custom, wrote out the rough draft of his confession. It took most of his free time. He worked all the next day completing it. "It is a dread thing to have around," he commented. No doubt the whole matter aroused his acknowledged scrupulosity. Immediately, he approached a confessor, James Rohan. Following the confession, Weigel, through Rohan's counsel, became perfectly aware of a block to his spiritual progress: "I have not yet surrendered to Christ, though I have surrendered to the god of Plato and Aristotle." Immediately after the confession, he burned the "text."

The problem of surrendering had a long and deep history with Father Weigel, a history that continued to distract and trouble him during the retreat. He admitted that "spirituality drags in Burke."

Francis Burke was a Jesuit, ordained in 1931 at Woodstock. Burke had an extraordinary mind with an excellent capacity for synthesis. He was also a remarkable personality who had a way of generating a degree of personal attachment that was quite beyond the normal. Burke had been an attractive person to the new class of theologians at Woodstock in 1930. John Murray and Weigel became especially close to him and were deeply influenced by him.[7] Weigel sat at his feet at seminars. Burke spoke of himself as the Socratian gadfly who prodded young Jesuits to think, argue and express themselves in philosophy and theology. He was especially critical of the traditional methods in apologetics.[8]

Burke was a man ahead of his time theologically. At Woodstock, at a time when the theological faculty represented a very conservative, manual approach to theology, Burke was reading and appreciating the "practically forbidden" books of Joseph Maréchal and Maurice Blondel.[9] He was also a deeply spiritual man who spoke at times as though he had had mystical visions.

About the time of Murray's and Weigel's ordination, Burke told his two friends that they should make an extraordinary private personal vow of fidelity to Christ. Weigel was deeply disturbed by the request of Burke whose personality, hypnotic influence on young men and cogency of mind made it difficult to refuse. Weigel feared that if he failed to make the suggested commitment he would be refusing a direct grace from God. Yet he decided against it. But the choice bothered him.

On Easter Monday, 1934, Francis Burke died suddenly and quite mysteriously in a hospital in Newport, Tennessee. He had apparently neglected to take insulin for his diabetes, went into a coma and died. This was a great shock to the Woodstock community and, in particular, to Gus Weigel, who sought to discover as much as he could about Burke's last days.[10]

References to this special commitment to Christ and to Frank Burke come up repeatedly in Weigel's retreat diary. The issue, as reflected in his remarks about his confession, was still bothering him. It proved to be his "chief distraction" throughout the spiritual searching of the retreat days.

On October 6, Weigel wrote extensive analytical notes on the theological and spiritual implications of the Incarnation and infancy of Christ. It was a scholar's impersonal approach to the mysteries of faith. The following day he was disgusted with his intellectualizing. Faith was still a matter of the intellect for him; the commitment was not yet made, he felt.

> I am not ready for surrender. It is no use to say, "No, I don't want it." That is untrue; I do want it; saying the opposite isn't going to change that. I need a powerful vision of the truth. It is not enough to see him doing things that show where the truth must be. I must see the truth! I can already see the "betterness" of the unselfish position in terms of logic—I cannot make the assent. I do not see—I do not see, the truth will make me free—but I must see it. Truth can give vision; I am not so foolish as to ask for an intellectual natural perception . . . What can give me to see what I want to see? It is not the study of Christ's life—useful though that may be. Christ's life as a lesson needs the ini-

tial vision—he alone counts. I suppose I must pray and have others intercede for me. . . .

These remarks point to Weigel's epistemological position: truth comes intuitively through a kind of innate vision. Also unveiled here is his approach to faith: the initial vision precedes any apologetic study in a man's coming to faith.

A beautiful testimony to Weigel's desire to "break through" and give himself to Christ in love as Burke had requested, yet his sense of powerlessness and unworthiness comes through in words written near the retreat's conclusion.

> I am so far from Christ and God . . . Suicide is the only solution that such an experience suggests. That betrays the spirit from which it arises. . . . I long so for a breaking through the thin barrier that separates me from Him. This again is pride and self. Faith is enough! God knows I do not even deserve that! I am at the present very desolate—alone, so alone, and miserable. There is no goodness in me, past or present . . . I resent it and dread the future. It is an empty life without love.

Early in the retreat Weigel had taken up the autobiography of St. Teresa of Avila. He gained much help from reading about her struggles with prayer, which ended simply in surrender, not to self but to the Beloved. Teresa knew and appreciated the Ignatian form of meditation but judged it too intellectual and not as good as a prayer of the will. This intrigued Weigel, who was not much taken with *The Spiritual Exercises* himself. Though he felt her "prayer of the will" had certain weaknesses, he wanted to study it carefully. Her approach seemed "less straightening" and more "sweet." But Weigel felt he should stick to Ignatius. "I am so fearful of my own judgment in these matters," he wrote. Yet he could not pull himself away from Teresa. His final mention of the Spanish mystic reflected an attitude he would eventually adopt in his ecumenical work: "St. Teresa says that we must be patient and let Christ do His work in His own way and in His own time. Let us hope—and *pray*."

Gustave Weigel's spiritual insights during his tertian retreat were coupled with a clarification of some of his own basic theological positions. During his theological studies at Woodstock, Weigel, probably influenced by Father Daniel Callahan, had read Maurice de la Taille (1872–1933), the French Jesuit theologian from the Gregorian University in Rome. His principal work, *Mysterium Fidei* (1921), is an original and comprehensive study of the Mass. De la Taille's theology, based upon patristic and scholastic evidence, is that the sacrifice of Christ is one, namely, that on Calvary. The Last Supper looked forward to this and the Mass prolongs it. His thesis was in opposition to many theologians who held that there must be a real immolation in the Mass. According to the October 23rd diary entry, Weigel had had his "eyes opened" the night he read de La Taille at Woodstock.

Lutz, the retreat master, presented a view of Catholicism as a moral union, a union of wills and yet he presented it as something more than this. He held that "it is a mysterious indefinable union with the mysterious Trinity." Weigel judged that this reduced the Church "to a semi-Pelagian Molinistic observance of the law . . . The absolute helplessness of the will to obey the law never bothers them. They speak of grace and picture it as an oil that takes out the creaks of a well-running machine." Weigel, with de la Taille, felt that Catholicism is more than this through the Eucharist. "Do I or don't I eat Christ? If I do, then I unite with him! I unite with him primarily as man—one cannot eat a spirit."

Weigel thought that his reading of the Gospel of John proved that Lutz' position was wrong and de la Taille accurate. And Weigel felt he must follow the insights of his own intellect. Yet he worried about the boldness of contradicting the position of his instructor. Revealed here is the inner tension Weigel always felt between authority which he needed and respected, and his own intellectual freedom which he valued so highly.

> He (Lutz) cannot declare me wrong or right. As a learned man
> he is deficient in my humble opinion. Hence, over my intellect

and its faith he has no authority either human or divine. I owe him authority, which I vowed; my obedience is illuminated by faith. It does not and cannot include in its scope the very light that makes it possible. God and his Christ speak to me as urgently through the halting words of a weak man. My talents, my time, my interests are his to dispose. My intellect which is my life is only God's and Christ's. I cannot surrender them—they are not mine.

During retreat, the exercitant has a chance to formulate his hopes and plans for the future. During the third week, Weigel, painfully aware of his human weaknesses, did so.

The past proves to me that of myself I can do nothing but evil. For the future I shall rely on Christ. He can take care of me from within and without. I give up all hope of saving myself—Christ must do that. What must I do? I don't know; I am setting out on the great unknown quite blind. My natural self has all sorts of Napoleonic dreams. My grossness already manifests itself with no protest sounded in the depths—there is a surface perturbation. It is enough to make me despair—but I hope and have even thin, faint visions of a holy life. Christ can do it. I am still of my first willingness—"in manus tuas, Domine, commendo spiritum meum."

Earlier during the retreat, while reading St. Teresa, Weigel reflected on the way in which Christ makes disciples. He wants to make them *him,* not like Weigel who wanted to make disciples *his.* "This must be the key to my work—make them share and expand my Christ-life—not serve and enhance my ambitions and love of power." As Weigel's life indicated, he not infrequently had problems with his "disciples" in that he would at times exert too much control over them to make them as he thought they should be.

Father Weigel's diary for the last days of the retreat records not only the depths of his spirituality and future hopes but also the vision of the Church which was developing within him. "Lutz conceived the Church under the Body figure—admitted physical union—but made it the consequent of grace union. He struck the life note and I was pleased. I need not fear. My vision is not wrong."

Finally, Weigel summarized the gains of his retreat. Admitting that he was not totally faithful in avoiding distraction in prayer, he professed his belief that only prayer would see him through his gamble of faith and dedication to Christ. He then assessed his progress:

> I have learned myself. I see what I am and I see what I need. I love with the frothy love I am capable of the Christ. I want Him to take me and transform me. I am willing to surrender all—at least so I say and seem to think. I shall arise, clasp his hand, and come. Perhaps on my putrid pride and proud putridity, I can rise to grasp that hand. He must do it. I am a great sinner and I am very proud. Self stands in the way and vaulting ambition prevents reform. However I must be—and am—patient. I am what I am and Christ knows it.
>
> As is clear I have courage—but not of myself. I leave with head erect because the Head is above the clouds and from it I have all power, all knowledge and all love. I do not relish the martyrdom that I know is coming but in Him I can stand it. Those lines terrify me. I wrote them at the dictates of the inside. What they mean I know not. God's will be done and through Christ I accept the whole future to fill up what is wanting. This is my surrender. Oh may I not be proved an "indian-giver!"

The remainder of the tertian year involved serving as chaplain in two hospitals: Hudson River State Hospital for the Insane and Metropolitan Hospital on Welfare Island in New York City, which was a general hospital. He spent one month in each place. In the hospital for the mentally ill, Weigel ministered only to the doctors and nurses, to his regret. He would have preferred contacts with those who were psychologically disturbed since he had a keen interest in psychic realities.[11] In addition to these hospital chaplaincies, Weigel preached a four-week mission in Middle Village, Long

Island, and the Novena of Grace at St. John the Evangelist Church in Scranton, Pennsylvania.

Daily life in the *Domus Probationis* was quite simple: a bit of clerical work, some library duties, waxing floors, helping an elderly priest say Mass, hauling stone, serving at table and a bit of study. Father Weigel saw the year as laboratory work in which he attempted to dissect himself.

Toward the end of tertianship, Otenasek wrote to Father Weigel about a friend of his who was planning to enter the Society of Jesus. Weigel's reply gives an insight into the conception of Jesuit life which he had at that time. He asked Frank if his friend had brains and an idealistic and unselfish spirit. He probed, too, about the man's willingness to surrender his own will in obedience to a religious superior.

Weigel's attitudes toward intimacy and sexuality at this time reflect the experience of one whose life had been lived more in the company of men than women. Some who knew Weigel well have stated that he was not comfortable with women, that he did not understand women.[12] Others have claimed this was not true.[13] Gus Weigel's experience with women in social, intimate situations had been slight. He had not dated in high school and then went immediately to the seminary where he was never one to "kick over the traces." As mentioned previously, he always regretted this. He felt inadequate as he tried to counsel his "boys" at Loyola about their dating problems.

Through the 1930s, Weigel urged his friend to go slow in his relationship with women, feeling they would get in the way of his dreams of success for Otenasek. Later, when he realized that marriage was to be Otenasek's path, Weigel insisted that he only wanted Otenasek to be happy and, if marriage would do that, he was for it. "Marry the Witch of Endor and you will still have my blessing."[14]

When Weigel met Mildred Buzek, the object of his friend's affections, he admitted:

I usually am not at home with things of the fair sex but your little lady quite overcame my reserve . . . It is good for me that she came. I never believed that one soul could be so attached to another.[15]

As Otenasek and Miss Buzek came closer to contemplating marriage, Father Weigel urged them to take joy in the idea of marriage because for them it was the only thing. However, "I do not want a wife and can't bear the thought of it." When Father Weigel had an opportunity to write to Otenasek's intended, he was "never more ill at ease." He didn't know what to say; it was like talking to a stranger, yet he said, "I do not look on Mildred as a stranger. Unfortunately I never had much to do with women and I find myself at a loss when I deal with them. Even my sister is much of a mystery to me in spite of our mutual devotion to each other."[16]

When, in late 1936, the two had not yet married because of Otenasek's school obligations, but wanted badly to marry, Weigel again counseled immediate, though private marriage.

Early in the summmer of 1935, Weigel preached at the first Mass of Leo Welch, S.J. Welch was one of many younger students at Woodstock with whom Weigel had become very friendly. In a letter to Welch, later that year, Weigel apparently engaged in what was becoming for him something of a hobby: psychology and analysis. Welch sent a piqued reply, indicating that he resented Weigel's "infallible" pronouncements. He felt that Weigel should not spend so much time criticizing his friends but should concentrate rather on their strengths, keeping "away from the contemplation of the thousand and one things which show what an ungrateful cur the other fellow really is."

No one is less able to influence a man's character than the one who starts off by holding up an ideal which is not fitted to the actual character of the man he is trying to influence. You must start from the bottom, and the bottom in this case is reality . . .

My advice to you, my dear Gussleheimer, is to contemplate the noble Agnes in Dicken's David Copperfield. She did not mom nor berate. I have no desire to take the place of David, no matter how well or poorly it fits. In your life there will be many Davids whom you will greatly benefit, if you can keep on playing the part of Agnes. Such is your destination. It is a brutally painful one, but one which will bring you intense joy, if you can be hero enough to play the part.[17]

Played the part he had and he continued to do so throughout his life. Many "Davids" there would be. He was a born mentor. Yet he always fought the tendency to make people into his image of what they should be like. His friendships did indeed seem to involve some form of control of the life of the friend, perhaps in a way similar to that control which Francis Burke had exercised briefly on his own life.

This was somewhat true in the case of Weigel's relationship with Frank Otenasek. Despite Weigel's persistent efforts to "help" his friend, Otenasek often had a mind of his own. Weigel pushed Otenasek to become a leader in the field of his choice, always urging him to harder and harder work in order to succeed. He told him that all this was in his grasp if he would just put out his hand and take it, will it.[18] And again! "Be big! Meanness and mediocrity are so common. Dare to do things! All that it means, is to set for yourself an objective, then work, oh so hard and so long and then make it your own. Never say die! Use the stubbornness that your German grande-mère gave you. You are as good as any of them and better than the most of them."[19]

Weigel urged Otenasek to fill his soul with scholarship rather than friendship.[20] "The head is more important than the heart. The one puts meaning and value into life—the other may but usually doesn't."[21] Later, when Otenasek seemed to be letting success go to his head, he modified his stressing of ambition, striving and success. "Work hard, indeed, but possess your soul in peace."[22]

Weigel's counsel to Otenasek unveiled something of his own mind on the tension between seeking success or seeking happiness—a tension most likely not satisfactorily resolved by him during his lifetime.

> Which is the more valuable for man; to reach his ambition or to be happy? Obvious answer is that one is contained in the other. However, that is not always true—in fact, it is rarely true. Then if the two cannot be had, which is one to suggest? Both of us I think are quite willing to sacrifice the happiness. Yet I think that herein we err and err greatly.[23]

Before leaving for two years of study in Rome, Weigel and Otenasek met for a two-day visit in Philadelphia, the first time they had seen each other since before tertianship. It was to be their last meeting for two years.

As he left for Rome in August, Weigel wrote to Frank a beautiful testimony of his faith and hope in the future God was holding out to him.

> I hope to do something real in my life, and when it is done, I want to die. What the real thing is, I do not know. It may be in the field of learning. It may be in the field of sacrifice. It may be in the field of prayer. Wherever it is, this is my prayer; Lord, let me do one great thing, good, real. Then let me die.[24]

Endnotes

1. Constitutiones of St. Ignatius, cited in John LaFarge, S.J., *A Report on the American Jesuits* (New York: Farrar, Straus and Cudahy, 1936), p. 75. Cf. also Joseph de Guibert, S.J., *The Jesuits: The Spiritual Doctrine and Practice* (Chicago: Institute of Jesuit Sources, 1964), p. 235.

2. de Guibert, *op. cit.,* p. 37.

3. Anthony Ruhan, S.J., "The Origins of the Jesuit Tertianship" in Raymond A. Schroth, S.J., ed., *Jesuit Spirit in a Time of Change* (Westminster, Md.: Newman Press, 1968), p. 100.

4. Weigel to Otenasek, August 19, 1934, and September 9, 1934.

5. WCA II F 303.22g.

6. Vincent A. McCormick, S.J., to Weigel, Rome, October 15, 1934, WCA II F 303.35v.

7. Interview with Edwin Quain, S.J.

8. Joseph A. d'Invilliers, S.J., to Patrick W. Collins, November 10, 1971.

9. Interview with Lawrence Atherton, S.J.

10. Interview with Edwin Quain, S.J. Weigel told Quain personally about Burke's request a few days after his ordination.

11. Weigel to Otenasek, December 1, 1934, and January 3, 1935.

12. Interview with Erwin Geismann.

13. Interviews with Mrs. Francis Otenasek, Sister Jeremy Daigler, R.S.M., Walter Burghardt, S.J. Dr. Richard Ferguson said Weigel understood the man-woman relationship as though he were married himself. This understanding came through his close contact with married couples both in Chile between 1937 and 1948, and when he returned to the United States in 1948.

14. Weigel to Otenasek, July 6, 1934.

15. Weigel to Otenasek, July 31, 1935.

16. Weigel to Otenasek, August 5, 1935.

17. WCA II F 303.35eee.

18. Weigel to Otenasek, September 7, 1930. Cf. also January 5, 1931.

19. Weigel to Otenasek, May 15, 1931.

20. Weigel to Otenasek, August 23, 1930.

21. Weigel to Otenasek, September 7, 1930.

22. Weigel to Otenasek, December 22, 1931.

23. Weigel to Otenasek, January 6, 1936.

24. Weigel to Otenasek, August 28, 1935.

The Biennium in Rome:
1935–1937

The Holland-American line ship, the *Veendam,* was a small vessel but comfortable. On board with Gustave Weigel when he sailed from New York on September 14 were about sixty passengers. He disembarked at Boulogne-sur-Mer and Weigel began a "barn-storming" tour of Europe, prior to reporting for studies in Rome.[1]

His first stop was London which he enjoyed immensely. The churches irritated him, however. Westminster Abbey, he felt, could not be a true church if such non-church-goers as Shelley, Byron and Darwin are buried there. St. Paul's Cathedral, though more of a church, was not for him a house of prayer. "This is true of all the famous European churches," he said. "The Bolsheviks are behind the times when they threaten to turn them into museums. They are that already."

After four days in London, he journeyed on to Brussels and to Paris, his "dream city." There he found real churches—"all Catholic." Of the modernistic art there, he judged it "awful stuff."

From Paris, Weigel traveled on to Strasbourg and Mulhouse where he visited his relatives. They took him to visit the birthplaces of his parents.

Crossing the Alps into Italy, Weigel visited Milan and Padua where he was "attacked" by mosquitos and also developed a painful boil on his neck. He was tiring of the "barn-storming" though he had found it an excellent education. "As fun it is poor stuff.

I always thought I was a cosmopolitan but I find to my chagrin that I am an American." Traveling alone was not good for him either, especially in places where he could not speak the language. Finally, on October 10, after nearly a month en route, Father Weigel reached Rome.[2]

Before classes began Weigel wrote of his impressions of Europe. He saw it as very restless, dangerously nationalistic and only superficially influenced by the Church.

> If I were not convinced of the supernatural and spiritual nature of the Church, I would say that the Church has failed. Everywhere you see her fighting—not to bring a Christian culture into the world—but to keep the little that is still left to her—and the fight is a losing one. Oh there are many Churches and many priests and nuns. Yes, there are people in the Churches—with plenty of room, however, for many more. In certain sections there is much piety—and some superstition. However, the faith is not a living force in society at large. Religion is like chewing gum. If you like it, you take it. If you don't you don't and it doesn't make much difference either way to society . . . What is wanted is a spiritual revival—and that is nowhere in sight. In Belgium they think organization will solve the problem. It won't. In France they think diplomacy will solve it. It won't. Europe needs an awakening in the soul. It needs a supernatural vision—and no human means can give that. God alone can give it anything—in fact, it is not even ready to receive the gift. To prepare the soul of Europe, needs not another Aquinas—but rather a Francis of Assisi.

Weigel's characteristic pessimism came through in his view of Europe. Perhaps it will muddle through, he wrote, "but I look forward to utter ruin in the near future." Only two things checked his pessimistic outlook: First, the losses of World War I seemed to have been repaired. "The point is that nature and humanity have great powers of rapid recuperation. Losses are not permanent. Out of losses gain is derived. Hence we can hope." Secondly, though the Church had no vital influence in Europe, "yet the

Cathedrals themselves stand manifesting the quondam existence of a mighty force which could rear these magnificent structures . . . Now the force that reared those Cathedrals is not dead. It is only sleeping. That it is still alive can be seen in the little groups that attend Mass in a little dark chapel of some big Church . . . The Church is the Mass and the Mass still lives in Europe."[3]

Father Weigel took up residence at the Jesuit House on the Piazza del Gesu, 45, together with two other confreres from the Maryland-New York province, Leo A. Cullum and John Courtney Murray. Nine other Jesuits from his home province were also in residence in Rome that year, including Vincent A. McCormick, the rector of the Pontifical Gregorian University where Weigel was to study. Weigel was assigned to study dogmatic theology and Murray, fundamental theology.

The Biennium program existed primarily to prepare professors for the scholasticates, universities and colleges of the Society of Jesus around the world. Some few students at the Gregorian, however, were assigned to professorships at the Gregorian itself.[4]

Father McCormick had the difficult task of building up the faculty there since the Society was greatly in need of more skilled and specialized scholars and teachers in its Roman university.[5] It seems to have been the intention that Gustave Weigel be assigned to study at the Gregorian in preparation for his assuming a teaching post there upon completion of his doctorate.[6]

From the outset, Weigel did not care for Rome. He had been warned of this possibility by a friend, Francis E. Shea, who had just completed his Roman studies.[7] He was correct in assuming that his friend would be initially disappointed with the Eternal City. All of the bad things which Shea predicted fell upon Gustave Weigel. He disliked the food, the lack of central heating, the lack of practicing Catholics in Rome—he disliked Rome in general.[8] Perhaps it was only his friendships with Murray and McCormick that helped make Rome bearable for Weigel.[9] Other Jesuits who studied at the Gregorian with Weigel and later achieved some kind of fame were Maurice Bêvenot, Edwin Healy, P. De Letter, Victor Sartre, Edmund Fortman, John Ford, Gerald Kelly, Stanislaus Felczak, Vicente Andrade and Muñoz Vega who later became a cardinal.[10]

The program of studies for the biennium students began in October. During his first year, Weigel took six courses and worked on one research assignment.[11] Father Weigel, as he had been at Woodstock, was not overly pleased with the quality of education at the Gregorian. In later years, he had little good to say about it. He felt Rome was a dangerous place for theologians and that there weren't many honest men there.[12] During these years of study, Weigel came to appreciate the German approach to scholarship more than the French. The latter he didn't trust.

> When a German writes he is hopelessly right or hopelessly wrong. You can tell at once. When a Frenchman writes he may be either but he always seems right and there you are in a pickle. You have to go to a German with his awful words and terrible sentences to find out whether the German can tell you if the Frenchman is right or wrong. It is always easier to understand the French writers but easy understanding does not necessarily make for truth—though it is a gift which the Germans might be more lavish with.[13]

Weigel suffered grief in his first year in Rome. Leontine Kieffer Weigel died on February 16, 1936. John Murray recalled that his friend cried when he received the news of his mother's death.[14] Later Weigel wrote to Otenasek of his reflections at the time and, with Weigelian pessimism, he speculated about his future.

> Poor woman, she had bad breaks in her life. She was completely wrapped up in me—and yet she saw me in all three weeks in 14 years. Health prevented her from visiting me and she could not even see my ordination. Then she died without me around. Perhaps it was better so. She could take pleasure in a dream child when doubtlessly the real thing was hardly as nice as she thought. She took my going to Europe hard and when by chance she dis-

covered that it might be forever, she was much disturbed. All my pious lies did no good. However, the future is just as dark as ever and I do not know where I shall teach. I rather hope it is America but I am not averse to Rome. What irritates me is to think that no matter where I am, even if very industrious, all my work will be as valuable to humanity at large as your discovery about feline pants.[15]

Father Weigel's doctoral dissertation was a study of the 5th century bishop of Riez, Faustus (c. 408–490). Weigel and Murray in their Woodstock days had worked together on the semi-Pelagian controversy, Weigel on Faustus and Murray on Prosper of Aquitaine.

Faustus, who was probably of British or Breton origin, was a monk at Lerins. He became abbot there in 433 and, in 459, was consecrated bishop of Riez in southern France. At the request of Leontius, archbishop of Arles, Faustus wrote a refutation of the predestinarian doctrines of a certain Lucidus. This work, *De Gratia,* was approved by the Council of Arles (472 or 473) but was later condemned at the Second Council of Orange in 529. Faustus, in his refutation, had adopted a semi-Pelagian position which insisted on the initial free will for the acceptance of that grace even when in sin.

In December, Weigel wrote that in two years he would be the "world's authority on an obscure theologian of Southern France . . . That is like being the World's Champion Hog Caller."[16] The next month he jokingly reported: "I am getting awfully learned. I even add foot-notes to my dreams at night. (I suppose some little American upstart of a theologian will read the book and say that it has all been disproved wrong. Just let him say it in my presence. I'll hurl umlauts at him.)"[17]

During the summer of 1936, Weigel traveled to France to visit the scenes of Faustus' labors and to research archives there. A letter from France indicated the beginning of a disillusionment with study and a restlessness with research that was to characterize the remainder of his life. He had learned little theology in Europe and the life of a scholar seemed futile to him, "writing articles that will never be read and finally publishing a monumental opus which everyone mentions but no one knows."

Looking to the future, Father Weigel remarked that his future was still uncertain. He hoped to return to the States because he disliked the thought of teaching at Rome. "The Roman teacher leads an uninspiring life. He directs too many students to do much work of his own. (My director directed 18 doctors-to-be this year!) The rector of the University told me he would break me in as prof by directing researchers and conducting seminars under the super-vision of an older prof. God help us! Reading theses in Latin, French, German, Italian and English; talking the same languages to uninteresting young hopefuls—ah no!"[18]

During the second year of the biennium, doctoralitis, a com-mon disease among advanced doctoral students, set in fiercely. In December, 1936, he wrote that he was sick of all classes and hated all teachers, "and even if they were good, I wouldn't like them." He was working diligently to finish the dissertation.[19] Yet pessi-mism persisted. Weigel wrote of himself at about this time: "The man you knew is dead beyond recall. Europe has worked havoc with me; body and soul. I belong to the 5th century. The 20th has not yet arrived for me—and it never will."[20] By the end of Febru-ary, 1937, he had completed it and looked forward to some leisure before the defense which he had expected would be in April, but was actually postponed until June. He told Otenasek: "I breathe again."

> It was one of those thankless jobs which does no good to any-one but the writer. I was introduced in the intricacies of method and the rigors of detail. It really makes no difference what has been said because no one is the slightest bit interested in the dark corner I chose for my research. It starts no revolution and there have been no startling revelations that will shake either theology or any other discipline. The thing is so academic and so unim-

portant even from an academic view-point that I shall have great trouble in finding a publisher.[21]

At the defense in June, the jury was composed of Ludwig Hertling, Joachim Salaverri, Clement Fuerst, Heinrich Lennerz and Charles Boyer. All graded it 10 except Boyer who granted a 9. Lennerz, in addition to his commendations, suggested that Weigel should compare the doctrine of Faustus in each of its parts with the doctrine of earlier semi-Pelagians so that the evolution of the heresy might be apparent. Boyer felt the speculative part could use some more profound consideration. He asked that, before publishing, the author make a more emphatic judgment on Faustus' doctrine, especially by more attentively studying the question of *gratia sanans* in Faustus.[22]

Opinions about Weigel's difficulties with the dissertation vary. John Courtney Murray wrote that Weigel had had some difficulties with the examiners of his dissertation. As he recalled it, Weigel "had written the history as it ought to have been, not as it was." To the end of his life this categorical mentality perdured. "History—not to say exegesis—always remained what Gus's scheme of thought required it to be."[23] Others contradict Murray's recollections. John J. McMahon, S.J., who arrived in Rome the year Weigel left there, recalled that it was the second and third sections that caused difficulty because "they smacked of unorthodoxy." A student-friend of Weigel's at Woodstock, Richard Cronin, S.J., remembered Weigel telling him that it was the analytical section of the dissertation that was criticized. The latter is probably correct since it was the historical, not the analytical section which was published after the defense, and Boyer had not been satisfied with the theological analysis of Faustus as presented by Weigel.

Part of the dissertation was finally published in 1938, entitled *Faustus of Riez: An Historical Introduction*. The author promised to produce a new analysis of the doctrines of Faustus at a later date. He claimed to have three distinct drafts of such an analysis at hand, none of which warranted publication.[24] The promised revisions were never completed. Weigel became too involved in his later teaching in Chile to do so.[25] However, in 1940, he did revise and expand the chapter on faith in a journal founded by Weigel, *Anales de la Facultad Pontificia de Teología de la Universidad Católica de Chile*.[26]

Immediately after completeing his dissertation, Father Weigel wrote to Frank Otenasek about his possible future, urging him, once again, to seek happiness over ambition.

> I have been "sold" to the Gregorian. As a matter of fact my own dreams are in terms of the American scene. However, as the result of this "sale" I am indefinitely bound to a Roman University for which I have no great affection. On top of this I discovered yesterday that the University is toying with a plan to "farm me out." The University of Santiago, Chile, is introducing a theological faculty, and it seems that the Gregorian University is to supply exchange professors until a native Chilean faculty can step in . . . Another plan in the minds of the powers that be is to put me into the University Library until they can form a real librarian. In other words, no teaching for some years. Both of these plans leave me quite limp. What value ambition? . . . At all events whatever happens will be for the best. There is a certain work appointed to me to do; it may not coincide with my own ideas, but that is the work that I shall do, and please God, I shall do it. I have known you and I have had my fingers in your soul. Therewith I content myself now and in the future. At least for one short period of my life I have lived. For the rest, my head is bloody—not very—but unbowed. "And if it be a sin to be ambitious, I am the most offending soul alive."[27]

The next month his hopes were higher because he had grounds to believe that he might be returned to the States to teach at Woodstock since one of the professors there had been taken ill quite suddenly and a replacement was needed.

Weigel's hopes for working in his native land did not materialize. According to Father Murray, the faulty analysis in Weigel's dissertation changed his future.[28] Through the arrangements of the Superior General, Vladimir Ledochowski, and Father McCormick,

Weigel was assigned to a chair of theology at the Catholic University in Santiago, Chile. Though he must have been disappointed at this turn of events, one of his friends from those days insisted that he accepted "libertissime!"[29]

August Weigel traveled to Europe in late June of 1937 to meet his son and travel with him through Europe, visiting the place of his own birth and marriage. Weigel was most solicitous for his father during the trip. On July 20 he and his father returned to the States. He visited in Buffalo with his sister whose marriage to Franklin Daigler he had witnessed in 1935.[30]

From Buffalo, Weigel traveled to Baltimore for a reunion with Frank Otenasek. Dr. Francis J. Otenasek and Mildred Buzek had been married in New York City on June 9, 1937. They sent an announcement to Weigel in Rome. Weigel returned it with an "announcement" of his own on the back side: "Gustave Weigel Ph.D., S.T.D., announces his arrival in the United States of America in late July; in anticipation to/of the assumption of the chair in theology at *The University of Santiago, Chile.*"[31]

On August 12, Father Weigel traveled by train to Miami where he boarded a plane for South America. Leaving his homeland again must not have been easy. He had written feelingly about his return from Europe.

"The thought of seeing America again even though for a few days is very sweet. It will he hard to leave, for I know what life in exile means."[32]

As her brother left for Chile, Louise Daigler wept as she had done when he had gone to Rome two years before, thinking as she had then, that they would not see each other again. That was to be true for August Weigel who died on October 6, 1939. He had faithfully written letters to his parents almost weekly since he had left home in 1922. After their deaths, however, Louise found she was lucky to hear from him twice a year, but always, no matter where he was, he would send her a cable on her birthday. Gustave Weigel's first full-time apostolate had begun and he threw himself into it so completely that he practically lost touch with his family and friends in the United States.

Endnotes

1. Weigel to Otenasek, September 15, 1935, and October 13, 1935.
2. Weigel to Otenasek, October 10, 1935 and October 13, 1935.
3. Weigel to Otenasek, October 13, 1935.
4. Edward Coffey, S.J., to Patrick Collins, Rome, December 1, 1971.
5. Vincent A. McCormick to Weigel, Rome, October 15, 1934. WCA II F 303.35v.
6. *One of a Kind*, p. 13; Daigler reflections; Weigel to Otenasek, March 1, 1937, and April 9, 1937.
7. Francis E. Shea to Weigel, Brighton, Massachusetts, October 2, 1935. WCA II F 303.35tt.
8. Daigler reflections.
9. Sister Mary Aquinas Neft, O.S.F., *An Annotated Bio-Bibliography of Gustave Weigel, S.J., 1906–1964*. A dissertation submitted to the faculty of the Graduate School of Arts and Sciences of The Catholic University of America in Partial Fulfillment of the Requirements for the Degree of Master of Science in Library Science, August, 1968, p. 11. Edward Coffey, S.J., mentioned that Weigel was also quite close to him, Tacchi Venturi and Theodore Daigler during his days in Rome. (Edward Coffey, S.J., to Patrick Collins, Rome, December 1, 1971).
10. Edward Coffey, S.J., to Patrick Collins, Rome, December 1, 1971.
11. Files of the Pontifical Gregorian University, researched and copied in Edward Coffey, S.J., to Patrick Collins, Rome, December 1, 1971. Cf. also WCA II F 303.22i and j for notes of classes he had with Pierre Charles, S.J., on Penance and *De Verbo Incarnato*. Sacramental Theology with Edgar Hocedez, S.J., graded 8; History of Theology, XIII century with Francis Pelster, S.J., graded 8; Sociology, with Gustave Gundlach, S.J., graded 9; Religious Psychology, with Alexander Willwoll, S.J., graded 10; Biblical Theology, with Alfredo Vitti, S.J., graded 10 and Missiology with Pierre Charles, S.J., graded 10. His research project was graded 10 by the director, Hocedez. In the 1936–1937 academic year, Weigel studied Sexual Psychology with Francis Hurth, S.J., and Sacred Art with Romano Fausti, S.J. Both were graded 10. Three courses were taken without credit and without grade: Academy of St. Thomas with Francis Gaetani; Church History with Silva Taruca; and *De Corpore Mystico Ecclesia* with Sebastian Tromp, S.J.
12. Interview with Erwin Geismann. Edward Coffey disagreed. He stated that Weigel was basically happy in Rome.
13. Weigel to Otenasek, January 6, 1936.
14. *One of a Kind*, p. 13.
15. Weigel to Otenasek, April 14, 1936.
16. Weigel to Otenasek, December 10, 1936.

17. Weigel to Otenasek, January 6, 1936. Again with humor, Weigel wrote that he had to return to Faustus: "They were as 'nutty' then as we are today. Likewise, they thought they knew it all."

18. Weigel to Otenasek, July 9, 1936.

19. Weigel to Otenasek, December 22, 1936.

20. Weigel to Otenasek, November 28, 1936.

21. Weigel to Otenasek, February 15, 1937.

22. Gustave Weigel, *Faustus of Riez: The Final Evolution of Semi-Pelagianism.* WCA II F 303.13; Neft, op. cit., p. 34; Edward Coffey, S.J., to Patrick Collins, Rome, December 1, 1971, from the archives of the Gregorian University.

23. *One of a Kind,* p. 13.

24. Gustave Weigel, *Faustus of Riez: An Historical Introduction* (Philadelphia: The Dolphin Press, 1938), p. 3.

25. Edward Coffey, S.J., to Patrick Collins, Rome, December 1, 1971.

26. *Anales de la Facultad Pontificia de Teologia de la Universidad Catolica de Chile,* No. 1 (1940), pp. 35-53.

27. Weigel to Otenasek, March 1, 1937.

28. *One of a Kind,* p. 13.

29. Edward Coffey, S.J., to Patrick Collins, Rome, December 1, 1971.

30. Daigler reflections; Weigel to Otenasek, May 25, 1937.

31. Weigel to Otenasek, LeHavre, France, July 1, 1937.

32. Weigel to Otenasek, LeHavre, France, July 1, 1937.

Apostolate in Chile: 1937–1948

In mid-August, 1937, Gustave Weigel arrived in the land he would come to love so dearly. His new assignment was not exactly to his liking[1] but at least it was an escape from being entrapped in a Roman educational and ecclesiastical situation which he detested.

Weigel expected to remain in Chile for perhaps three or four years. Then he thought he would return to the Gregorian University as a professor. Humorously he wrote to Otenasek:

"Oh hell! I wish people would not think me quite so brainy. They would be nearer the truth and I nearer to contentment. However, as you know, I have always held that happiness is not a legitimate ambition."

With less humor but with his usual sense of realism, Weigel told his friend the real meaning of his new assignment as he understood it.

> Let there be no delusions about Chile. My going there is a matter of expedience. Politics motivate the whole appointment and I am merely a pawn in the game. There is no compliment in the matter, for Santiago is not an intellectual center. The Gregorian University had to send someone, and an immature untried prof. whom they suspect of radicalism is a logical choice. They trust me enough to hold up the honor of the Society of Jesus, but they can quickly correct a failure, should there be one. I am decidedly curious just how I am considered at headquarters in Rome. The General—an exceptional man of great capaci-

ties whom one admires—was very nice to me. He gave me a fifteen minute audience without my asking for it. He said kind things— and sent me off.[2]

Gus was quite unprepared for the changes he found his new life required. It is said that, when he heard about his assignment, he and John Murray got out an atlas to see where Chile was.[3] He spoke no Spanish. In his interview with the Superior-General of the Society, Vladimir Ledochowski, the dialogue at the time of the appointment is said to have gone something like this:

Weigel: "They do not like Americans in Chile."

General: "Make yourself liked."

Weigel: "I do not speak any Spanish."

General: "Learn Spanish."[4]

He did learn to speak Spanish, but slowly. One of his students recalled his first appearance in the patio of the College of St. Ignatius. There he was, "the Gringo"—"tall and disheveled, making incredible efforts to make himself understood in a rudimentary Spanish."[5] He later said to his sister, Louise, "I talk Spanish like Ma talked English."

Weigel took up residence with the Jesuit community at the Colegio de San Ignacio. No doubt he was surprised at the comforts of the house. He had expected quite primitive conditions in Chile. One friend had offered him an electric shaver to take with him to his new country and Weigel refused, fearing that they might not have electricity there.[6]

Why had Gustave Weigel come to Santiago? The rector of the Catholic University, Don Carlos Casanueva, had written to the Father General in Rome, telling him of the sad state of affairs in his theological faculty. He asked for "new blood" to be assigned by the General. Weigel was one of those sent to assist the Chileans with their problems.

His primary duties were as professor of dogmatic theology at the University. He taught the tracts that flowed from St. Thomas Aquinas' *Summa Theologica,* Pars III, which included Christology, soteriology and sacraments. Every third year he would offer courses in Oriental theology, religious psychology and Thomistic metaphysics. He also gave courses on Catholic culture at the University. From 1942 until 1948 he served as dean of the theology faculty.[7]

In addition to his teaching at the University, Weigel assumed the position of professor of philosophy and English at the Colegio de San Ignacio, a high school, and teacher of religion at an English-speaking Catholic high school for girls, Villa Maria Academy.[8]

The capacity to communicate which he had hoped he would have when he was at Canisius High School and which he exercised with success at Loyola College stood him in good stead in Chile. He soon won the esteem of clergy and university circles for his vast knowledge, his profundity in philosophy and theology and for his uncommon common sense.

One of his disarming qualities which impressed Chileans was his frankness and simplicity, traits which he attributed to his Alsatian background and to characteristics of North Americans in the Great Lakes region. One of his favorite students from those days, who was sometimes called "Gus' natural child," according to Walter Burghardt, was Juan Ochagavia. He described Weigel as one who avoided empty formality and sought the genuine, the authentic, the meaningful in relating to people. When he encountered phoniness, he could scarcely disguise his ill-feeling. Though this jolted some, Ochagavia saw Weigel's ironic candor as reflective of the ceaseless questions of Socrates who brought into question the false security of Athenians. However, Ochagavia felt "Father Weigel had much more heart and goodness than did the Old Greek philosopher."[9] This is reminiscent of Weigel's own educational experiences as he sat at the feet of Frank Burke who looked upon himself as being "a Socrates gadfly."

Father Weigel's classroom style was reminiscent of his days at Loyola. Debater that he was, he loved to provoke a good discussion that would make the students think out the deeper implications of the problems being considered. Ochagavia remarked that

78

naturally the quick wit and profound mind of Weigel always triumphed in these discussions.[10] His presentations, chiefly in a semi-Latin, full of Spanishisms and Chileanisms, glowed with wisdom, mimicry, humor and human sympathy. His insight into deep questions and his ability to wade through the clutter of academia to the heart of the matter, expressing the core of problems with keenness and clarity, made him especially popular with the students. Though a progressive theologian, he was always careful to be true to Church tradition.[11]

In tributes to Weigel following his death, two of his former high school students in Chile recalled his days with them. One said that he often appeared very tired but would never admit it. His description is vivid:

> He was tall, narrow shouldered, with long arms which ended in large hands, fingers which were stained by cigarettes and were as strong as pliers. His head was small, topped with fine, very fine hair that would remind you of a bird, capable of flying to great heights. As far as features go: strong teeth, a high aquiline nose, but most dominant were his eyes of steel, clear grey eyes; vibrant expressions, with the irony of being carelessly affected, with a penetrating smile and indisputably intelligent.

Although he taught philosophy and English to these students, English usually turned out to be philosophy in disguise. The youths learned to look for "the disinterested truth among perplexing formulas, doing away with prejudice and myth, until we had encountered and confronted stark, naked truth."[12]

Weigel confessed to Otenasek only three months after his arrival that he had the students eating out of his hand. He said he told them all he knew "but in such a way that they think there is much more that I could tell them. It is the old trick and you saw how it works." In the classroom he felt "the old Gus Weigel at work." "One could safely say," he told Otenasek, "that he . . . (Weigel) . . . is content in Chile and that he is willing to stay there if not all his life at least for some years."[13]

Gustave Weigel's philosophical and theological stances were basically Augustinian with the structure of St. Thomas. Ochagavia commented on this paradoxical situation:

> Though his heart was more in tune with the rhythm and fullness of the genius of Augustine the ideal of his intellectual life became the rational and architecturally woven thought of Thomas Aquinas. But he was far from that archaic "Thomism" which returns a thousand and one times to the formulae of St. Thomas as though one were going to contemplate the objects in a museum. St. Thomas was for him much more a quarry to which he would go to find inspiration to face on his own terms the problems of today. In this he always felt the vital Thomism of his two confreres, the French Jesuit Pierre Rousselot, and the Belgian, Joseph Maréchal.[14]

Weigel's treatment of the sacraments was quite in line with the tradition of his day, with one exception. Thesis V in his treatise on the eucharist contains an orientation to the mystical body ecclesiology. For Weigel, the mystical body was identical with the Roman Catholic Church. And his ecclesiology stresses the notion that the reception of the eucharist *physically* incorporates a person into Christ. In the ecclesiology which he later developed at Woodstock, this notion played an important part.

Father Weigel's influence in Chile spread far beyond his classroom and the printed pages of academia. He became involved in the *life* of the people of Latin America. Before discussing some of these involvements, it is important to see what made him so well-fitted for such work. It was simply his personality. He was totally open and available to others. People felt he was so understanding and so human. He went out among the people, shared their lives and became one of them in a way other priests there did not. Only by immersing himself in all the dimensions of reality, he felt, could one elevate them and offer them to God.[15]

Already in November of 1937 he had organized the English-speaking Catholics into a group for monthly Mass in the chapel at the university. Once each week he heard their children's confessions as well of those of some English-speaking nuns. He told Otenasek:

I float about in English and American circles. I lead a strenuous social life. I have dined with many of the "best" local families and have met all the "big-shots" except the president of the Republic, who however, nodded to me quite graciously one day. I doubt if he knew who I was, however. I have met all the members of the cabinet and many of the various ambassadors and I take tea with this gentry at will. (I don't will it as much as you can guess.) The Americans and English of Catholic persuasions come to see me often and I have an old English lady who is preparing for her reception into the church. That in brief is my life here.[16]

His sister, Louise Daigler, agreed that her brother gave of himself freely but "he gave not wisely but too well." She recalled:

Some nights he slept in his clothes—not time to undress. But he loved it all. The rich and the poor adored him. The young and the old clung to him. It was all very simpatico but very exhausting. . . . My father died while he was there. The regular letters ceased and I heard from him seldom. I was jealous of Chile. Hated the place that had consumed him. A bishop from Santiago came to Buffalo and looked me up—Oh, no! Santiago could NOT get along without Father Weigel. Emphatically not. I felt he was being "used" by many. He gave his warm coat to a bum, he gave money to others, he gave his rest, all his time, to the people. He loved going up to the mountains on horseback. . . . He was driving himself but enjoying it.[17]

This human warmth and selflessness showed itself at the university as well as in the community. In addition to his teaching duties, Weigel was a friend to his students as he had been at Loyola College in his regency. His room at the College of Saint Ignatius became practically a "club" where philosophy and theology were debated "in a cloud of smoke." Very often, in order to speak with him in private, it was necessary to ask him to leave his room.[18]

The pressure of his activities—at the University, the Colegio and at the Villa Maria Academy—prevented Father Weigel from spending much time in serious scholarship. He regretted not being able to keep abreast of theological developments. Though he felt uneasy about this, he judged that the urgency of people's problems came first.[19]

Though he was basically an apolitical person, having no innate sense of the *politique,* his interest in people propelled him to become involved in political and social problems in his adopted homeland.[20] Chile was a land suffering from great inequality of wealth. Weigel felt that the Church usually aligned itself with the wealthy and participated in a politico-socio-economic system that made the poor get poorer. He had always been sympathetic to the poor especially since he felt that his hard-working father had never been properly paid. He felt this was a grave injustice, crying out to heaven for vengeance.[21] In Chile, however, Weigel had contact primarily with the middle and upper classes.

Weigel described Chile and its culture as "spotted with something shabby." The homes, even of the best families, were tacky, usually made of mud blocks covered with paint. "The college here," he wrote, "which is one of the oldest and best in the city is an ugly affair, far worse than anything you have ever seen." He described going to dine with some rather poor farmers. He was shocked to discover that someone had already used the napkin he was given.

Politics, he sensed, were corrupt and mainly in the hands of the Catholic conservatives and Masonic liberals. These two groups usually worked hand in hand politically. Neither were willing to develop radical social programs for sharing land with the poor farmers, for raising wages or offering universal education to the lower classes. Younger Catholics, he felt, were developing a deep social spirit but "they lack leadership and a radical program of activity.

The Communists are at work but the material they work with is not promising and likewise they have no real leaders." He judged: "The older Catholic leaders—clerical and lay—are opposed to radical reforms and the younger men, though active are not yet secure as to their objectives and they are inclined to mend measures by compromise rather than by radical reform. I think in general that we can say the Church has failed the people."

The root of the problem was foreign domination. Americans, Germans, French, Syrians and English controlled the natural resources and basic industries as Weigel saw it. Why? "I have yet to meet a learned man here who is a native. The Chilean is bright enough but I think he lacks the capacity of working hard . . . It seems that the Chilean cannot run anything well. He lacks technicians and energy."[22]

Weigel soon made friends with priests and laity who were working to change Chile and the Church's role in it. One of these was Alberto Hurtado, S.J., a socially-conscious young Jesuit who wrote a book, *Es Chile un pais Católico* in which he criticized the Church for its lack of sensitivity to the human problems so evident in their country. Because Hurtado had attacked the comfortable established system, conservatives were enraged. Weigel came to Hurtado's support and they became great friends.[23]

By 1941, Weigel had a rather clear picture of the Church's situation in Chile. "The country is supposed to be Catholic but the Church has not the influence nor strength that she has in the United States." This is true, he said, first of all, because there is a distinction between religion and religiosity in Chile. In the whole nation there was a genuine spontaneous religiosity of a low intellectual content and of a very liberal moral code. But it was not Catholicism. Catholicism had no influence on the majority of the people.

Weigel asked, "Is Chile a Catholic nation? Yes, if by that we mean that it accepts Catholic forms to express whatever religiosity is present. No, if by that we mean that it accepts a Catholic vision of life." The Catholic vision of faith does not always square with the institutionalization of that faith. At times those in charge of the Church organization do not understand or care about the vision, and the institution becomes unbalanced. Yet it is judged, not on its obscured vision, but on its visible and perverted institution. The Chilean Church was much like that, Weigel thought. Its institution was clerically dominated and this created a certain antagonism and anticlericalism toward the Church.

Weigel insisted that the United States needed to win the trust of the Chilean Catholic Church which had assumed an ambivalent attitude toward Pan-Americanism at that time. Why? America is a Protestant country, they thought. Protestant missionaries, with the exception of Anglicans, had tried to convert the Catholic South Americans and this had been resented by the native Catholics. They also feared Americans who had come to the South with clear anti-Catholic prejudices. They lived by "liberal" ways in the United States, ways suspect by the Church in Chile. In criticizing those American Protestants who came south with these offensive tactics and attitudes, Weigel revealed a posture he would later assume in the ecumenical movement.

It is never wise to overlook the positive values in the adversary's position. If these are recognized and admitted, it is usually not difficult to come to terms with the adversary. But if we shoot for his head, it is obvious that he will fight every advance that we make to get at his head.

One of the things the Catholic Church in North America should do to foster Pan-Americanism, Weigel felt, was to send clergy and religious from the North to Latin America by way of experiment as he himself had done. Due to this approach, suspicions were weakening, he said. However, the experiments had not always been felicitous.

Weigel penned an extensive letter, commenting on the Catholic Church in Chile, to Norman Armour, the United States Ambassador to Argentina, whom he had met the previous fall. His observations obviously were grounded in his own "Gringo" experience.

The American priest or nun frequently cannot bear up under the load of restrictions to which he or she must submit. The result is then open friction and the South American Church authorities become confirmed in their suspicion there is something wrong with American Catholicism. However, where the specimen under study had enough sense of humor and enough sagacity to conform in indispensables and go his own way in the rest, the results have been excellent. . . . In all such experiments—and many more must be made—the subject must be carefully chosen. He must have enough flexibility to understand that abrupt changes produce only malaise.[24]

This is an excellent description of the situation the American Weigel was finding himself in at the opening of the 1940s. The tension was growing between him and those Chilean Jesuits who were puzzled by his approach. Yet he was an excellent "subject" because of his ability to be flexible without undermining his principles.

Gustave Weigel's involvements with people concerned about Chile were rather extensive although he himself never became very directly active in national politics. However, he was friendly with the group of Catholics who broke from the Conservative Party to form the Christian Democratic Party. Old politics and older views of religion characterized the membership of the Conservative Party. Progressive Catholics such as Hurtado, Alejandro Magnet (later the Chilean ambassador to the Organization of American States) and Eduardo Frei Montalva (later president of Chile) felt something new was needed. Conservatives sought to have the Vatican impose sanctions on those who became involved with the new party.[25] In 1947, this inter-party fighting caused difficulties at the Catholic University. The vice-rector and several teachers were forced to resign. Weigel too became involved but was not forced to leave.[26]

By late 1946, Father Weigel's views on the Church in Chile had changed somewhat. He was more convinced than ever that Chile was not a Catholic country. It was simply caught up with the Spanish culture which happened to be Catholic in name. To remedy the situation, Weigel said those who truly want to be Catholic in Chile, and he felt there was a strong core of these—these should be catechized. All the Church's efforts should be directed toward them, according to Weigel, and the Protestant gains in South America should not disturb Catholics greatly. The ones converting to Protestantism were "nothing" as Catholics anyway. "If we are not able to attract them to our Church, let them go to the church that they want to. That Protestantism is not a true solution is a sad reality which history will manifest. That Chile will go Protestant is as possible as the U.S. going Shinto."[27]

One of those English-speaking diplomats with whom Father Weigel formed a close friendship was the American ambassador to Chile, Claude G. Bowers. Bowers, years later, recalled that he had been impressed by Weigel's humorous realism and his brilliant and deep mind.

> His eloquence was that of sober thought on fire. His popularity transcended religious lines that divided Catholics and Protestants. He was a prime favorite among the English and Americans. I found him hard to contact quickly, since he hurried from one engagement to another with such rapidity it was difficult to overtake him. He knew most phases of Chilean life intimately and I found him invaluable as a source of information about people and events. Nature had made him a clever diplomat.
>
> During the war I had heard him deliver a sermon, apropos of the times, that impressed me as extraordinary both in substance and phrasing. Since he has a delightful sense of humor and loves a joke, I was surprised to find, apropos of this sermon, that one of my jokes may have annoyed him. At the conclusion of the sermon, a number of people, all friends, were on the veranda of St. George College, where he had preached, and I approached him with the remark, made solemnly, that he had the most remarkable memory of any man I had ever known. He seemed puzzled. The audience drew closer. "Yes," I said gravely. "I followed your sermon closely and you did not deviate one

word from the manuscript as I had handed it to you." The audience laughed. Some time later he told me I should not have said it. Astonished, I reminded him that everyone who heard had a sense of humor and knew I was joking. "Well," he said, "the British Ambassador heard it and the English have no sense of humor." I knew his remonstrance was another joke.[28]

Father Weigel's many friendships with non-Catholics, like Bowers, were occasions for ecumenical involvements. Weigel was always quite at home with those who did not share the Catholic faith, as seems to have been the case ever since his youthful friendship with the Lutheran boy in Buffalo. One of his Chilean friends, Dr. Carlos Eyzaguirre, said that Weigel knew Portestant thought. He considered them to be humans seeking God, but in a different way. Protestants were generally poorly treated by priests in Chile. Weigel's concern and respect for them did not always go over well with the local clergy.[29]

Weigel's sympathy for Protestants caused him to be invited to participate in ecumenical gatherings. One such was an unusual memorial service for Franklin Delano Roosevelt in the Santiago cathedral. The popular United States president had died April 12, 1945, of a sudden cerebral hemorrhage in Warm Springs, Georgia. Chileans were grieved and honored Roosevelt as the great statesman who had had a special friendship for Chile. Weigel gave the eulogy.[30] Bowers commented that it was a most unusual event in Chile to memorialize a Protestant in a Catholic cathedral. The cathedral was crowded with the public and there was a great gathering outside. Weigel preached again at another memorial service arranged by the Embassy in conjunction with the American Society of Chile and the American Women's Association of Chile. It was attended by large numbers from the American and British colonies at Santiago and was held at Santiago College. Bowers claimed the sermon was a masterpiece.[31]

A Protestant service was held in Santiago, too. Weigel was invited to lead a prayer, which he obligingly did. Some Catholics were shocked. They considered it to be *communicatio in sacris*. One such was Monsignor Maurilio Silvani, the Papal Nuncio in Santiago, who reported the matter to Rome.[32] Weigel's protector and personal friend in Rome, Vincent McCormick, apparently defended his action as not being truly *communicatio in sacris*.[33] After all, the service was more of a civic gathering than a Protestant religious service. Yet this action did not sit well with traditional Catholic authorities in Santiago.

Gustave Weigel's early understanding of ecclesiology can be seen in two conferences which he gave to Chilean bishops, probably in 1938. "Though the Church is a society, it is more than that. It is the Mystical Body of Christ. Each member, because he eats Christ's eucharistic body, becomes somehow the Body of Christ himself. Because of this, Catholics are different from all other men. They do their duties not by reason of some written law but by reason of the rules of the Christ life in them."

Weigel's "Church" was, in line with the tradition of that time, heavily hierarchical, finding its fullness in the episcopacy: The Church is the episcopacy and the episcopacy is the Church. Bishops alone are the teachers. Others are simply their delegates. Whereas Christ is the head of the body and "his admirable Mother is its neck, I would suggest that the episcopacy can be seen as the spinal column of this body—according to the teachings of specialists, the spinal column is the prolongation of the brain; it is the most essential part of the body, as it joins the body to its head and all of its parts. It is that part of the body which gives it its characteristic and distinctive form." The bishops, in some way, contain the whole, according to Weigel.

The pope, because he is the episcopate in its concentrated form, holds supreme jurisdiction within the episcopate. "In him the episcopate is fully realized, and as long as he exists, the episcopacy exists fully and perfectly." Bishops are extensions of this fullness of power, though not as delegates of the pope but as the materialization of the same power in a determined and concrete situation.

Weigel's placing of the papacy clearly within the episcopacy was something of an advance over theology of that time. It reflected a view of episcopal collegiality later developed at Vatican II. Yet his view of the relationship between pope and bishops needed more explicitation.

For Weigel the Church was a "splendid miracle," as was mentioned in *Pastor Aeternus,* Vatican I's Constitution on the Church. Yet, in Chile, the miracle was often obscured because of the Church's flaws. But, Weigel insisted, if the Church is Christ incarnate, it will always have flaws. Those who look with bodily eyes alone will see only the defects. But those who see with the eyes of the Spirit can perceive her radiating divine force. Weigel urged the bishops to determine which defects in the Church were too human and to eliminate them. "Holiness in whatever form always excludes that which is 'too human.' " As a theologian, Weigel said he could answer the Church's critics only with theory and abstract words. The bishops, on the other hand, must answer with a living testimony and actual words. "In this," he said, "lies the greatness of your position and the formidable responsibility of your mission."

In the face of "clouds of uncertainty" present in Chile in those days, Father Weigel counseled courage to the bishops who were united in the Spirit.

> This is the courage that we need the most, the courage which sees the nobility and the greatness of putting one stone on top of the other. It is the word which can be said courageously and truthfully by each Chilean Bishop when he is tempted by discouragement, and looks for consolation in human conveniences. "I am engaged in a great undertaking and cannot come down."[34]

Weigel's popularity among Chileans prompted the Coordinator of Inter-American Affairs at the Commerce Department in Washington, D.C., to invite Father Weigel in March of 1944 to lecture on Latin America in the United States. Referring to Weigel as "young, vigorous and enthusiastic," the letter of invitation said that, according to a member of the United States Embassy staff in Santiago, "Father Weigel is certainly one of the greatest assets this country has in Chile . . . and that the American community in Santiago, in general, holds him in high esteem."[35]

In writing to his New York provincial about the matter, Weigel gave a rare reflection on his personal state of being. Out of contact with his province for some time, he at last gave this account of himself.

My Dear Father Provincial:
Your letter arrived and gave me a pleasant sensation; not so much for the content which was certainly pleasant, but for the fact that you wrote it. I often feel that as far as my Province is concerned, I am practically dead. The fault is in great part my own, because I never write to anyone. Let me say a few things about myself, for you ought to know something about your only South American. My health is excellent and I have never been sick—an occasional cold does not count. I am reaching the venerable age of 40—the next birthday makes me 39. I get along beautifully with my local superiors who trust me and like me. Here at the university my position is also excellent. The Rector has absolute confidence in me and my professors all are on my side. Even with the Hierarchy my relations are good. With the local Archbishop I could not stand better and I have been invited to give the priests' retreat three times—once in the Archdiocese of La Serena and twice in Santiago. I have another invitation to go to a southern diocese next summer—your winter. In the last convocation of Bishops, they chose me to give them their day of retreat. I gave it and they were satisfied. Being an American, one or other Bishop and one who is more than mere Bishop or Archbishop, look on me with some doubt, but they respect me and never show any opposition. I have personal faculties in almost all the dioceses and many have given me the faculty to confirm, including the Nuncio. This lovely situation may change over night, so it means very little, really.

I have little or nothing to do with the local government and I do not meddle with politics in any form. I know various political figures and from all I have always received respect, courtesy and kindness. A famous ex-president entered into a contract whereby I could go to his house as soon as I should hear of his illness in order to hear his confession. (He does not use this institution at present.) My relations with the embassy are cordial and extremely active. De facto sum intermediator ex officio—sensu amplio—in rebus ecclesiasticis. I was sent to Quito on a little mission last January. Cum fac. sup.

I love the Chileans and, except for the anti-American group, they like me. I have been very happy here, so happy that I frequently want to leave before this happiness should find a flaw. There is too much work. I am a professor of theology, a professor of philosophy in various institutions, including our college, a frequent lecturer, a parish priest for the English-speaking Catholics, a chaplain to the American nuns, a counselor of hundreds of Chilean youths and a representative of American Catholicism. It is a full life and I am normally very tired. But very, very happy. Spiritual life? Well, with all I do, there is little time left for that, but I fulfill my Easter duty.[36]

Father Weigel's popularity in Chile was not universal, as has been suggested above. Anyone so widely traveled and widely known is bound to have enemies. He represented a kind of priesthood that was quite foreign to the Spanish spirituality of the Chilean Church and the Chilean Jesuits in particular.

In the aforementioned May, 1944 letter to his provincial, Weigel had made reference to an anti-American group who had opposed his appointment as dean of the theology faculty. They were working to get him out. His appointment as dean reflected his successful position within the university, not his relations with the Chilean Jesuits.[37]

His life with the Chilean Jesuits was not easy. He was not about to follow their way of life which he felt kept them away from the people they were to serve. They waited for the people to come to them, according to the Spanish way of ministering. This he had always detested. Weigel went out to the people first. He smoked, drank, told jokes and did not always wear a cassock. At times he would come home late at night and find himself locked out since priests were to be in the house by an early hour in the evening. He would then have to bunk with some friends nearby who offered him a bed anytime he came home too late to get into the priests' residence at the college.[38] Typical Weigelian independence refused to capitulate to the Chilean Jesuit way of life. Throughout his life he resented anyone tampering with his freedom. He knew he was doing the Lord's work, bearing witness to Christianity among the people as best he knew how. That was enough. But it was not enough for his superiors in Chile.

Tensions reached a high level late in 1944. Weigel was aware that they could not rise indefinitely. On September 14, he wrote to his friend in Bogota, Juan Restrepo. This letter is not available but in Restrepo's reply of September 26 it is apparent that Weigel was exploring the possibility of a transfer from Chile. One alternative was for him to become a member of the theological faculty at the Catholic University in Bogota, together with Restrepo. However, Restrepo, who said he held Weigel's friendship "as the dearest thing I have," feared that Weigel's "mannerisms" might be offensive to people of a Spanish temperament, as they had been in Santiago, and Weigel could lose the liberty he had in Chile. The other alternative would be to ask the New York provincial to have him returned to this country. Restrepo feared, however, that that could be a situation in which Weigel would still be "intranquil."[39]

The agony of the divisive situation was tearing Weigel apart and prompted him to write a pointed letter to the New York provincial asking to be removed from Chile. For several years, he said, he had worked and been happy in Chile. But the differing outlooks on life of the Society of Jesus and the Church in Chile had become more than he could bear. The complaint made to Rome against his ecumenical involvements, which had since been settled, and the constant struggle with superiors made the situation impossible. He listed four "judicial reasons" to justify his leaving Chile:

1. Whatever may have been the necessity for my initial coming, today the university has enough equipped doctors in theology to fill the posts I occupy. I am not of this Province.

2. Constant friction between myself and my environment, which with the best of will on both sides, does not diminish, but rather increases.

3. A consequent permanent malaise of spirit which embitters me no end, producing a continuous irritability, which in the long run—perhaps not too far off—will produce a complete collapse.

4. A discontent, which in the present moment, is most acute. . . .

I merely ask that you get me out of here before something happens that will make my removal inevitable. That danger is not just something in the order of the possibles. In my present state of mind, anything is possible.⁴⁰

When his Chilean friends got wind of his feelings, they took steps to see that he would stay with them. Jimenez spoke to the Chilean Vice-Provincial in Santiago, explaining how valuable Weigel was to the country and to the Church, and how disastrous his withdrawal would be. The Bishop of Talca, Manuel Larrain, a close friend of Weigel's, wrote to him in broken English, advising him to stay: "This is your way of the Cross and you have not still arrived to the last station."⁴¹

Nevertheless, the tensions continued to build. Weigel performed his ministry to the people in freedom and the Chilean Jesuits became more irritated and, it would seem, increasingly jealous of his success and popularity.

In 1947, Weigel celebrated his twenty-fifth year as a Jesuit. He had been in Chile for ten years and had made his final solemn profession there on August 15, 1939. On the occasion of his jubilee, many of his friends in his adopted land heaped accolades upon him. Not least of those was Claude Bowers who wrote:

> You have become an institution here in Chile, not only to the members of your faith but to all North Americans without regard

to creed who share in a profound admiration for your great ability as a thinker, your never failing courtesy and helpfulness . . . I hope you enjoy your coming sojourn among our own people but we would all look upon it as a serious misfortune were you not to return.

Toward the end of 1947, in conjunction with his jubilee, Gus Weigel, aided by a collection of 5,400 pesos from his English-speaking friends in Santiago, returned to the United States for a visit.[42]

Part of Father Weigel's reason for going to the United States was to accompany the young son of a prominent, old Chilean family, Manuel Ureta, who had studied under Weigel at the Colegio in 1944. The parents of the twenty-year-old young man had decided to let their son have a look at their northern neighbor and could imagine no better traveling companion than "The Gringo." They too helped to pay his expenses. The Chilean Jesuits urged him to make the trip. With some reluctance, since he felt there was so much work to be done "at home" in Chile, he did leave for the States with the Chilean lad on January 3, 1948.[43] He was supposedly to investigate the university situation in the United States for the Chilean Catholic University.[44]

The first stop was in Panama, then on to Mexico City. After five days there, Weigel and his companion flew to Houston, took a train to Kansas City and then visited a friend of Weigel's at Fort Leavenworth, Kansas. It was on their next stop in St. Louis that Gustave Weigel received the most bitter pill of his life. He received a brief telegram from the provincial telling him that he was not to return to Santiago. Ureta recalled that Weigel became very sad, yet he was controlled. It wasn't until their next stop in Chicago that Weigel broke the news to his young companion. He was visibly angry and puzzled.[45] At Notre Dame, he received a letter from Vincent McCormick, his old friend and patron. McCormick, who had become the American assistant to the Superior General, John Janssens, explained the situation.

94

Our Superiors in Chile do not wish you to return. You are to remain in your Province. Certainly no American Province is going to impose anyone of its members on another Province. The local Superiors carry responsibility for their Provinces or Missions. You have put in some ten years of your life, working hard for the good of the Faculty and the Church down there. You are going to be missed very sorely; there will probably be some protests against your being removed. You will do what you can or need to do, in order to smother them. Obedience will now assign you another field for your activity and the use of the more than ordinary talents that the Lord has given you. Accept the assignment with your usual elan, in the spirit of a devoted religious who seeks only to do the will of God and gives himself whole-heartedly to accomplishing it once obedience points it out.

Superiors do not wish you to return, because they do not approve of your method of conduct. You accepted corrections very humbly, but did not benefit by them. It is not for me to enter into the merits of these charges. It is of course something of a personal sorrow for me to have to think that you did not give satisfaction on all counts and that your religious observance was not what Superiors had a right to demand. I trust to you to correct what needs correction. However, I was quite ready to agree to your return to the Province for other reasons also. I rather believe it will be for the greater good of your spiritual and intellectual development just at this period to change your ambiente and live for a time among those who know you and whom you know. Such an ambiente will supply stimulus not without direction and restraint. Both will be helpful to you. Hence however regrettable may be the causes of your leaving Chile, your return to the States seems to me AMDG. I have informed Fr. Provincial through Fr. Socius that you are to remain in the Province, without giving any reasons. You will be very prudent and kind in all you may say about down there.[46]

From Notre Dame, Weigel and Ureta traveled to Buffalo for a week to see Weigel's sister, her husband, their two children, Mary Louise and Earl. He was seething inside at the way in which he

95

had been sent into "exile." Mrs. Daigler recalled that he had been too many things to too many people in Chile and so his superiors thought it better that he stay in the United States. Though overjoyed to have her brother home again, Louise sympathized with his "hurt" and "livid anger"—"and his anger was something," she said.[47]

The first Jesuit to whom he spoke about this was his old friend from student days, Edwin Quain, who was at Fordham University in New York City. Quain clearly recalled the conversation. According to Quain, Weigel was "extremely upset because his heart was in Santiago and he wanted to stay there. He felt that some of the Jesuits in Santiago had profited by the occasion of his being out of the country to manage the situation to get rid of him." Perhaps Weigel was most hurt because he did not have a chance to close out his deep personal relationships with his many Chilean lay and clerical friends.

Quain was sympathetic to the pain Weigel was feeling. Yet he was so glad to have him back in this country that he urged him to forget Chile. If that was the way he was going to be treated there, Quain said, the Chileans didn't deserve him. Weigel strongly disagreed. With passion, he insisted that he did not want to interrupt his Chilean work. He also said he no longer felt at home in the United States. He had adopted Chile as his home. Quain recalled that Weigel's English showed that he was no longer an inhabitant of this country. Many Spanish idioms came through and he had trouble understanding some of the English expressions of the day.[48]

After about a week of visiting in New York, Father Weigel and Manuel Ureta traveled on to Baltimore where he had a reunion with Frank Otenasek and other Baltimore friends. For a time he lived at Loyola College where he had lived and taught during those happy days of his regency. It was not yet clear what his new assignment would be.

In February he received a letter from the Chilean Vice-Provincial, Alvaro Lavin, who explained why he had had Weigel removed from Chile.

The reasons are brief and almost exclusively for fear of the great "liberty" which you radiate, perhaps innately from your temperament and formation and the lack of adaptation to the many customs and manners of being and working which is [*sic*] ours and which can be dangerous especially because of the influence that your Reverence has due to your great talents and qualities which few others possess. I well know the number of criticisms which will fall on me when I publicize your not returning. I also know very well (and I am saying this sincerely) what they would be able to criticize in Your Reverence and which is not your fault, as there is something natural in your manner of being and education which is distinct from what we have here.[49]

In his reply to Lavin, Weigel showed the magnanimity and depth of spirituality that always made him "larger" than any situation in which he found himself. He was able to focus on the deeper reasons for his exile: jealousy and threat. It revealed, too, the pragmatic vision Weigel had of customs and traditions. All must serve the Christian witness!

Dear Father Provincial:

I suppose that you realize that the person writing this letter to your Reverence feels somewhat annoyed and uncomfortable but that can take care of itself: this letter is not being written through bitterness nor anger. I feel anger towards no one, much less your reverence, for whom I have always had a sincere relationship, even though it has never been that deep. I realize that you are known for your kindness and I think well of you and have no reason to feel the contrary. Even though the letter has arrived from Rome, and it is evident that it is the work of your reverence, my first reaction was to blame someone else and I'm still doing it.

But your letter, kind to say the least and the elucidating mood in which I find myself, has stimulated me to have a conversation with your reverence, which in reality, should have been done a long time ago. This was not possible for several reasons—the principle [*sic*] reason being the lack of cordiality in our relationship. Ever since I came to Chile, a lack of confidence existed between us, even though I suppose you yourself have done nothing about it. I well remember the time that I was standing in the vestibule of the students' dormitories, talking with Livingstone and I can't remember who else, when your Reverence arrived and you sent them to the dining room and you "let me have it" in German. Strange how such an insignificant incident stays in one's memory. It is not your custom to get after people, especially in public. God only knows why you did it that day; maybe you heard something disagreeable during an especially hard day or it could have been that you were spontaneously defending your vision of "Jesuitism" which you inconveniently found threatened in this "rare bird," this Yankee Jesuit.

As your Reverence can see, I am writing . . . without bitterness and resentment, but with all the profound objectivity of which I am capable. I humbly beg that you read what I have to say with patience and with an open mind. I am not defending myself. My case lies in the past, dead and buried. I see no great gain in my returning to Chile to continue my activities in Santiago. I do hope, however, to return to Chile after a long time, to see some of my dear friends, who are the only reason of my feeling badly, this being separated from them and from a country that I have loved and continue to love. Your letter, without wishing it, had a Chilean air about it, plus something new. This something more, and this fills me with satisfaction, is your concern to take away the pain and intranquility for the past. But it was also very Chilean in your suavity, in passing over some truths, for example, instead of saying, as you did in your letter to Rome, that I leave and not return, you told me favorable things for not returning. How Chilean and how gentlemanly!! What are we to learn from the Weigel case? I wish to answer this question. You said in your letter that I have talents that few possess. Another example of Chilean amiability; the truth is that my talents are not rare there! And so my conclusions have the recommendations of my not being the irresponsible nor inept type.

Why did you really throw me out of Chile? According to the letter from Rome and yours, it's not because I am bad, nor lazy, nor an egoist, nor for lack of success in my work, nor for not being a "Jesuit" in the true sense, but for my not being able to adapt sufficiently to the form of being and working of the Jesuits in Chile. According to your letter, it's not really my fault, but because my temperament and education have made me incapable of adapting. I don't know if there are other accusations which are hushed up in the letter and I don't see the possibility of other faults. I accept the prior exposition and I admit that you have given an exact and objective description.

Now comes the analysis of this act and I do hope that it will be of value for your Reverence, because for me it is no more than an academic exercise that will not affect me at all. I didn't adapt. That is true. But, there are some non-Chileans in the Province who have adapted themselves much less than I—and they continue there. Moreover, there are Chileans who have not adapted—and yet they stay on. Why then does there have to be a distinct solution for the Weigel case? For a double reason; one which is hushed up, which frankly speaking, lacks dignity; and the other a valid reason for a Jesuit who is a Jesuit. And the hushed up reason? The subject was, by happy coincidence, in your province and for that reason it was possible to liquidate the point with maximum expediency, economy and psychology and with a minimum of fear and frustration. Your Reverence will be indignant for my saying this, but your very indignation proves the point that this reason can't be talked about and I would recommend that a sincere examination of conscience would bring out that this reason weighed on you in your solution of the case.

Regarding the other reason, what is valid for a Jesuit? A triumphant lack of adaptiveness—Your Reverence has expressed it this way: "Lack of adaptivity produces a harmful effect, greater because of the depth of influence he wields with his great talents held by few others." Really, it wasn't mere lack of adaptation. This can be seen in the tolerance for others' inadaptability, even if they aren't gifted with great talents. You really don't find lack of adaptation in them, but you tolerate them for other weighty reasons; for example, the cost of sending them back to their respective provinces, the impossible practicality of such a method, the positive contribution that they make despite their defects, because this does not have a very harmful effect. But a triumphant inadaptation is intolerable, precisely because it is triumphant. For a Jesuit, this is so common that it is no distinction. A subject who causes trouble and bothers his superior has to go. This is common and a fundamental principle of our life. The superior sends and directs, not only by direct precepts but also by tacit and understood insinuations. The subject obeys and if with fault or without fault he does not obey, you have to liquidate him in the most charitable form possible. I am completely in agreement with this. This is how the Company of Jesus has always been and thus has been able to render great service to the Church and to souls, A.M.D.G.

For this I recognize your right and clear duty in asking that I do not return. And for this reason I do not complain. But this puts a grave responsibility on your Reverence, that you cannot excuse a person for reasons of his formation and accepted traditions. I had to leave, not for inadaptation but because the inadaptation by its success was a very powerful criticism of the Jesuit's manner of being and working in Chile. Such a criticism can be harmful in that it can produce an immediate response in us and in the people with whom we work. It could be that the best solution at a given moment is to suppress the root of the criticism. Whether or not it is the best, I don't know and neither does your Reverence, but being the superior, you had to resolve the concrete case immediately and, as the subject, I have to accept the solution. But as for the criticism, it merits your thorough consideration as it is your duty to guide the activities of the regiment in the continual and actual battle for the Greater Glory of God.

If my activities in Chile were successful, who can negate such an evident work? Therefore my methods were rational, or better said, adaptable to this end. If the Jesuit's manner of being and working do not permit the use of such methods (with the supposition that they were morally good) then it is the Chilean

100

way that is not adaptable to the end. Then it is the duty of the Jesuit superior to change this manner, not only with prudence, but with courage. This duty is not to defend nor maintain traditions which were justified at their inception, and to promote the maximum of success for the works of service for the Church and for souls. This idea is completely Ignatian because St. Ignatius fought traditions all through his life, traditions good in themselves and for other times, but which he considered obstacles for a fruitful work. Perhaps it is wrong to console myself with this reflection that our Holy Father confirms the solution of your Reverence, because one should defend the authority of the superiors; but it does make sense out of my way of thinking.

From the time that your Reverence entered the Company until today, the manner of being and working of the Company in Chile has changed greatly. It is enough to compare Jesuit activities in Chile with those of Peru. They will continue to change. In 50 years it will be seen why Weigel had to leave Chile. Your Reverence will not be able to evade this evolution. I cannot give enough thanks to God for the charity and understanding which has been given generously, delicately and humanly by my superiors that they have received me with much love. And laugh if you will. I admire that they have put up with letting me be among the Latins for nearly eleven years, which is a record among us!—and don't forget that this speaks equally or more eloquently on the part of the Latins.

I will finish this long letter with a petition and an offer. The letter from Rome insists that I do not speak badly of Chile and that I help the superiors there keep the calm in my case. Actually, I cannot speak badly of Chile—I love it too much. As for the superiors, the best I can do is to do nothing . . . There will soon be a thousand fantastic explanations about my leaving, around which there will surely be a certain amount of truth—but I am not responsible for any of these explanations. So, I do not wish to be accused falsely to Rome, and I hope that your Reverence will defend me in such a case. The offer that I am making is that if you need anything that I can do, I am at your orders. Ask without fear. As for the rest, thank you for everything.[50]

Weigel's Chilean friends began to react immediately to his dismissal. Julio Jimenez, who eventually took Weigel's place on the university faculty, wrote to the Superior General in Rome, pleading that Weigel was indispensable for the university work.[51] The Cardinal Archbishop of Santiago, Jose Mario Caro Rodriquez, also wrote to the Father General praising Weigel and regretting his departure. He stated that Weigel had performed his duties "with singular ability" and that "he was highly esteemed and appreciated by the professors and students and by the Board of Directors of the University and in general by all the social classes in our country."[52] Carlos Casanueva, the rector of the university, was surprised and crushed by the move since Weigel had promised to remain until the end of his term as rector. He, too, sought to contact the General but Lavin advised against this "given the circumstances and the customs" of the Society of Jesus.[53]

By early March of 1948, word of Weigel's departure began to reach outside the university and the Jesuit community. In a letter addressed to Vincent Keelan, Weigel's provincial, Claude Bowers begged that his friend be allowed to return to Chile where he was so greatly admired and appreciated among all peoples.[54] In reply the New York provincial, John J. McMahon, assured the ambassador that Weigel was more needed in the United States than in Chile.[55]

On March 28, *El Diario Illustrado*, a Santiago daily newspaper, published an editorial tribute to "The Gringo" which makes no mention of the intrigue involved in his reassignment.

> By knowing him we have learned to esteem much that is valuable in the North American character: his love of the truth, his manly frankness and his criticism of some rules and his anxiety to better them. Those of us who saw him in action can appreciate the vehemence of his noble desires, which did not always agree with our own sluggishness.
>
> Typically Saxon, he often became irate with our constantly putting things off till tomorrow. And he was accustomed to manifest his thoughts with sharp sallies.[56]

By April 6, however, the popular Santiago magazine, *Ercilla,* carried a story of the intrigue entitled: "Phantom at Catholic University: Dispossession, Expulsions and Resignations." It accused the Chilean hierarchy of unjustly removing eight university professors, including the vice-rector, Panchito Vives Estevez; the future president of Chile, Eduardo Frei Montalva; and Weigel. The article alleged that this was part of the Church's continuing effort to stifle the movement toward socialism.[57]

Six days later the National Catholic Action Board of Chile responded to the charges of the magazine. They insisted that Weigel's withdrawal was the work of his own Society and had nothing to do with his university assignments. It is "totally false," they added, that he lost his posts "due to his socialistic tendencies."[58]

During his first months back in the States, Gus Weigel was given no assignment. Brooding at Loyola College and St. Ignatius Church in Baltimore, his bitterness and inner turmoil increased, though he did not allow this to surface publicly. It did come through in a letter written to Alberto Hurtado on May 10.

> My dear Alberto:
>
> The reason why I write to you in English is not that I cannot or do not wish to write in your tongue. It is merely because I know that anything that I write to Ours down there is opened with care and diligently read before it reaches the person addressed. They will not understand in this tongue and they trust you sufficiently to give you my letter.
>
> As the months go by I am getting worse. I long only to be down there and all my thoughts are directly toward the south. The point is this: was an injustice done or not? Secondly, what are we going to do about this injustice? To be told that the Lord Abbot laments my absence is just silly. Not only that; it is insulting. If he regrets that I am gone, then, why in heaven's name did he send me away? He was not forced to listen to the man who runs the noviceship. I receive letters from my superiors down there, the men who expelled me from their houses, and they tell me that I have charity, or so much charity, and that I have

the apostolic spirit, and that my apostolate was successful. It was too successful because since my way of life was so different from the consecrated traditions of down there I was a temptation to our young men to depart from those holy customs. Now, I ask you, what is demanded of a good Jesuit? I think it is that he have charity and that he be apostolic and that he exercise his apostolate at the orders of the superiors. I do not claim that I was so good as all that, but they tell me that I was just like that. If this is true, wherein lies my awful sin? Are our heads here to defend anachronistic traditions which are melting away before our eyes, or are they to make effective apostles? If the Lord Abbot cannot see that he has made a great mistake, he can see nothing—nor will he be justified because the boss of the noviceship gave him such counsel, and he will be much less justified because of his personal dislike for me. It is useless for him to deny such a thing and more than useless for you to try to tell me that what I say is false.

Let us have one thing clear in our minds. You always insisted that I was an intelligent fellow. How intelligent I am is something that I do not know, but at least I am intelligent enough to be able to see facts. My character does not allow me to hide the truth from myself and from others. I tell the truth—and therefore I am "imprudent"—the greatest of all sins in one of Ours. The fact that hundreds of people in your city are at present without a guide whom they badly need, and without whom they will cease to be the Catholics that they were, seems to be something of no consequence. This may be Jesuitical but it is not human.

Now I want you to be honest and sincere. No more letters like the one that you sent me. I want a letter from you, but if your interest is to console me by being sugary or by defending the thing done, I would rather not have the letter. You know how I am—intelligent enough to see through all that. It is completely silly to speak of my going to Chile for the summer vacation. It costs too much. Likewise, how on earth would superiors give me that permission when they know that I am a *persona non grata* down there? Either I return to Chile soon while my love for those people is still ardent, or I never go back at all. There is much work to do here and work that is pleasing to me. With time I shall forget the persons whom I loved and the thought of going back to all the heartaches and obstacles of that country will be repellent. Therefore all question of returning is now or never. To which your good Jesuitical heart answers—never, oh never.

You see that I am very bitter and you *paga el pato*. The dirty thing that was done will never be right as far as I am concerned. God in His own wisdom knows what He is doing and I have faith in Him—but only God can make good come from evil. The men who do the evil must pay, even to the last centavo. I am not interested that they pay; I do not wish to see them suffer. I have suffered too much in this whole question and I have no desire that others go through all this.

May God bless you in your work. Pardon me for writing to you so bitterly—but I had to say something; I cannot keep all this inside forever. You can do me much evil by betraying my confidence in you, if you divulge what I have written. If according to your Jesuitical training it is A.M.D.G. and right to do this evil, well, so be it.[59a]

Very sincerely yours,

GW

Weigel had written to McCormick, in answer to the painful letter telling him he was not to return to Chile. Unfortunately that letter is not available. McCormick's reply, however, is extant. Written on the same day Weigel wrote to Hurtado, it counseled a spiritual approach to the whole ugly matter.

More than a month has passed since your letter came in answer to mine and my intention to write you at once went the way of so many other good intentions, leaving you too much alone in a moment of real trial and perhaps bewilderment. Thus God hastens our souls and draws us to lean more heavily on Him.

It is not true that my position prevents me from deploring the manner in which you were relieved of your work in Chile.

My immediate reaction, emphatically expressed, was that the method used was indeed deplorable and offensive to a Jesuit who is seeking only to do the will of God, when and where He wishes it. But there were palliating circumstances, it was explained. Because of your influence down there and the high respect in which you were held by so many persons of authority, it was feared that obstacles might have been placed in the way of Superiors carrying through their wishes. No doubt all wanted to do what they thought best. The trouble was not in the will. Let it be. What was feared, came to pass; for some did express their intense regret when informed that you were not to return. The very successes registered become the occasion of suffering and internal struggle. That has done you no harm. One period of your active life has closed. From all accounts, it has been productive of great good. You did a fine job and many appreciate it. Time will tell us more of it, and of its worth.

Now you begin activity in the home country. It will take awhile to orient yourself. Once you receive your assignment give yourself and the best that is in you to the new work. Forgetting the things that are behind, stretch forward . . . and day by day let Christ take firmer hold of all your troubles and ambitions and eager desires to accomplish great things for his glory. Praeclara de illo speramus.[59b]

Gustave Weigel's days in Chile were at an end but what he had done there continues to this day, both in the religious and the politico-social realms. In the fall of 1948, he was honored by the Chilean government decorating him as "Officer" in the Order "Al Merito," an award for foreigners who contributed to the cause of Chilean freedom and welfare.[60] The Father General of the Jesuits acknowledged Weigel's great honor.[61] Two years later, Senator Millard Tydings of Maryland, speaking before Congress, lauded Weigel's Chilean work.

"Unlike many North American residents in a South American capital, he understood that his vocation required that he know and like the Chileans, not simply the socially-conscious members of the

106

English-speaking colony in his community. Dr. Weigel became an adopted son of the Republic."[62]

Juan Ochagavia, who knew Weigel's work so well, wrote of his friend's lasting influence in Chile:

"Throughout his courses and conferences, he stamped his personal mark on an entire generation of our country's clergy, communicating to it his spirit, which was open to progress, realistic and hardworking. Many of the qualities that have signalized the bishops of Chile during the (Vatican II) Council reflect the judgments and ways of seeing things that Father Weigel passed on to those fortunate enough to have been his students.[63]

Weigel, never much impressed with "honors,"[64] began to forget the things of the past. As the tributes rolled in, Gus tried to cope with his natural bitterness, to readjust to life in his native land and at his *alma mater,* Woodstock College.

Endnotes

1. Juan Ochagavia, S.J., "The Gringo," *Catholic Mind,* LXIII, June, 1965, p. 23.

2. Weigel to Otenasek, LeHavre, France, July 1, 1937.

3. Ochagavia, *op. cit.,* p. 23.

4. Neft, *op. cit.,* p. 23.

5. Ochagavia, p. 20.

6. Julio Jimenez, S.J., to Sister Olga Neft (Neft files), hereafter referred to as Jimenez reflections.

7. *Ibid.* There are no records of Weigel's Chilean assignment in the Archives of the Curia Praepositi Generalis in Rome according to a letter to the author from Vincent T. O'Keefe, S.J., November 11, 1971. Cf. also interview with John Courtney Murray, S.J., June 15 and 17, 1967 (Neft).

8. Ochagavia, *op. cit.,* p. 24.

9. Ochagavia, *op. cit.,* p. 21.

10. *Ibid.,* pp. 22–22.

11. Jimenez reflections.

12. Herbert Muller, "Father Gustave Weigel, S.J.," *El Mercurio,* Santiago, January 12, 1964.

13. Weigel to Otenasek, Santiago, November 10, 1937, and November 15, 1937.

14. Ochagavia, *op. cit.,* pp. 22–23.

15. *Ibid,* pp. 23–24.

16. Weigel to Otenasek, November 10, 1937.

17. Daigler reflections.

18. Ochagavia, *op. cit.,* p. 24.

19. *Ibid,* p. 24.

20. Interviews with John Courtney Murray, S.J., and with Mildred Otenasek.

21. Daigler reflections; Interview with Erwin Geismann, November 4, 1971.

22. Weigel to Otenasek, Santiago, November 10, 1937.

23. Alejandro Magnet, *El Padre Hurtado* (Santiago: Editorial de Pacifico, 1954), p. 223.

24. Weigel to Norman Armour, Santiago, November 24, 1941. WCA II F 303.

25. Reflections of Jaime Guzman (Neft files).

26. Magnet, *op. cit.,* p. 320.

27. Weigel to Humberto Munoz, Santiago, November 14, 1946. WCA II F 303. 35z.

28. Claude Bowers, *Chile Through Embassy Windows* (New York: Simon and Schuster, 1958), pp. 254–255.

29. Carlos Eyzaguirre to Patrick Collins, Salt Lake City, December 3, 1971.

30. Claude G. Bowers to Secretary of State in Washington, D.C., Santiago, April 21, 1945, pp. 1–4. WCA II F 303.35p. The entire text of Weigel's eulogy of Roosevelt is in this memorandum.

31. Bowers, *op. cit.,* p. 255; WCA II F 303.34p.

32. Jimenez reflections.

33. Vincent A. McCormick to Weigel, Rome, January 17, 1948. WCA II F 303.35r; Jimenez reflections.

34. WCA II F 303.24d. Two updates talks to Chilean bishops.

35. Walter T. Prendergast to Paul A. McNally, S.J., Washington, D.C., March 22, 1944. Archives of the New York Province, Society of Jesus.

36. Weigel to James P. Sweeney, S.J., Santiago, May 4, 1944. Archives of the New York Province of the Society of Jesus.

37. *Ibid.*

38. Interview with Edwin Quain, S.J.; Ochagavia, *op. cit.,* p. 24.

39. Juan M. Restrepo to Weigel, Bogota, September 26, 1944. WCA II F 303.35kk.

40. Weigel to McQuade, Santiago. WCA II F 303.35jj. This letter in the Weigel papers is undated. It may not have been sent.

41. Manuel Larrain to Weigel, Santiago, undated. WCA II F 303.35d.

42. Claude Bowers to Weigel, Santiago, July 28, 1948. WCA II F 303.34p.

43. Interview with Edwin Quain, S.J., and with Sister Cleophas Costello, R.S.M., and with Manuel Ureta.

44. Jimenez reflections; Interview with Edwin Quain, S.J.

45. Interview with Manuel Ureta.

46. Vincent A. McCormick to Weigel, Rome, January 17, 1948. WCA II F 303.35r.

47. Daigler reflections.

48. Interview with Edwin Quain.

49. Alvara Lavin, S.J., to Weigel, Santiago, February 16, 1948. WCA II F 303.35e.

50. Weigel to Lavin, undated. WCA II F 303.35e.

51. Jimenez reflections.

52. Jose Maria Cardinal Caro Rodrigues to Father General, Santiago, February 20, 1948. WCA II F 303.35pp.

53. Carlos Casanueva to Weigel, Santiago, February 26, 1948. WCA II F 303.34v.

54. Bowers to Vincent Keelan, S.J., Santiago, March 5, 1948.

55. McMahon, S.J., to Bowers, New York, March 18, 1948. (Archives of the New York Province of the Society of Jesus).

56. Pedro Urquieta, "Father Weigel," *El Diario Illustrado,* Santiago, March 28, 1948.

57. *Ercilla,* April 6, 1948, p. 11.

58. *The Daily Illustrated,* Santiago, April 12, 1948, p. 1.

59a. Weigel to Hurtado, Baltimore, May 10, 1948. WCA II F 303.34vv.

59b. Vincent A. McCormick to Weigel, Rome, May 10, 1948. WCA II F 303.35r.

60. Felix Nieto de Rio to Weigel, Washington, D.C., October 27, 1948. WCA II F 303.35bb.

61. John J. McMahon to Weigel, New York, December 9, 1948. WCA II F 303.35t.

62. *Congressional Record,* April 1, 1950, pp. A-2857-2858.

63. Ochagavia, *op. cit.,* p. 23.

64. Carlos Eyzaguirre to Patrick Collins, Salt Lake City, Utah, December 3, 1971.

The Woodstock Professor: 1948-1964

Starting life anew is not an easy task for anyone. Gustave Weigel found his first year back in the United States extremely difficult. He had felt he was engaged in a great undertaking in Chile and that he should not "come down" from that task of putting one stone upon another, as he had once exhorted the Chilean bishops.

Yet Weigel was a deeply spiritual man who looked for God's hand in the mysteries of everyday life. He knew that God often writes straight with crooked lines. Though he felt his exile from Chile had been the most "crooked" line of his life, he continued to look for the designs of Providence. Perhaps something he had said in his address to the Chilean bishops served as a lamp to enlighten those first dark days back in the States.

> The actual moment has its own rules which man does not understand. The valiant man is the one who acts when the moment presents itself. There are many geniuses and outstanding men who are not known because they were not ready to take advantage of the moment . . . The poet Milton . . . says in a poem of great depth, that they also serve who only stand and wait. We should never lose our spirit, because there is a great divine plan developing in our activities.[1]

One "actual moment" for the "great divine plan" in Weigel's life came through the intense personal suffering caused him by his removal from Chile. As he would say years later, however, that

110

forced return to the United States was "a providential act of God." His work in Chile had drained him physically and mentally. His scattered life there did not allow him to produce things of greater theological value to which he felt called. Now he felt a need for study and reflection in order to answer the great problems with which the present-day Church was faced. As Juan Ochagavia, one of his Chilean friends, recalled, he laughed at his days in Chile when he ran hither and yon, speaking about everything from theology to the flowers on the Alps.

Friends in the States surrounded him to heal his "broken heart." According to John Murray, 1948 was spiritually perhaps the most difficult year in his life. Murray, who had not communicated with his old friend since they had parted in Rome in 1937, only gradually came to know of the "substantive and procedural injustice" Weigel had suffered. Not being the "cry baby type," Weigel was most reluctant to discuss the affair with his friends at Woodstock. Murray said his greatest problem was not that of "bidding the past goodbye," but rather that of finding himself in the present. "He was at a loss—in fact, lost."[2]

During those early days back in the States, he frequently complained of being tired. A doctor's examination uncovered no organic problem. The doctor told him, "You don't need sleep. The trouble is that you refuse to face this new reality."[3] The uncertainty of his future must have plagued his mind. Father John J. McMahon, the New York provincial, suggested to Weigel that he assume the post of *socius,* assistant to the provincial, but he wasn't interested.

At first his interests continued to be directed southwards, toward his adopted land. Father Walter Burghardt, S.J., recalled that he first met Weigel at Mt. St. Agnes College in Baltimore shortly after his return. He was giving a vivid lecture on the geography, culture and religion of Chile. Burghardt detected no bitterness in Weigel's public remarks or tone, which gives some substance to Murray's claim that Weigel was no "cry baby" about his problem. Weigel's

111

writings immediately after returning also centered on Latin America. His heart was still there.[4] His first article appeared in *Theological Studies,* edited by Murray, in December 1948. In April of the next year, he delivered several addresses on Latin America.[5]

Father Weigel's longing for Chile lessened, however, as he began to find himself "at home" at Woodstock. There had been no opening for him on the forty-two-member faculty to teach theology, so, in the fall of 1948, he was assigned to teach cosmology, German and special disciplines. He was also appointed an examiner of the students and a *censor librorum.*[6]

Cosmology was not exactly Weigel's favorite interest; in fact he could not have cared less about it.[7] It was, however, a chance for him to lead students in the quest for truth and he began with vigor. He had had his philosophical tools sharpened the previous spring, when, in residence at Loyola College, he gave some lectures in philosophy. He used no text but simply went in his own direction, often leaving some of the slower students lost in the complexities of his thought.

A young Baltimorean, David L. McManus, was passing the classrooms at Loyola that summer and heard a virile voice boom out: "There are no atheists. Those we call atheists are fighting and arguing against false images of God, but on analysis, not the idea of God . . ." McManus, a Loyola College student, was intrigued and returned again and again, though he was not registered for the course. Weigel noticed him, as he did all bright students in his teaching career, and struck up a conversation with him. He asked McManus if he were interested in "The Real." "Yes" was the reply. This encounter was the starting point of a friendship that appeared to equal Weigel's deep relationship with Frank Otenasek.[8] McManus and Otenasek were often referred to as Weigel's "natural sons," though the latter always kept the title, "first-born."[9]

That summer McManus rode his motorbike to Woodstock nearly every other day. In the fashion of Socrates, sharing wisdom with his chosen pupil, Weigel expounded on Plato. This was education in the European mode, with personal communication between teacher and student. "I'd get out there in the morning," said McManus, "and we'd go over what I'd read, have lunch and then go down to the quarry for a swim. Then we would talk some more and I would go home." The next summer they studied Aristotle together.[10]

In the fall of 1948, Weigel began his classes in cosmology at Woodstock.[11] The Jesuit philosophy students were swept up by the "breath of fresh air" that began to change life at the Maryland house of studies.[12]

Weigel was eclectic as a philosopher, borrowing from sources which suited his *Weltanschauung*. This drew criticism from professional philosophers. Some claimed his philosophy lacked depth; others that it had too many loose ends; and still others that it was contradictory. But those who appreciated Weigel's philosophical positions were aware that it was his unique view of reality that allowed him to be the open-ended person that he was.[13] It was a combination of Platonic and Augustinian epistemology.[14]

One can easily be confused when reading Weigel's philosophy. Although he was a Platonist at heart,[15] he wrote and spoke with an overlay of Thomism which he had come to appreciate through Maréchal's transcendental method. Weigel's Platonism, therefore, was expressed in Aristotelian form. Yet Norris Clarke, S.J., recalled Weigel saying once that he "vomited Aristotle out of his intellectual mouth."[16] Aristotle was too abstract and ignored the intuitive, thought Weigel. "Man has a potency—obediential—for an intuition of God. . . . Thomistic epistemology puts a definite 'intuitus' at the heart of the judgment."[17]

For Plato, Augustine and Weigel, universals are not abstracted from the concrete. They are immediately intuited. Like Plato, Weigel founded them ontologically through the doctrine of participation. The ideas are real. In his cosmology, Weigel taught that the hylomorphic theory was not proved but arrived at by intuition. This caused his cosmology students some trouble in their ex-

113

aminations because the examiners did not hold to his explanation and were not aware that Weigel was so teaching. Weigel called this metaphysical intuition.[18]

Norris Clarke, S.J., who began teaching existential Thomism at Woodstock at that time, clashed with Weigel on philosophical matters. Influenced by Suarez, Weigel held that all possible ideas had an existence. Weigel's explanation was that this was an "exhalation of possibles" from the Divine Mind eternally and with necessity. This did not satisfy Clarke. He felt this left a metaphysical impossibility and was consistently Platonic. For Clarke, this exhaling the being of possibles from the Divine Mind without the mediation of the Divine Mind itself was a "metaphysical monster."

Weigel, in turn, did not approve of Clarke's input at Woodstock. He resented Clarke's poisoning the scholastics' minds with existentialism. Weigel wrote to Clarke, stating that he had released the "irrational id" through his existential Thomism. Existence, according to Weigel, was added on to the essence which was real. Existence was the "irrational" and was to be feared. For him, if something could not be conceptualized, it escaped rationality; its essence could not be grasped.[19] Sister Cleophas mentioned that Weigel distrusted existentialism because it lacked a metaphysic.

There seems to be a consensus that Weigel was not a systematic philosopher. McManus said he could not have been a philosopher in the true sense at all because he was not searching for the answers. He knew all the answers from Catholic doctrine and only used philosophy to justify what he believed by faith. For him there were no "open questions" as there must be in philosophy, yet Weigel was convinced that he *was* a philosopher because he could grasp "The Real." It is probably correct to say, with Arthur Madden, that Weigel, though not a philosopher, used philosophy for his own purposes.

Weigel's "breath of fresh air" in Woodstock's philosophy faculty was definitely a break in the tradition. He felt that things were too tight and too tied to past ways. His intention was to loosen up the tradition and make people think rather than merely to memorize.[20] Yet to the "fresh air" of existential Thomism he was quite closed.

One of those who took Weigel's course in cosmology in his first year at Woodstock was John Giles Milhaven who said: "He made me think more than anyone I ever had, and the kind of thinking he stimulated in me brought me to more insights . . . than any other teacher came near to doing." He recalled that Weigel's flair, colorful expression, vivid and provocative descriptions and great sense of humor immediately made him extremely popular and successful among the students, though some did claim they felt he was "superficial."

Insight for Weigel was as Plato had described it, "a sort of spark that flashed out after much discussion and questioning and rubbing of words and arguments back and forth together, but was not anything that could be expressed in words." It was in dialogue and the give-and-take of deep discussion that these intuitions emerged. That, Milhaven felt, is why Weigel loved to discuss and play with words, infuriating people in order to make them think more deeply. In this dialectic, intuition was born and insight was gained.

Weigel taught him also that the insight of the intellect had basically little to do with sense experience. Insight "basically comes from the dynamism of the mind and the drive of the person." Insights cannot be easily verified nor can they be systematized or expanded. "There is just a way of saying it over and over again, as Plato does."

As Milhaven said:

There was no way except to set up the situation for the spark to fly, but there was then, no way for verifying or corroborating it in any kind of a simple factual objective or verbal way. The only way possible of verifying it . . . was converging with others who had perhaps gone through that same experience and had the flashing of the spark. There was a sharing and a strengthening and a broadening of the insight.

Milhaven also recalled that Weigel had little use for American pragmatism and existentialism. Notions of the relativity and historicity of thought such as Bernard Lonergan or Avery Dulles propose today would have shocked Weigel, according to Milhaven. His philosophy paid lip service to the empirical, the pragmatic and the historical but was basically quite essentialist.[21]

Gustave Weigel's teaching of philosophy extended beyond the confines of Woodstock College. Between 1955 and 1961, he, together with Sister Cleophas and Arthur Madden, initiated a summer Philosophy Institute for female religious.[22] Between 1955 and 1956, he taught courses in epistemology, metaphysics and religion at Fordham University during the summer sessions.[23] According to Burghardt and Quain, these were basically the same courses taught under several different headings. They were whatever the professor wanted them to be.

Philosophy was not, however, Weigel's primary interest. He was a theologian by training and by temperament and the teaching of cosmology and German literature in the 1948–1949 academic year were merely stop-gaps. As Murray put it, "in 1949 he was stripped of all distinction; he was no longer a name. And he needed to be a name, not out of personal vanity, of which he was devoid, but simply because he was himself, conscious and confident of his powers."

As editor of *Theological Studies,* Murray was able to make a concrete suggestion. Needing a specialist in Protestant theology, he suggested that Weigel could focus on that for his journal. Since no other American Catholic theologian had taken up that field, Weigel could become the expert. Murray reported that "he plunged into the area with mounting zest." There was no significant American ecumenism at that time. Weigel, more than anyone else, initiated the change.[24]

After one year of teaching cosmology, a position opened in the

Woodstock theology department. Father Joseph Bluett had been transferred, leaving vacant a position in fundamental theology. Specifically, there was need for someone to teach the tract *De Ecclesia* to the first year theology students. Though Weigel would probably have preferred to teach a course on grace[25] or on the sacraments which he had taught in Chile, he undertook the new tract with his accustomed enthusiasm and drive. In that same year, 1949, Weigel was appointed to teach a course in Oriental questions, something he had been deeply interested in since his days at the University in Santiago. During the 1951 and 1952 academic year, Weigel was assigned to teach the tract *De Actu Fidei* to the first year theologians.[26]

Gustave Weigel was, above all else, a theologian. It was in this discipline that he was professionally trained and it was as a theologian-among-men that he made his greatest contribution to the Roman Catholic Church in transition. Theology was, for him, "the science of the real."[27] It was a difficult discipline for beginners because they bring much common sense to the undertaking and become discouraged when they discover that the discipline presumes no common sense but insists on demonstrating everything.[28]

The data of theology is "all reality." The particular point of view adopted is that of "reality as revealed to us by God." The data are reduced "to the categories used by the teaching of the living Catholic Church." And the sources for the data are numerous: 1) the teachings of the episcopate, past and present; 2) the Scriptures as understood by the Church; 3) the consensus of theologians accepted by the Church, especially the Fathers; 4) the liturgy of the Church; 5) the laws of the Church; 6) the living faith of the Catholic people, "in as far as it is indicated by a consensus."[29] Philosophy, personal revelations, scientific findings or personal religious experience were not, for Weigel, sources of theology. Weigel was aware that theology could "use" other sciences. Yet these were not theology, but tools for theologians.[30] Nor could theology truly be biblical, mystical, liturgical or patristic. So he said,

"There is certainly a place for these but it will always be inadequate."[31]

Weigel tended to treat Scripture also as a theological tool. Those who studied under him and who taught with him at Woodstock generally felt that, although he had some understanding of the new historical-critical method used in scriptural studies, he was not truly conversant in this field. Francis McCool, S.J., the New Testament professor, believed that, for Weigel, Scripture was ultimately unimportant since it was the Church's teaching that was crucial. Weigel felt the Church could go on without the Bible, according to Dulles. Scripture was "decorative" to the magisterium since the Church, knowing revelation by introspection, could interpret it. Scripture was seen as a tool of the magisterium.[32] Despite the "ground work" scripture technicians would do, the problems ultimately had to be handled by theologians. McCool felt this represented a Catholic rationalist position. George Glanzman, former professor of Old Testament at Woodstock, judged that Weigel was not concerned enough about historical detail to appreciate the painstaking work being done by modern exegetes. He interpreted the text to suit his own purposes. He was basically analytical in his approach and, if facts didn't always fit into the analysis, they were not of ultimate importance.

Weigel made it quite clear that theology is not faith. Theology is faith's discipline. As he said in one public lecture, "I still live the faith I learned from Sister Claudia in fourth grade; my theology had nothing to do with it."[33] However, he doubted that one could be a theologian and not be a believer. Personal sanctity helped the process of theologizing.

Each theologian forms his personal synthesis, according to Weigel. In doing so, he may err and be condemned by the Church. "There has been no theologian of great renown who has not taught propositions which the Church at a later date rejected."[34] As Weigel once told a student, you know you're a theologian when you've been condemned by the Church. He goes out and out until he gets "sand-bagged."[35] Weigel himself seldom went out and out, being basically a conservative theologian. However, some thought that he was extreme.

Theological schools form around different synthetic structures. All admit the same data but unify it according to different principles. Showing his sense of the historicity of Christian theology, he wrote: "The different tones of different theologians always have cultural roots." The choice of one unifying principle rather than another "is usually determined by cultural pressures."[36] Elsewhere, Weigel said that theology is influenced by the time and place in which it is formulated. This historical influence shows itself in the terminology used, in the tacit assumptions made, and in the questions asked at a given time. Theologies will always differ for those three reasons, but faith never differs.[37] Yet, according to Glanzman and Murray, Weigel was never as aware of the historical factors as his theory holds.[38]

Father Weigel's personal approach to fundamental theology is outlined in "Introductio in Theologiam." He rejected the late 19th century rationalistic apologetic, developed as a polemic against subjectivism, rationalism, historicism, idealism, positivism and liberalism. The weakness of this method was that it gave the impression "that the postulates of theological method could be demonstrated with rationalistic rigor." He rejected this non-theological apologetics in favor of a newer approach which began in the third and fourth decades of this century. It asked that fundamental theology be itself rather than a pretense at philosophy or history. It sought apologetical answers from theological sources rather than mere reason.[39]

In conclusion Weigel categorically declared, probably as a means to stimulate discussion and deeper insight, that theology is an end in itself. It should be studied simply because it gives knowledge. Only secondarily is the student enabled to present revelation more clearly, though this is an authentic by-product of theological study. "This is why," he said, "the Church demands that all its ministers be trained in theology. However, the Church neither demands nor

119

expects all, or even a great part, of its ministers actually to be true theologians, any more than it expects every cult-agent to be a liturgical artist."[40]

It is very interesting to read what Weigel considered to be the current trends in Roman Catholic theology in 1956.

1) the theologians are doing their best work in articles and monogaphs rather than in series of classroom manuals, which latter are now secondary manifestations of theological activity;

2) vitality rather than abstract schematism is now the quality sought for in theology;

3) metaphysical thought is highly realistic in opposition to an earlier nominalistic logicism;

4) there is an exuberant return to the Scriptures studied in themselves by strictly scholarly methods, not to refute non-Catholics but to rediscover for our time the biblical way of expressing the message of the magisterium;

5) in like manner; there is a return to the organic thought of the Fathers and the Medieval Doctors;

6) as a price for its historical consideration of the diverse elements of the deposit of faith, current theology is not so easily reducible to succinct, simplified, schematic outlines.

Here Weigel revealed several things about his own theology which have been implied above. The Bible was expressing "the message of the magisterium." And Weigel personally felt that the loss of schematization was "paying a price." Analysis and structure were always very dear to him. He acknowledged that what existentialists call "subjectivity" is alive in modern theology. "It is not hostile to schemes made in the abstract, but it does want to know how much schemes enrich and are actualized in man's lived experience. In place of schematic divisions and subdivisions of terminology, the psychological significance of faith is studied by preference." In a post-script to this article, Weigel mentioned that in the United States, "Paradoxically enough, stand-patism is stronger than in most places. Therefore, the evolution in theology is here not so notable as in other lands. Yet there has been a slow evolution."[41]

In the process of changing theological methodologies, Weigel feared the "theologasters." They were "men who know the use of the theological language and the arts of theological dialectic. Such men are glib and write glibly, but they rely on the verbal structure of dogmas rather than on the revelation to which the dogma is attached." Those who are uninitiated find it difficult to distinguish between a true theologian and a theologaster. But, with typical realism, Weigel concluded: "There is no need to rail against it. It must be accepted with resignation and equanimity."[42]

Father Weigel felt deeply that the Church at that time needed theologians but that they must be carefully controlled by the hierarchy, the living Tradition of the Church. Theologians can be useful to the Tradition in the development of dogma. They are not a luxury but a necessity for the Church.

> By their efforts the theologians recognize submerged elements in the total tradition and bring them to view. They synthesize what Scripture and tradition affirm in a way adequate for the age and place they live in. They deepen the understanding of already existing dogmas. They can be a defense for the Church in her encounter with error.[43]

During the 1950s Gustave Weigel spoke several times about the theology that was highly regarded in Catholicism at the time: Thomism. In 1954 he declared: "We cannot understand our own time without an understanding of Thomas."[44] Later he said: "Extremely ardent Thomists seem to think that Thomism is everything. This is certainly an exaggeration and we can dismiss it." Weigel saw Thomas' greatest contribution to have been in epistemology. For Thomas helped the Western World to realize that it can know "that man's mind is not doomed to chaos nor rendered sterile by a native blindness . . . That problems are capable of solution by thrusting them under the light of reason."[45]

Gustave Weigel once told some friends that a school changes when its faculty changes. His own appointment to Woodstock was a part of a basic shift in theological approach there. He felt that the "Denzinger approach" to the Church and to apologetics was "mindlessness." He opposed the proof-text methods of Anthony C. Cotter, S.J., which were being taught in other courses.[46] Weigel resented an apologetic which treated all men in the same way. His long experience with psychology and counseling, combined with his Kantian-like approach to truth, convinced him that men's needs and capacities are different and that, at different times, the same man will have quite different faith-needs.[47]

Some considered Weigel to be a maverick because of his "sensationalizing" newness. One professor, fearing Weigel's method, sought to have him removed from his post by reporting him to Rome. The "old guard" felt Weigel's stress on the Church as Mystery rather than the approach of rational and historical apologetics undermined the faith. To his critics, Weigel was always kind, though he considered them passé. He would never fight about his positions—just state them and refuse to become embroiled in the polemics of defense.[48]

To the students of those early years, Weigel's approach was an eye-opener. He prepared them well to resist Woodstock's rigid and narrow approaches to theology, for example, the theological notes method. Weigel's lively approach to the subjects made them exciting for the students. They felt he "knew what theology was all about" and was able to draw clear contrasts between old and new methods.[49]

With the coming of other Jesuit faculty members who had studied in European schools, Woodstock's academic face continued to change during the 1950s. Such professors were Francis McCool, the New Testament scholar; George Glanzman, the Old Testament professor; and Vincent O'Keefe, whose field was apologetics.

Despite the new and fresh approaches which Weigel took in the early 1950s, he was and remained basically a highly conservative thinker.[50] One student described him as "a conservative in sheep's clothing."[51] As the years went on, he seemed to move from a liberal to a conservative position but that was simply because the times continued to change and Weigel, according to his own testimony, remained basically the same. To those who would ask him how things were going at Woodstock, he would frequently reply with a typical Weigelian aphorism: "Many changes, no improvements."[52]

Gustave Weigel's Woodstock classes were memorable. He was a consummate teacher. All of the pedagogical traits which he had first developed at Loyola College and further fostered at the Chilean university served him well at Woodstock.

His early years of teaching at Woodstock saw him totally engrossed in preparing his class notes and in the give-and-take of the lecture hall. He loved to challenge the students, making outrageous statements, without qualifications. This would force the students to attack his positions creatively. He would then make the necessary distinctions to prove that his sweeping generalizations had not, in fact, been completely wrong.[53] Walter Burghardt said of his teaching method that he was not just giving data to students; he was "relating" to them. In the dialogues, he expected, wanted and needed opposition in order to clarify his own intuitions about reality and truth. It was in these exchanges that he hoped that his students too could more fully grasp "The Real." Yet he was enough of an intellectual "snob" to think that only about five percent of them could do so. In his more pessimistic moods, he would despairingly ask if it was really worth teaching "The Real" since so few could grasp its depths.[54] In such moods one could catch the contrasts in his personality: idealism tempered by realism, which often came out as pessimism.

Weigel took great pride in being present for all his classes. Even in later years, when his speaking engagements were taking him all over the country, he would be at Woodstock for his lectures. Sometimes he was poorly prepared, due to his travels, but he was always there. Burghardt remarked that his classes were either brilliant or horrible, depending on his preparedness. Several former students recalled him rushing in at the last minute, with his Alitalia bag in one hand, saying, "What class is it I'm teaching now?"[55] Weigel's retentive memory served him well in those times when he was not prepared.

"Gus was inseparable from his style." It was dramatic and humorous, making him a "great showman" on the lecture platform. His class in ecclesiology was termed "The Golden Book with gestures." It was humorously said that the theological note attached to Thesis I, the moral miracle thesis which Weigel felt most convincing, was "Rhetorice Certa." He made his points with a booming voice and with clever stories, not infrequently of a quite "earthy" nature. He was also known for choosing unusual pronunciations. Students would challenge him on this, only to discover through a dictionary-check that Weigel was, as usual, correct, though he may have chosen a second or third pronunciation.[56]

Weigel the teacher and Weigel the person were one and the same. He was always "teaching" and he was always "himself." Perhaps he did his best teaching at Woodstock when he gathered his close "disciples" in his third floor room late in the evening. At times, though, he could be quite cold to those who did not appreciate him and therefore were not in his coterie.[57] As he had done in Santiago, his room became an open house for students and faculty.[58] There, sprawled on his couch-bed with students sprawled in the chairs and on the floor, he would hold forth until the early hours of the morning, usually on serious topics and usually on theology. The teacher-student relationships there became man-to-man as theology became truly engaging. Again, his philosophy conditioned him to think that truth came intuitively, through the give-and-take of dialogue, more than through any kind of logical deduction or empirical induction. It was at the level of the personal that "The Real" was to be grasped. And personal he was. Hidden beneath a gruff exterior mask was the "real" Weigel—sensitive and kind. All who knew him seem to agree that he was "a great human being."

Simple people were drawn to him, and he to them, such as the

Woodstock kitchen workers. He also made friends with the bus driver who used to take him from Woodstock into Baltimore. Weigel didn't drive and was either chauffered by the students who loved to have the opportunity to talk to him or else he took the bus.

One of the best descriptions of Gustave Weigel, the teacher-person, was written by John L'Heureux, who studied under Weigel in the fall of 1963, his last semester of teaching.

> Gus is a great soul, hearty and a little vulgar, and altogether without pretense. He's a huge gruff man who woofs and gargles when he talks. He looks and even walks like a disappointed bear. I find his classes stimulating, offbeat; many don't like him, feeling that he's just bazzooing when he should be teaching. To an extent they're right. I suspect, however, that he himself feels— as I did when I taught school—that the only really important stuff he says is the persiflage, the obiter dicta struck from the flinty texts of Denzinger. Gus loves the Church incredibly and so he chastises it, as indeed I suspect he chastises himself. He is brutally honest. He says wonderful, amusing things too: "I've always felt that the man who invented the distinction between mortal and venial sin must have gone to hell." And others, which would never survive the perilous passage through censors. He is a great man. It's a privilege to study under him.[59]

L'Heureux mentioned that Weigel had a great love for the Church. Nothing could be more true. It was in the Church that Weigel had found The Infinite, "The Real," "The Truth." His life was risked upon faith in this Truth. And yet he knew the Church's miseries as well as its ever-new and transforming message.

To those who rebelled at seeing stains and sins in the Church he taught patience to accept it as it was and not to be scandalized. "If it is good enough for God, it should be good enough for me," he would say wisely, with one of his habitual understatements.[60]

L'Heureux's recalling Weigel's comments on the distinction between mortal and venial sin says much about Weigel's basic attitude to moral theology and law. Some might call him somewhat risqué in this regard. Others might consider him lax. It is probably best to call him a realist in these matters.

John Murray wrote about Weigel's comments on moral problems at a conference in Cambridge, Massachusetts. Weigel had sat at the meeting for two days without saying a word. Finally the chairman addressed him directly. His reply was simply: "I take no interest in morality." Murray added: "That was true—and that was the end."[61] McManus remembered, however, that years later, Weigel did have a fondness for the moral theology of Fritz Tillmann which was scripturally based and pastorally oriented.

Moral theology seemed quite unreal to Father Weigel, dealing as it so often did in abstractions and rules. What he dealt with was the real problems of real people. And he did this endlessly in his many counseling sessions with students at Woodstock and with friends outside the Jesuit community. Joseph Doty recalled that Weigel's counseling was marked by a keen sense of human psychology which he had had since his formative years. In Chile, Weigel underwent psycho-analysis. Years later both Weigel and Murray submitted to a controlled experiment with LSD.

Although as a counselor, he was a good listener, who gave his total attention while listening, his counseling tended to be quite directive, as it had been with Frank Otenasek. He probably operated quite intuitively here too. He could feel where the person was going and was often able to complete halting sentences of his counselees. Sometimes, though, since Weigel loved to talk, it would be hard to get a word in during a counseling session.[62]

Weigel's knowledge of psychology and psychiatry allowed him to approach sin subjectively. He did not deny the objectivity of sin. But it was "out there" someplace. Subjective guilt was something else, as was traditional in Jesuit confessional practice. Some felt his practice in this area bordered on situation ethics but more likely, because of his acceptance of the "out there" objective reality of sin, he was within the tradition of his Society.

In matters of sexuality, especially with adolescents, Weigel was

126

quite mild and non-condemnatory.[63] In these matters, he was more concerned with human growth than with sin.[64] One friend from Chile related that Weigel did not pay much attention to sins of the flesh and was more interested in the intellectual development of the young people.[65]

David McManus recalled a conversation with Father Weigel regarding the sacrament of penance. Weigel said he thought everyone should go to confession—about every nine years. He was aware of his own defects and seemed to enjoy not hiding them. His Augustinian approach to grace made him trust deeply in the overcoming power of divine grace. He believed that it is in human weakness that the strength of Christ's grace manifests itself.[66]

A deep but not obviously pious spirituality informed Gustave Weigel's life. Dulles wrote that he spoke rarely of his interior life but that it was vigorous and intense, involving a progressively greater love for the psalms and hymns of the breviary. His spirituality was a combination of strict orthodoxy and total freedom. He found God knocking at his door in the person who came to him for help, and so was immersed in the divine twenty-four hours a day, as Burghardt described him. His Augustinian-influenced spirituality was "child-like" according to Murray. It was simply: God's Will will be done, no matter what we do. Perhaps this is best summarized in the three final points of a retreat which he gave in 1958:

> I. Live in faith and hope. See God in every moment of the day
> . . .
>
> II. Have a great toleration of the limitations of the world, neighbor and self. Only God is God, all else is imperfect. Don't expect too much; be satisfied with what is there. We are called to give constant witness but not to change things except as God wants.
>
> III. Live in good humor. Do not be angered by the contrarities of life. Learn to laugh at them. Smile at the defects in others. Laugh at your own deficiencies. Humor—another word for intelligent tolerant humility.[67]

When it came to the vow of poverty, Weigel was a "penny-pincher," according to Burghardt. After delivering a $500 lecture, he would walk twenty blocks to save bus fare. Generous to a fault with those in need, he seldom spent anything on himself, especially not on clothes. When going to Baltimore to visit friends, he would take a bus and seldom would he allow his friends to drive him home. He preferred to go the "common" route.[68]

The member of the Woodstock community who probably influenced Weigel most and was closest to him during those years was John Murray. Though they disagreed on many things and would argue with each other frequently, both had implicit trust in each other. Quain recalled Weigel making one of his startling statements to Murray who would retort, "Gus, don't be such an utter damn fool." And the argument was on. In this dialogical way, Weigel would learn something.[69]

It could not be said that Weigel really depended on Murray. Although loved by most he was personally intimate with few. He depended on no one but God though "he did set a great value on loyalty." For Weigel, Murray was always around to give him his loyalty and that was enough. Murray contended that his friend was so confident in himself that he felt no dependence on anyone. For example, Murray usually showed his writings to Weigel for comment but Weigel never reciprocated.[70]

The relationship between these two Jesuits should be studied in detail. But suffice it to say here that they were two quite different people who complemented and challenged one another. Murray was more the scholar and researcher; Weigel was more the activist and popularizer. Murray was more consciously reflective; Weigel spoke out more quickly on any and every subject. Murray enjoyed formal social occasions; Weigel was uncomfortable in similar situations.[71] Murray was Aristotelian-Thomist; Weigel was Platonic-Augustinian-Thomist-Kantian, etc.—an eclectic. Murray found difficulty in expressing the complexity of his thought with clarity; Weigel's basic insights were always luminously expounded. Both were highly intelligent but in two different ways. Murray's intelligence tended to be categorized and abstract; Weigel's, though always searching to be systematic, was more free-wheeling, more intuitive and insightful.

Gustave Weigel wrote extensively and lectured widely across the country. After conducting a retreat for the Sisters of Mercy at Mt. St. Agnes College in Baltimore in 1950, he became very close to this community and especially to Sister Cleophas Costello, an English professor who eventually became the college's president. He once said that if he could have a community like that behind him, with their prayers, he could do anything. It became a mutual admiration society between Weigel and the sisters. They enjoyed his brilliance, wit and humanity. When it came time for his niece, Mary Louise, to go to college, he urged her to go to Mt. St. Agnes where "the sunshine comes in through the windows."[72]

In the fall of 1953, the United States government sent three American clergymen to Germany on a two-month goodwill tour. The tour, sponsored by the State Department's Intellectual Exchange Program, was designed to help remove misunderstandings in regard to the place of religion in the United States. Dr. Nathan A. Perlman, a Jew; Rev. James C. Flint, a Protestant; and Weigel were asked to undertake the task. Weigel enjoyed the trip immensely, especially because he established a friendship with Perlman.[73] While in Germany, Weigel scrupulously tried not to spend much money on food. He bragged of having had wurst for his meals two or three times a day. He returned tired, and, after eating, complained of having pains in the lower abdominal region. His sister, knowing of his ridiculous diet and overwork, suggested he might have ulcers.

In the spring, Father Weigel reluctantly took his problem to the Woodstock house doctor, Harold Burns, who hospitalized him in April in Baltimore's Mercy Hospital. X-rays revealed a tumor. Doctor Burns planned to operate. Friends urged Weigel to have a specialist but he, typically, wanted no special treatment.[74] Dulles remembered that when Weigel went to the hospital, he wished him well. Weigel replied, "This is the kind of examination for which one doesn't prepare." As the time for surgery drew near, he feared for the worst. Yet the sisters who nursed him recalled that he had a splendid attitude and was very resigned to God's will.[75] Murray wrote of this "whole painful episode."

> The night before his first surgery he was quiet and serene, free of all apprehension. But I also came away with the strange impression that he did not want to live and did not intend to. He later corroborated the impression; but he never explained his sense of having reached the end. In some psychological sense it was a reaction to what he—a strong man who had never been ill—considered an aggression and an injury. In the deepest sense I think it was a resignation—to the point, as it were, of a capitulation—to the Will of God. An instinct for the will of God was the cornerstone of his spirituality, on which was erected an edifice of striking simplicity and enormous solidity. But for once he had forgotten the hypothesis.[76]

On May 6, he underwent a bowel resection and a tumor was discovered in the colon. It was a polypoid benign tumor, which ordinarily would not have been terribly serious.[77] However, complications set in. The incision refused to heal and Weigel's life hung in the balance. All-night vigils were organized in the Woodstock chapel during the times of the most serious crises. When Murray later told his sick friend of this, Gus burst into tears.

Weigel's attitude towards death came out during those days when he, in the words of an attending nurse, "came so near to death, stayed there, and yet survived."[78] His sister, who was at Mercy Hospital much of the time, recalled her brother's philosophy on dying. "He would say: 'A man's no good after 55. They ought to shoot him then.' This, needless to say, was not always happily received by the 55-plusers that he told it to. Yet he meant it."[79] Walter Burghardt, too, told of his friend's attitude toward death during his illness.

Gus was a realist about death, about his death. He was not afraid to die. Not that he yearned for it "as the heart pants after the fountains of water"; Gus did not do much panting. It was simply that death was a fact of life, a Christian reality, a significant stage on the way to God. There it was and so he faced it. One day it would come; but in contrast to most of us, he did not greatly care whether it came tomorrow or at the eschaton.[80]

Perhaps Weigel's willingness to die yet his desire to live can further be interpreted through some words he wrote about death during his tertianship retreat.

Death I can only see as a passing through heavy, dark, thick silent hangings. I would not care to go through them, not for fear of the other side, but because I feel that there are some things still to be done on this side. I don't know—there is something soothing, alluring, quieting about heavy, high, dark, thick, silent hangings.[81]

On May 15, Weigel's prognosis was favorable. The radical surgery had consisted in removing about three-quarters of the colon, together with considerable adjoining tissue and the appendix. Dr. Burns was optimistic since the protuberance in the colon which had been revealed by the x-rays had not broken which would have caused internal bleeding. Since part of the colon remained, there was no need for a colostomy. An examination of the liver and adjacent organs showed no trace of metastasis. It was felt that the carcinoma was localized in the removed section of the colon and had not spread to other parts of the body. Though the first week after surgery had been "utterly miserable" for the patient and he was very weak and needed special nurses, this was not unusual for such radical surgery. The rector of Woodstock, Joseph F. Murphy, S.J., wrote a report to the New York provincial saying: "there is no reason why he may not enjoy twenty years and more of fruitful activity."[82]

Murphy's letter had barely been finished when he received an emergency call from Mercy Hospital. Weigel had unexpectedly gone into shock. His kidneys had stopped functioning and it was almost impossible to get his blood pressure. He was anointed. In a few days, the critical period passed but it was a definite setback, reversing much of the progress made during the preceding week. On May 22, he suffered another severe relapse and was rushed to the emergency room. Dr. Burns, assisted this time by Dr. Walter Wise, performed a second operation. Again it was thought that his life was near the end. Yet through it all his wit and humor prevailed over the intense pain.[83] Murray recalled that he and Father Murphy were once called to the hospital in the middle of the night. Doctors and nurses were laboring over him. "Almost unconscious, he caught sight of us and growled with gasping breath, 'It was hardly necessary to call out the Marines!' "Murray remembered that he once threatened his long-time friend: "Gus, if you die on me now, I'll never speak to you again." Weigel later blamed Murray for having brought him back from death's door.[84]

Another humorous incident from this period was recounted by Ochagavia.

> When the situation prolonged itself, a friend told him in jest that they had already opened a grave for him in Woodstock cemetery but that, since in the meantime another Father had died, the Rector wanted to ask him if he would be so kind as to yield it to this other Father. His answer was typical of his ever sharp sense of humor: "The proposition seems very unfair to me, but, oh, well, since it's for an old friend he can have it."[85]

Though Father Murphy told Louise Daigler that the prospects for her brother were bright, he was pessimistic in his letter to the New York provincial. The physicians attending Weigel were divided on the prognosis. One felt Weigel had a long life ahead but three others said it would not be surprising to see metastasis within a year which would mean further hospitalization "for the purpose of easing the pain at the end."[86]

There are some events in a person's life after which one is never again the same. For Gustave Weigel, the months of May, June and

July 1954, were such an event. He referred to it as his passing through "the Valley of Death." When, through God's grace, he came up on the other side, he had a sense of "living on borrowed time." He believed that God had spared him to do ecumenical work[87] and he became "a man in a hurry" to set about this task for he felt he had only a few years left.[88] He set out to do the "something Real" which he had told Otenasek he had hoped to do when he finished his studies at Rome; "then, let me die." Thereafter he would never refuse an invitation to speak if he could possibly get there. He would go anywhere and everywhere without discrimination. He was a great drawing card both for important and for trivial occasions.[89] Burghardt wrote that there was a single principle operative in his life at that time:

"His conviction that, if he *could* do what he was asked to do, this was God's way of letting him know that he *should*. I disputed the principle, but as we look back now on his life and its influence, he may well have been right."[90] Robert McNally compared the Weigel of this period with St. Paul. Paul, thinking that the world was going to end at any minute, raced around the world trying to convert as many as possible before the Parousia. Weigel, who expected his own end, did likewise.[91]

Weigel became again the restless man of the people that he had been in South America. Not that he was ever anything but a "peoples' priest" but now this took absolute priority and the quiet scholarship he had looked forward to on his return from Chile was left behind. For the most part he lived on his accumulated intellectual capital which was considerable. Murray said Weigel's motivation was complex. Part of it was his sense of the Will of God which for him was concretized in the task at his elbow, in the call that came from someone. Part of it was related, in some way, to a sense that his own life, lived under the impulse of inner dynamisms, had come to an end.[92] Murray counseled moderation but Weigel turned a deaf ear. The former wondered if his friend really enjoyed that kind of busy life. Murray doubted that he did but the question was really irrelevant to this man of Alsatian-Jesuit-Kantian obedience.

"His fundamental disposition came out in a remark that he often made when confronted with something he did not want to do but had promised to do: 'I've married the witch of Endor; I'll be faithful to the witch of Endor.' "[93] As the years rolled on between the 1954 Valley of Death and the 1964 actual death, Weigel felt that he was doing his best work, perhaps that "most real" work he had hoped to do before his death.

Although his lectures and travels did not keep him from his accustomed fidelity to his duties at Woodstock, his teaching did suffer.[94] He was not developing his ecclesiology; he was not preparing his classes; he was not doing the reading and the scholarship that his role demanded. Instead he devoured more and more mystery novels, especially Rex Stout's Nero Wolfe stories.[95]

Father Weigel told John Giles Milhaven that, during those last years of his life, he had lost interest in teaching, had lost the energy to prepare classes. By his own admission he was just putting on a "show" and "hamming it up" in the classroom. Within a year before his death, he admitted to Milhaven that his real interest was in having informal conversations with intellectuals.[96] To McManus, also, he confessed his boredom with teaching and yet how true to form was this final interest in dialogue! Did not Weigel always hold that truth came by intuition and that intuitions were unveiled and clarified through the give-and-take of dialogue? His position in these last years was consistent with his epistemology, his personal approach to truth. And, after all, truth was what he was after. "I would rather be right then President," had been his high school motto.

Gustave Weigel saw himself as the kind of teacher he described in the model Platonic Academy. When he once described a Jesuit scholar, he described himself. He had said that a scholar of the society must be a creative scholar who meets truth, assimilates it and shows it to others in his own unique way. The teacher, after his personal assimilation of truth, must communicate it through personal contact with the students. They are first won over to the professor by his classroom presentations and then subjected to his influence outside the classroom.[97] Those who studied under Weigel and were favored by his personal "touch" have testified that his practice of this theory of pedagogy was what made Gustave Weigel a consummate teacher.

Teaching and lecturing from his intuitions and insights did not always work out too well for Weigel. Sometimes his speeches indicated that he really wasn't terribly familiar with the topic. One such area was liturgy. He knew little or nothing about it. In one talk, he said, "I gladly admit I know nothing about liturgy; I am almost proud of it." As Father Godfrey Diekmann, O.S.B., put it, Weigel was in favor of the liturgy but did not understand it or care to become involved in the movement for its renewal. "I'm all for it but leave me alone," was his attitude. Displaying his usual "good sense of irreverence," Weigel felt the desire to restore primitive liturgy was pure antiquarianism.[98]

Despite this indifference to liturgical renewal, Father Weigel had a special chapel, a "Qahal," at Woodstock where he would celebrate his own particular brand of Eucharist in the late fifties and early sixties. The chapel, also termed "The Protestant Chapel," had been appointed by various friends with an altar and candlesticks. Celebrating at odd hours and attended by his "disciples" Weigel faced the people and used the vernacular before this was permitted. Why, one might ask, would he go to this trouble if he was not *au courant* on the liturgical movement and didn't really care about it? It was because it helped people. His pastoral orientation rather than a scholarly understanding or reformer's conviction moved him to do this.[99] Weigel told the Fergusons and Mrs. Otenasek that he wanted vernacular liturgy, not for himself, but for people. He feared, however, that priests would butcher the English language during the Mass whereas in Latin the butchery was not so noticeable.

One of the types of addresses which Weigel gave most frequently during those years after his bout with cancer was the Religious Emphasis Week address on college campuses across the nation. This was his "bearing witness."[100] This was, for Gus Weigel, what being a Christian and a Jesuit was all about—"bearing witness."

Several universities honored Gustave Weigel with honorary doctorates: Universidad Católica de Chile, Lit. D., (1956); University of Vermont, LL.D. (1960); Georgetown University, LL.D. (1962); Yale University, D.D. (1962); Alfred University, D.H.L. (1963); St. Mary's College, Winona, Minnesota, LL.D. (1963); and, in 1960, he was given the Christian Wisdom Medal at Loyola University in Chicago.

The citation which Father Weigel received at Yale is a terse avowal of the esteem in which he was held in the Protestant community.

> Gustave Weigel. Priest, theologian and author. You have become a foremost interpreter of American pluralistic Protestantism to members of your own Church. You have broken through the Reformation wall and pioneered in Catholic-Protestant dialogue. Your critical, yet sympathetic presentation of the beliefs of those with whom you disagree has already helped to create a new ecumenical climate in our country. Yale is honored to confer upon you the degree of Doctor of Divinity.[101]

Weigel received his Yale doctorate the same day President John F. Kennedy was so honored. Kennedy invited the Jesuit to fly to Washington with him and then he had him driven to Woodstock in a White House limousine. Excitedly, he went into Murray's room to report the whole episode. Murray interrupted the story to ask him when he had last gone to the bathroom. Weigel, thinking this a rude, personal question, continued his story. Murray again interrupted. "Was it before your honorary degree?" Weigel thought it was. "Well, your shirt front is zipped into the fly of your pants and you went through all that looking like that?" It was true and no one laughed harder than Gus himself.[102]

Gus Weigel's renown earned him several offers for jobs. One was as editor-in-chief of the *Natural Law Forum* at Notre Dame University. He declined.[103] Another which he accepted but never fulfilled because of his death, was that of editor of *Sacramentum Mundi* with Karl Rahner and Juan Alfaro.[104]

One post for which Weigel was considered within his own province was that of editor of *America,* the Jesuit weekly magazine. This was in the early fifties. Weigel himself opposed the choice. His memo to the provincial lists reasons against the appointment and also gives valuable insights into Weigel's own self-image:

1. My opinion is that it would not be a wise choice. The reasons are:

   a. *Formal and material incompetence:*

      i. Formal incompetence—the editor must be a man who can command men. This is his first function. Weigel can get along with men, but he cannot command them; if he cannot win them to his views by friendship, he is helpless to invoke authority. Not all men will be friends of the leader. That is impossible.

      ii. Material incompetence—the editor of "America" should be an exceptionally well-informed man. Weigel's knowledge of the world, with the exception of South America and the U.S.A. is quite thin, nor has he ever shown anything but a superficial interest in current events. Nor should we be deceived of his knowledge of languages: his command of French and Italian is weak; he speaks an Americanized German and his Spanish is not Peninsular. Whatever work he has done in observing the local scenes, manifests a power of reporting, not a power of editing, but an editor should be more than a decent reporter.

   b. *Wrong training for the post:*

      i. Weigel's interests have always been in the field of universals and not in the field of particulars. He likes

137

synthetic reductions of a manifold to a theoretic formula. This is proper to the schoolman, but not desirable in an editor.

ii. He is genuinely in love with theology. He has given satisfaction to his academic superiors both in South America and here. His students find him stimulating and to their liking. He himself is at his best in the work of teaching and writing on themes of his discipline. Yet the editor of "America" could use such interests only rarely and would have to keep them rigidly in seclusion. Yet it seems wrong for a man with such interests not to develop them. Theology is a most important field of work and we do not have too many men who are spontaneously zealous for theological meditation. To lose an enthusiastic theologian in order to gain a dubiously effective editor seems a poor gamble.

c. *Personal shortcomings by reason of character:*

i. Weigel is impetuous in act and utterance. In the restricted area of the classroom this defect can be compensated by other qualities but in an editor of a responsible journal like "America," such a handicap is very serious.

ii. Weigel is prone to exaggerated statements which he makes to win adherents to his views which he feels too strongly, in spite of a simulated indifference and scepticism. In a paper like "America" statements must be cautious and prudent even in the defense of a good cause.

2. All this is stated sincerely but is given as points to be considered by superiors rather than restricting the freedom of superiors. Non recuso laborem sed credo me aptum non esse ad laborem.[105]

Amongst his many travels during the last ten years of his life, Gustave Weigel particularly enjoyed an official return visit to Chile and Colombia in the summer of 1956. Many old wounds had healed and he was welcomed by Latin American officials as well as Chilean Jesuits. In a report to the United States government, who had sponsored his sixty-two-day tour, Weigel wrote:

"The tour was fatiguing, but that in itself was the best sign of its value. Contacts were numerous, easy and sympathetic. Everywhere requests were made to extend the visit or at least to return soon. Interest and sympathy for the United States are pronounced in many sectors, and the latent hostility so characteristic of Latin America is not as strong today as it was ten years ago."[106]

Gustave Weigel was a true Jesuit, yet he never allowed his life to be circumscribed by Jesuit relationships. His love for people took him far beyond the structures of the Society and the grounds of Woodstock College. On his return to the States in 1948, he reestablished his relationship with his sister, Louise, and became better acquainted with her two children, Mary Louise and Earl. Though he visited them only about twice a year, always at Christmas, "his visits were the milestones of the year." His visits were brief, three days. Once he stayed a week and vowed never to do it again. After the third day only Louise sat around, hanging on his every word. He often quoted Ben Franklin: "Fish and company after three days stink."[107]

Old friendships were renewed around Baltimore with the Loyola class of '33 and their families after he returned from Chile, especially the Raymond Kirbys and the Frank Otenaseks. Every Thursday night that he was "at home" he spent with Frank and Mildred Otenasek, having the same meal of steak, baked potato and salad. Though he was their intimate, he was always "Father" to them. It was at the quiet friendly dinners of these few Baltimoreans that Weigel frequently relaxed and showed the greatness of his humanity. If "outsiders" were invited, however, he would become restrained and reticent. His conviviality was catching. Aided by a few scotches before dinner and brandy after dinner, he would tell tales into the night on almost any subject.[108]

Another insight into Gustave Weigel's personality comes from the recollections of his friend, Sister Cleophas Costello. With her he frequently shared the joys and sorrows of his Woodstock years. Yet she never felt free to pry into his life. This he would not have allowed. No one could encroach on his personal inner freedom. She merely held with sympathy whatever he entrusted to her. She felt that her friend had a tremendous intellectual power that could overpower people. He had the unique ability of both being able to see the whole panorama of a problem and also being able to penetrate to the minute core of a problem and resolve it. She saw his chief weakness as an impatient cynicism when he had to "suffer fools," something which he never did "gladly."[109]

Every Friday evening that he was available David McManus came to Woodstock to see his old mentor. The Jesuit urged McManus to enter the Catholic book publishing business which he did when he established Helicon Books in Baltimore in 1957. Weigel attended the board meetings regularly as a consultor. McManus repeatedly attempted, without success, to get Weigel to settle down to write a four-volume work on ecclesiology which Helicon would publish. Weigel put him off, always joshing that there were more important things to do and that that was not the right time for such a job.[110] Burghardt, too, had urged his friend to write a complete work on the Church. But nothing was forthcoming. Now Burghardt admits that Weigel was probably right. It was not the time. Vatican II ideas were ripening but could not yet be gathered in for the harvest.[111]

This chapter, the most detailed in the biographical study of Gustave Weigel, shows a man deeply and zestfully in love with life; yet a man who could be quite pessimistic about life. A man whose stance could be described as "sardonic."[112] This dual streak came from his deep insight into life's meaning—an insight gained by constant and consistent company-keeping with the ever illusive "Real" and "True" which he saw as his God. In one of the innumerable dialogues through which he intuitively sought Truth, Weigel spoke these telling words:

You cannot deal with truth on any level whatsoever, without being in a continuous line with God. Any truth, the smallest, most insignificant truth, is itself only a participation and manifestation of the great truth which is God himself. Any truth at all is of its very nature, an introduction to piety, but not if the man's going to use it in order to convince somebody of God. No, no, no. Love the truth for itself and this will bring you to God. All things bring you to God if you look at them in terms of truth.[113]

Endnotes

1. Gustave Weigel, Address to Chilean Bishops, WCA II F 303.24d.
2. *One of a Kind,* p. 15.
3. Ochagavia, *op. cit.,* p. 25.
4. Interview with Walter J. Burghardt, S.J., November 1, 1971.
5. In April of 1949, he spoke at the National Catholic Education Association annual meeting in Philadelphia on "The American Citizen's Obligation to South America." In the following April, he again addressed this organization's annual meeting on "Problems of North American Students in Latin America." At the same meeting he talked about improving international understanding through the use of modern languages. An article on priestly vocations in Latin America appeared, too, in April. (These references are in Neft, *op. cit.,* numbers 103, 30, 106 and 104 respectively.)
6. Interview with John Courtney Murray, S.J., June 15 and 17, 1957 (Neft); Interviews with Francis McCool, S.J., September 9, 1971, and Walter Burghardt, S.J., November 1, 1971; Maryland Province Catalogue, 1949, pp. 41–44; Interview with Avery Dulles, S.J., June 21, 1966 (Neft); NY Province Catalogue, 1949, p. 111.
7. Interview with Edwin Quain, S.J.
8. Interviews with David L. McManus (Neft).
9. Interviews with David L. McManus (Neft) and Raymond A. Kirby (Neft).
10. Michael Long, "Bookman," March, 1964, pp. 3–4 (Neft files).
11. Interview with David L. McManus.
12. Interview with Joseph Doty.
13. Interview with Arthur Madden.
14. Weigel to Otenasek, August 27, 1930. Cf. also Ochagavia, *op. cit.,* p. 28, for Weigel's devotion to Augustine.
15. Interviews with Robert McNally, S.J., and John Courtney Murray, S.J. (Neft).
16. Interview with Norris Clarke, S.J., September 20, 1971; Sister Cleophas also testified that Weigel "detested" Aristotle's thought. Geismann stated that Weigel was "suspicious" of Aristotelian categories.

17. Gustave Weigel, "The Supernatural and Philosophy," *Proceedings of the Eleventh Annual Convention of the Jesuit Philosophical Association; the Philosophical Implications of the Recent Controversy on the Natural Desire of the Beatific Vision,* held at Boston College, Boston, Mass., April 18, 1949. Edited by James I. Conway, S.J., Woodstock, Md.: Woodstock College Press, 1949, pp. 44–47.

18. Interviews with Norris Clarke, S.J., and Arthur Madden. Cf. also Gustave Weigel and Arthur Madden, *Knowledge: Its Values and Limits* (Englewood Cliffs, N.J.: Prentice Hall, Inc., 1961), pp. 19–24 and 37.

19. Interview with Norris Clarke, S.J. John Murray, a dedicated Thomist, also objected to Weigel's Platonism. (Taped comments of John Giles Milhaven, October 28, 1971.) David McManus, who tended to be sympathetic to Plato himself, called Weigel a Platonist one day and it made the Jesuit quite angry. He disclaimed the accusation but McManus always questioned how Weigel could be a Platonist and yet hold to the Incarnation.

20. Interview with Richard Cronin, S.J.

21. Taped comments of John Giles Milhaven, October 28, 1971.

22. Interviews with Arthur Madden, and Sister Cleophos Costello.

23. Gustave Weigel, S.J., and Arthur G. Madden, *Knowledge: Its Values and Limits,* p. v. The course notes were used by Madden at Mt. St. Agnes College and at his suggestion and the prompting of Prentice-Hall publishers, Weigel collaborated in publishing them with Madden. (Interview with Arthur Madden.)

24. *One of a Kind,* pp. 16–17.

25. Interview with Robert McNally, S.J.

26. In the following year, 1953, Weigel was assigned as moderator of spiritual exercises and sermons (*Ibid.,* 1953, p. 107). In 1954 and 1955 he became a special censor of scriptural books and custodian of the grounds at Woodstock (*Ibid.,* 1955, p. 113). One of his few hobbies was mowing grass and looking after the beautifully wooded campus at Woodstock. (Interviews with Robert McNally, S.J.; Walter J. Burghardt, S.J.; Richard Cronin, S.J.; Paul Cassidy, S.J.) His duties remained the same for the rest of his life except for the fact that, from 1957 on, he was listed as a corresponding editor for the Jesuit magazine, *America.*

27. Gustave Weigel, "The Historical Background of the Encyclical *Humani Generis,*" *Theological Studies,* 12, (1951), p. 230.

28. Gustave Weigel, "Introductio in Theologiam," WCA II F 303.17a, p. 2.

29. *Ibid.,* p. 6.

30. *Ibid.,* pp. 6–7.

31. *Catholic Theology in Dialogue,* p. 96.

32. *Catholic Theology in Dialogue,* p. 92.

33. Gustave Weigel, "Teaching and the Word of God," *Communications and the Word of God* (Toronto, Ontario, 1959), p. 48. Sister Claudia had attended Weigel's First Solemn Mass.

34. "Introductio in Theologiam," p. 7.

35. Interview with Richard Cronin, S.J.

36. "Introductio in Theologiam," p. 8.

37. WCA II F 303.21, unfiled, typed address, June 27, 1958.

38. *One of a Kind,* p. 17; Interview with George Glanzman, S.J. In 1956, Weigel wrote: "Today's theologian is lovingly conscious of history and he refuses to treat a formula of faith without studying its historical genesis and vicissitudes. Current theology is less Euclidean and more Augustinian." (Gustave Weigel, "Theology:

(1900–1956)," *Catholic Encyclopedia,* Supplement III: (New York: The Gilmary Society, 1957), no pages.)

39. *Ibid.,* p. 11. An undated lecture, "Contemporary Catholic Thought," explains this in greater detail. Cf. WCA II F 303.19u.

40. *Ibid.,* pp. 13–14.

41. Gustave Weigel, "Theology: 1950–1956," *op. cit.,* no pages.

42. *Catholic Theology in Dialogue,* p. 98.

43. *Ibid.,* pp. 97–98.

44. Gustave Weigel, "The Debt of 20th Century Thought to Thomas Aquinas," Third Annual Aquinas Lecture, March 1, 1954, Kings College, Wilkes-Barre, Pennsylvania; this was slightly revised for the Aquinas lecture, March 9, 1959, Manhattan College, New York City, and entitled "Is Thomism Everything?" The change of title is significant for his change of emphasis regarding Thomism. WCA II F 303.19n; also in the same file, probably from the 1950s, is "Scholasticism in the Modern World" and "The Thomistic Conception of Man."

45. Gustave Weigel, "The Debt of 20th Century Thought to Thomas Aquinas." Weigel said the Thomistic "balance" has been the basis for American democracy and religious liberty. "Our American pro-judgments unconsciously derive from Aquinas and from no one else." This would seem to be a far-fetched observation.

46. Cotter was a German theologian, teaching at the Jesuit school in Weston, Massachusetts, and was a personal friend of James Griffin, S.J., who taught *De Revelatione* to the first year theologians.

47. Interview with Walter Burghardt, S.J.

48. Interview with Robert McNally, S.J.

49. Interview with Donald Campion, S.J. Campion was a member of Weigel's first ecclesiology class.

50. Interviews with Francis McCool, S.J., Richard Cronin, S.J., Avery Dulles, S.J., Walter Burghardt, S.J., Erwin Geismann, and Donald Campion, S.J.

51. Interview with Richard Cronin, S.J.

52. Interview with Erwin Geismann.

53. Interviews with Arthur Madden, Edwin Quain, S.J., James A. O'Brien, S.J. (Neft), David L. McManus, and Ochagavia, *op. cit.,* p. 21.

54. Interview with David L. McManus (Neft). Interview with Walter Burghardt, S.J. Father Dulles wrote in tribute to Weigel: "A dynamic teacher with a flair for the dramatic, he delighted in making challenging statements that would arouse passionate disagreement. Like others I used to raise my hand and object until, after a few skirmishes, I found out that Father Weigel's debating tactics were invincible." *Catholic Review,* January 10, 1964.

55. Interviews with Dominic Maruca, S.J., James Hennesey, S.J., and Paul Cassidy, S.J.

56. Interviews with Thomas Green, S.J. (Neft), Donald Campion, S.J., Donald Moore, S.J., James Hennesey, S.J., James A. O'Brien, S.J., and Francis McCool, S.J.

57. Interview with Joseph Doty.

58. Interviews with Walter Burghardt, S.J., Robert McNally, S.J., Richard Cronin, S.J., Paul Cassidy, Edward Mooney, and Dominic Maruca, S.J.

59. John L'Heureux, *Picnic in Babylon: A Jesuit Priest's Journal, 1963–1967* (New York: Macmillan, 1967), pp. 11–12.

60. Ochagavia, *op. cit.,* p. 28. Cassidy and Campion in their interviews also referred to Weigel as "a great man of the Church."

61. *One of a Kind,* p. 14. Yet Carlos Eyzaguirre recalled that Weigel in Chile waxed eloquent on moral problems in those delightful after-dinner sessions. (Carlos Eyzaguirre to Patrick Collins, Salt Lake City, December 3, 1971).

62. Interviews with Edward Mooney, William Lamm, S.J., Paul Cassidy, S.J., Joseph Doty, and David McManus.

63. Walter Burghardt, *op. cit.,* pp. 604–605; Carlos Eyzaguirre to Patrick Collins, Salt Lake City, December 3, 1971.

64. Interview with David L. McManus. Cf. also Gustave Weigel, S.J., "Scrupulosity from Other Points of View: Moral Theologian," *Personality and Sexual Problems in Pastoral Psychology* (New York: Fordham University Press, 1964) pp. 84–90.

65. Carlos Eyzaguirre to Patrick Collins, Salt Lake City, December 3, 1971.

66. Ochagavia, *op. cit.,* p. 28; Interview with David McManus.

67. WCA II F 303.19z. This retreat was given in June 1958 at Notre Dame University and again that August at Berchmans Hall in Sunapee, New Hampshire. Weigel gave many retreats all across the United States from the time he arrived in 1948 until his death.

68. Interviews with Walter Burghardt, S.J., Dr. and Mrs. Richard Ferguson, Mildred Otenasek, and Raymond A. Kirby.

69. Avery Dulles, S.J., felt that their disagreements were not just a game. They were deep and serious. Murray tended to criticize Weigel more than vice-versa. Robert McNally, S.J., agreed with Dulles.

70. Interview with John Courtney Murray, S.J. Erwin Geismann says Father Weigel was not truly close to anyone on a personal level. McCool, McNally and Glanzman concur that Weigel depended on no one but himself and God. Perhaps Weigel's friendship with Frank Otenasek would be an exception. Letters from Weigel to Otenasek contain expressions of great human warmth and intimacy.

71. Weigel to Otenasek, July 6, 1934, expresses Weigel's early attitude towards social activities. Murray had taken Weigel to his family's home on Long Island and Weigel reflected: "For a day I was in an atmosphere foreign to me after all these years. An exclusive beach club; its concomitant luxuries; people whom one meets and really never knows; sophistication; the glamor of refined display. John had taken care of me for four years at Woodstock. I soon fell in love with his mother and sisters. However, I met many others. It takes too much out of you. Dear me no, I do not want that sort of thing. It is quite unreal." Quain recalled that Weigel had told him how uncomfortable he had been when he and Murray were guests of Clare Booth Luce, Murray's friend.

72. Daigler reflections; Weigel to Mary Louise Daigler, March 25, 1955. It was at Mt. St. Agnes College that Weigel helped to initiate and direct the summer Philosophy Institutes from 1955–61.

73. *The Catholic Review* (Baltimore), January 22, 1954; WCA II F 303.11c. Interview with Avery Dulles, S.J.

74. Interview with Francis J. Otenasek.

75. Interviews with Sister Thecla Lancaster, R.S.M., and Sister Brendan Murphy, R.S.M.

76. *One of a Kind,* pp. 17–18.

77. Interview with Dr. Russell Morgan.

78. Interviews with James Griffin, S.J., Richard Cronin, S.J., John Courtney Murray, S.J., Robert McNally, S.J., and Sister Kathleen Smith, R.S.M.

79. Daigler reflections.

80. Walter Burghardt, *op. cit.,* p. 606.

81. WCA II F 303.22g.

82. Joseph F. Murphy to John J. McMahon, May 15, 17, 18, 1954, New York Jesuit Provincialate Archives.

83. Interviews with Sister Jeremy Daigler, R.S.M., Sister Kathleen Smith, R.S.M., and Sister Brendan Murphy, R.S.M.

84. *One of a Kind,* pp. 18–19.

85. Ochagavia, *op. cit.,* p. 26.

86. Joseph F. Murphy, S.J., to Thomas Henneberry, S.J., July 31, 1954; New York Jesuit Provincialate Archives; *One of a Kind,* p. 17.

87. Daigler reflections; Interview with John Courtney Murray, S.J.

88. Burghardt, *op. cit.,* p. 606. Avery Dulles, S.J., reported that Weigel lectured so often to make money to pay his own 1954 medical bills.

89. Burghardt, *op. cit.,* p. 606; Interview with John Courtney Murray, S.J.

90. Burghardt, *op. cit.,* pp. 606–607.

91. Interview with Robert McNally.

92. *One of a Kind,* pp. 19–20.

93. *Ibid.,* p. 120.

94. Interviews with Robert McNally, S.J., Walter Burghardt, S.J., John Courtney Murray, S.J., John Giles Milhaven, Paul Cassidy, S.J., Avery Dulles, S.J., and Donald Moore, S.J.

95. Interviews with Walter Burghardt, S.J., and David L. McManus.

96. Interview with John Giles Milhaven.

97. Gustave Weigel, "The Heart of Jesuit Education—The Teacher," *Jesuit Educational Quarterly,* XX (June, 1957), pp. 7–16.

98. Gustave Weigel, "Impact of the Liturgical Movement on Catholic Ecumenism," *American Benedictine Review,* XIV (June, 1963), pp. 194–197; interviews with Walter Burghardt, S.J., November 1, 1971; David L. McManus, October 22, 1971; Godfrey Diekmann, O.S.B., May 16, 1966 (Neft); Joseph Doty, October 23, 1971.

99. Interviews with Richard Cronin, S.J., Avery Dulles, S.J., Thomas Green, S.J., Sister Jeremy Daigler, R.S.M., Dr. Richard Ferguson, David L. McManus. In 1962, Weigel was cautioned by the Maryland Provincial to be "a bit more cautious about the questions of the vernacular in the liturgy in the course of your excellent public speeches. Shades of the Denver Register." (John M. Daley, S.J., to Weigel, May 28, 1962; Maryland Jesuit Provincialate Archives.)

100. Interviews with Richard Cronin, S.J., and Sister Cleophas Costello, R.S.M. Among the campuses visited were Harvard, Yale, Stanford, Lehigh, Pennsylvania, Purdue, Georgetown, Fordham, Notre Dame, Marquette, Catholic University, Johns Hopkins, Loyola of Chicago, Rutgers, Carnegie Tech, Brown, Smith, Ohio State, Wisconsin, Vanderbilt, Goucher, University of Michigan, North Carolina, Northwestern, University of Minnesota and the Universities and Colleges of Utah. The latter visit was made at the personal invitation of Weigel's good friend, Bishop Duane G. Hunt of Salt Lake City; William F. Maloney, S.J., to Weigel, March 14 and June 5, 1956; Maryland Jesuit Provincialate Archives; Interview with Walter Burghardt, S.J., November 1, 1971.

101. Neft, *op. cit.,* p. 25.

102. Interview with Thomas Green, S.J.

103. Weigel to Thomas Henneberry, S.J., Woodstock, August 12, 1959; Henne-

berry to Joseph O'Meara, New York, Feburary 9, 1960 (New York Jesuit Provincialate Archives).

104. Karl Rahner to Weigel, Innsbruck, Austria, June 9, 1962; John M. Daley to Weigel, June 12, 1962 (Maryland Jesuit Provincialate Archives). Cf. *Sacramentum Mundi,* V.I. (New York: Herder and Herder, 1968), pp. 19–21, for Weigel's single contribution, "American."

105. Weigel to Jesuit Provincial, undated, New York Jesuit Provincialate Archives. A post which Weigel did accept was that of Catholic Consultant for the *Encyclopedia Brittanica* from 1959 until his death. (WCA II F 303.22a.)

106. WCA II F 303.25d. "Report of Father Gustave Weigel, S.J., on IES Grant, 581–6."

107. Daigler reflections.

108. Interviews with Raymond Kirby, Frank Otenasek, Mildred Otenasek and Dr. and Mrs. Richard Ferguson.

109. Interview with Sister Cleophas Costello, R.S.M.

110. Interview with David McManus.

111. Interview with Walter J. Burghardt, S.J.

112. Interview with Sister Cleophas Costello, R.S.M.

113. "Teaching and the Word of God," *op. cit.*

Ecclesiology

When Gustave Weigel began to teach at Woodstock College, he had never taught a formal course in ecclesiology. Therefore, when he was appointed professor of fundamental theology at Woodstock in 1949, replacing Joseph J. Bluett, S.J., he had to prepare a totally new course. During his first year teaching ecclesiology, Weigel worked intensely, putting his course notes together from week to week. Students often helped him with typing and collating materials.[1] He produced very little else in those first years of teaching.[2] He was too busy preparing both this course and the *Actus Fidei* course which he was assigned to teach in 1951.

The first typed edition of his *Summula Ecclesiologica* differs only slightly and non-substantially from the final edition which was produced in 1954. Weigel usually knew what he wanted to say and how he wanted to say it. After that, not much changed. *Summula Ecclesiologica* means a little summary. It is subtitled *Tractatulus Ecclesiologicus,* again in the diminutive.[3] In the style of a traditional manual of theology (Thesis, Status Quaestionis, Partitio, Definitiones, Adversarii, Nota Theseos, Probatio, Scholion and Excursus), it is written in a mixture of Latin and English. This was a departure from the exclusively Latin tradition at Woodstock.

Father Weigel listed the sources he brought together for his *Summula* at the beginning of each of the thirteen theses in the body of the work. They are, without exception, Jesuit authors. Six sources are used extensively: Michael d'Herbigny, S.J., *Theologica*

147

de Ecclesia, 1921; Hermann Dieckmann, S.J., *De Ecclesia tractatus historico-dogmatici,* 1925; Peter Lutz, S.J., *Tractatus de Ecclesia Christi,* 1924; Joseph de Guibert, S.J., *De Christi Ecclesia,* 1928; Timothy Zapalena, S.J., *De Ecclesia Christi,* 1940; and Anthony Cotter, S.J., *Theologia Fundamentalis,* 1947. The latter two works, according to Weigel, represent in method and tendency the nineteenth century's approach to ecclesiology.[4] This was the apologetical method definitively in vogue after Vatican I, in which natural reason was used as a propaedeutic to the graced act of faith. History and reason were summoned to prove the truth of the Church's faith-claims.[5]

Weigel's ecclesiological method is somewhat different from this rationalistic approach. For him the theology of the Church is a scientific discipline in which a correct and adequate vision of the organ of divine revelation is proposed through a certain historical method, proving with philosophical certainty that the Roman Catholic Church is that organ.[6]

Recognizing, as he so regularly did, the uniqueness of every individual, Weigel stated that the human approach to faith should not be the same in all cases. Since it would be impossible to piece together arguments for each person, he proposed the position that he judged most compelling, not for the individual perhaps, but for his age.[7]

Ecclesiological method, until the time of Robert Bellarmine, had been dogmatic, its principles being drawn from Revelation alone. Due to the polemic against the Reformers of the sixteenth century, Bellarmine's treatise on the Church, the first complete work of this kind, was apologetic rather than dogmatic in nature.[8] Weigel tackled his task in this apologetic manner.

Stemming from *Dei Filius,* Vatican I's Constitution on Catholic Faith,[9] Weigel's apologetic examines the Living Church. The Church's existence is so miraculously conserved and enlivened that it must be from God and its doctrines must be divine.[10] Used also by Augustine,[11] this analytical method, without trying to prove

148

too much, still lays a rational groundwork for the faith that is already within Christians.[12]

Father Weigel stated that the Roman Catholic Church is the authentic, infallible and unique organ of Divine Revelation for the human race, and is itself the infallible and exclusively indestructible witness of its Divine Legate.[13] This was Weigel's favorite thesis, termed by his students, "Rhetorice Certa."[14] Weigel empirically examined that religious body, spread throughout the world and united by a common ritual, doctrine and morals, living under obedience to the local bishop who is united to the Roman pontiff, the ultimate and decisive authority. Because this *coetus* has been authentically designed by God to communicate divine revelation to the human race, it cannot err and, *de jure*, it exclusively communicates this revelation. Weigel admitted that, *de facto*, other religious bodies can communicate partial revelation.[15] Father Weigel admitted, too, that his position appears to involve a kind of "olympian security" for the Catholic Church.

"It requires no little courage to face the world and declare that one is the official only mouthpiece of God and incapable of error in this role. Not only is this claim made but it is further stated that no one who does not belong to the Catholic Church can achieve the end of mortal human life."[16] Yet the Catholic Church makes these claims and sticks by them, he said. In the light of Vatican II's ecclesiology, a more modest claim would be made for the Roman Catholic Church which must be always in a state of reformation.

In his examination of the life of the Church, Weigel began by stating that the Church is a society, i.e., "a union of human beings, consciously striving in terms of authoritatively planned and imposed coordination, for an end deliberately conceived." In fact, the Church is the highest type of society. This is so because it is "a *directed* collaboration in terms of officials who must be obeyed." Unlike other societies which do not attempt to make their members think certain things, "the Catholic Church . . . excludes nothing that is human from its field of directed collaboration." However, he states the limits to this openness. Inner coercion is exercised by authority to make all members "accept intellectual positions declared by the society through its officials to be necessay for this union. There is no activity that is excluded from this type of legislation." If this inner conformity is lacking, the individual automatically ceases to be a member.[17]

"Weigel's Church" therefore, was heavily authority-oriented and centered around the acceptance of juridically imposed intellectual positions and truths. How fitting a vision for one who would rather be right than President and whose life was an on-going pursuit of "The Truth" and "The Real"! How convenient that his search found satisfaction in this "society" which, as he believed, really possessed truth authentically, uniquely, and infallibly! The old maxim has it that we see what we want to see and need to see. And, as we see things, so they become for us.

For Weigel, the Church appeared as a moral miracle in its very existence, for three reasons: 1) It is a supernatural society, spread throughout the world, involving great variety of cultural expression and personality. Yet, by inner assent, all members are one in creed, code and cult. Over all this variety, the Church "claims directive power over any phase of their lives." By comparison with other societies, the Church is superior in this way.[18] 2) The Church, despite its geographical spread and variety, has a true and substantial unity. All "share the same vision exactly." Differences are only accidental. When compared to other societies—e.g., the Masons—its unity is quite unique.[19] Weigel seemed to confuse the one vision of faith with a uniform theological union. 3) The stability of the Catholic Church, too, is incomparable. This is true, even if the Church is only considered as it has existed from around 500 A.D., the date at which some Protestant critics say the Roman Catholic Church began. Despite its ups and downs, "it lives and lives as always around the Pope of Rome."[20]

Weigel pointed out that, historically, societies tend to dissolve from external opposition, such as coercion or ideological attack, or from inner decadence. In the light of these laws of the dissolution of societies, the Catholic Church's unity and stability appear as a moral miracle.[21] Weigel's lack of concern for historical details showed itself here when he stated that all of these attacks were repulsed without an army, only by spiritual force. Until 1870, the pope did have an army. His troops drove off the Turks in the Battle of Lepanto. Weigel noted too that decadence has been a constant factor in the Church's internal life. Yet the Church has not perished.[22] The Catholic Church is a moral miracle, then, for Weigel, because its survival contradicts the very laws of the dissolution of societies.

In the final section of his phenomenological investigation, Weigel commented on the vitality of the Catholic Church as further proof of the moral miracle.[23] In this section, the chauvinism of his investigation of the life of the Church is obvious. He listed the well-known saints of the Church, saying that it is the peculiarity of the Catholic Church that it produces such holy figures in all times. "It is true," he added, "that there are great and good men outside of the Catholic community, but their number is not so constant nor so typical . . . The Salvation Army is not Catholic and is a splendid organization, but somehow its work is not the same as the work of nuns in asylums and hospitals. Buddhist monasteries can make for contemplation, but the air of a Cistercian monastery breathes something different and more energetic." Weigel's rhetorical skills could sometimes extend the truth.

The Catholic Church, he claimed, is also more fruitful than other societies in all fields of beneficence: hospitals, universities, art and music and learning. This is especially true of Catholic philosophy which is able to assimilate into the Catholic scheme the good things in other philosophies, yet cast aside those elements which are non-assimilable. High deeds of adventure are ornaments of Catholic history too. The discovery of the New World, the Crusades, and missionaries are mentioned. Social services are provided by the Church

151

by religious women. His exalted description of these dedicated women bears full quotation:

> They receive no salary; they have no home in the sense of family life. They are necessarily saints. They may be cross, unpleasant, inclined to laziness, practicing intrigue in the little politics of their little communities, yet their life is built on unselfishness. Their food at best is good but hardly luxurious; at worst frugal and simple. Their accommodations at best modest; at worst poor. Their work long and hard; their pleasures few. They are generally mediocre people; small in their virtues and small in their vices; but they do a work that no one else does quite in the same way. They are paid nothing for their labors; frequently enough receiving no gratitude from their charges. Catholicism made them possible and where Catholicism goes, they go too . . . Some are small souls, spreading the poison that distills from small minds, but they are sustained with humor by the others. It all works out calmly.
>
> In ordinary life, Catholics have the benefit of 'little comforts' distributed by the Church to meet life's needs. The hard-working housewife finds consolation in her devotion to the Virgin. The adolescent, tempted to experiment with his 'manhood,' is strengthened by the Catholic ideal, no matter how often he may fail. This makes him 'better' than his fellows. Sickness, poverty and death are easier to bear because of the Catholic ideal.
>
> It is good to be a Catholic. In joy and sorrow it is an aid and a prop. If its doctrines were carried out by all men, this earth would be a very pleasant place indeed. Even as things are, it gives a vision whereby the individual can be effective and happy even though the world we live in is slightly mad even in its best days.[24]

All this is typical Weigelian pessimism and realism tempered by a Catholic hopeful optimism. Reading these pages with contemporary ecumenically-oriented eyes, one has the impression they were written by a Roman Catholic triumphalist. The Catholic Church's holiness and fecundity are extolled as better, existentially, than any. All others pale before it. Who would guess Gus Weigel to be this nation's Roman Catholic pioneer in ecumenism!

Thus, through an examination of the Church historically, psychologically, philosophically and personally, Gustave Weigel judged that he had shown persuasively but not demonstratively that the Roman Catholic Church must be what it claims to be. His method attempted to justify the Church *as is,* validating what a person already believes about the Church. The closer the person is to the institution, the more persuasive will be the "moral miracle."

One of Weigel's students offered a telling critique of this moral miracle argument. Weigel had supported the approach by an analogy with a certain European cathedral. If you stand in one spot, he said, you have a view of beauty which you get from no other position in the building. That was similar to seeing the Church from the vantage point of the moral miracle. The student said that seemed like seeing something which wasn't really there.[25] Indeed, Weigel's vantage point does seem to piece history and facts together in a way which at times is not really there. Yet Weigel's sense of the lived reality of the Church being the primary witness to God's revelation is basically sound although he tends to ignore, in print, the Roman Catholic Church's flaws.

An interesting point in Weigel's ecclesiology is his treatment of Church and Kingdom. His position is that there is a continuity between the Kingdom of Israel and the New Kingdom preached by Christ which he is already inaugurating. It has different stages: 1) the Kingdom of Israel; 2) the New Kingdom begun by Christ which now grows among us; 3) the glorious, risen Kingdom at the end of time. Between stages 2 and 3, there is a community of the elect of the Kingdom which is called, *Qahal, Ekklesia* or Church. "To this community is given the task of announcing the glad tidings of the Kingdom to all and maintaining a new life of man in accord with the laws of the new Kingdom."

Weigel showed a clear advance over some earlier Catholic thinkers when he stated that the *Ekklesia* is not coextensive with the Kingdom. The latter is the reign of God over all, even those who do not recognize the presence of the new Kingdom. The Kingdom is, therefore, more inclusive and extensive than the Church. The Church "is the visible human nucleus of its evolving reality."[26] Though he did distiniguish Kingdom and Church, Weigel did not, however, show clearly the inchoative Kingdom at work in the world outside the Church. For Weigel, God's action toward us is centered almost entirely in the Roman Catholic Church, as was the common emphasis in his day.[27]

Thesis V presents the operative vision Weigel had of the Church from his seminary days: the Mystical Body of Christ.[28] John Murray said that Weigel's synthesis on the Mystical Body was his only original contribution to ecclesiology. It was in reading the work of Maurice de La Taille in his student years that Weigel had sensed the Church as a mystery. Later, in reading Karl Adam's *The Spirit of Catholicism* and Dom Odo Casel's *The Mystery of Christian Worship,* this vision was deepened. The Church is a mystery and an object of faith. Therefore it cannot be adequately or perfectly understood by reason alone.[29] As a professor of ecclesiology at Woodstock, Weigel expanded this vision of the Church. By then the Mystical Body had become only *one* of the images of the Church, though it was still an extemely important one. This was in contrast with his predecessor, Joseph J. Bluett, S.J., who had stressed the Mystical Body metaphor almost exclusively.[30] In his treatment of the Mystical Body, Weigel noted the difficulties found in the word *union,* which were left unsettled by the encyclical, *Mystici Corporis,* thus leaving theologians free to speculate on the nature of the union. Gustave Weigel did just that in a very unique way.

The union, as he understood it, between Christ and the faithful is neither hypostatic nor substantial, neither physical nor moral. The union, which is *sui generis,* is accidental and supernatural. The accident is in all the members objectively real and is the same specifically in all the members. It is a relation, "a relation of sharing actively his concrete existent human nature to the members."[31] This sharing in Christ's concrete existent human nature is a position unique to Weigel. The source of his thought could not be determined. The originality of his position is seen clearly in the short formula he gave to describe this *unio mystica*.

> The mystical union is a supernatural, accidental, ontological union, superceding the moral order, by which the concrete humanity of Christ is communicated to men although not resulting in one physical composite physical being but elevating man to a higher state of being and acting on account of a certain physical modification of the whole man, so that through a certain *communicatio idiomatum* is truly but analogically predicated of men the attributes which are properly said of Christ.[32]

According to Father Weigel, the concept of *Soma tou Christou* in Paul means a supernatural union of men into a social fellowship which is knitted together by an all-pervading and permeating Spirit of Christ, "so that speaking in terms of analogy, the new linking makes men parts of Christ as members of a body."[33]

All of this is caused efficiently and formally by the Spirit, the Soul of the body. The accident produced in the members by the Spirit produces an exigency for participation in the human nature of Christ.[34] Satisfied in the Eucharist, "the formal effect of this modification is the transfusion of the *vis* (potentia activa) of Christ's human nature into the human nature of the member."[35]

Weigel said that this exigency and its consummation are never outside of the ecclesiastical context and unity. "Therefore the complete sanctification of man is in terms of the Church and never beyond it."[36] Thus his interpretation of the doctrine ends up with a very "churchy" Church. Its relation to the world is not clear and the action of God to save man going on in the whole of humanity is not specified.

Weigel concluded the section on the scriptural images of the Church[37] by saying that all described one and the same reality. No one image can give the whole view of the mystery that is the Church. "The *Ecclesia* image shows us a visible society; the Body shows us a supernatural, vital union; the Bride-and-Groom image shows us a union of mutual communication in terms of love."[38]

In the latter image, Weigel added the notions of Augustine[39] and Chrysostom[40] to make clear that the union between Christ and the Church is "carnal" in a quasi-physical union, effected and sustained by love.[41]

In *Pars Tertia* Father Weigel assembled all the essential elements for the definition of the Church and arranged them in hierarchical order.

> The Church of Christ, or the Roman Catholic Church, is essentially a mystical union between the living Christ and the faithful taken singly and collectively. This appears visibly as a true, universal and hierarchical society, established by Christ for the purpose of giving instrumentally to its members the new life and a share in the divine nature through the application of the redemption effected by Christ to the human race, and of infallibly communicating the Christian Revelation to all men until the end of time.[42]

Weigel said this definition managed to hold a balanced view of the Church in which both the visible and invisible elements in her nature are preserved in an "ontal" unity, with priority being given to the spiritual. He saw his definition as a distinctive progression in ecclesiology.[43]

Having identified the Church of Christ with the Roman Catholic Church and having investigated the nature of that Church, Weigel then proceeded to study dogmatically what he considered to be the most important part of that Church: the hierarchy. All jurisdiction in the Church is situated exclusively in the episcopal order, as the successor of the apostolic college.[44] In this, Weigel was a man in advance of his time, foreshadowing the teachings of Vatican II on collegiality in #22 of *Lumen Gentium*. For Weigel, primacy had to be seen within the episcopal order. Speaking in this way was uncommon in Weigel's day. Even in *Lumen Gentium,* #22, papal power is treated before that of the episcopal college.

Weigel entered upon a lengthy defense of the use of the term jurisdiction. Those, such as Protestants, who stress the primacy of the spiritual in the Church, are not comfortable with the material consideration of jurisdiction. It is this element that distinguishes Catholic Christianity from all non-Catholic Christian groups, according to Weigel. Weigel insisted on the importance of jurisdiction.[45]

Having concluded the section on the power of ruling, Weigel considered the power of teaching in the Church. Again, he placed it first in the episcopal college. The episcopal college, teaching the Revelation of Christ either through the solemn and extraordinary magisterium or through the ordinary magisterium, is the authentic magisterium in the Church and is infallible.[46] The magisterium, then, does not extend beyond the episcopal college which includes the pope as its primate, according to Weigel. This is a notion which he would come to reconsider at Vatican II.

The final *scholion* is particularly interesting in the light of Weigel's later participation in the Second Vatican Council. In no way can a council oppose the pope. One might ask: what value is a council then? It is never absolutely necessary but it can be useful and relatively necessary. It can advise the pontiff and it can make clear to adversaries that a certain doctrine is patently the teaching of the entire church. However, since the definition of papal infallibility by Vatican I, Weigel judged that councils would be no longer as important as before. Because of the defining power of the pope, there is no need for recourse to a council for this work unless the pope so chooses.[47] Weigel personally felt there would be no more ecumenical councils after Vatican I.[48] This opinion did not, however, reflect his position at Vatican II where Weigel supported the development of the doctrine of collegiality.

The predominant impression from Gustave Weigel's ecclesiology is that the Church is extremely top-heavy. Weigel's Church is super-hierarchical. One could say that, since the higher contains the lower within the Church, there is no necessity for the faithful. One only needs the episcopal college united with its head. Thus, although Weigel was in advance of his time on collegiality, he was not abreast of his time when it came to a theology of the laity, at least as expressed here. His development of *laos tou Theou* was slight.

After this heavily hierarchical ecclesiology, Weigel at last turned to the question of the members of the Church. "Extra Ecclesiam Nulla Salus" was, for him, the "first principle" directing the consideration of the members of the Church. Weigel summarized the Catholic meaning of this age-old principle: Only Christ can save and the Church is Christ prolonged. The Church applies Christ's redemptive work through the sacraments with which she was equipped by Christ himself. The Church *per se* administers the sacraments only to her own and therefore membership in the Church is *per se* necessary.[49] This rather negative and exclusivist position is especially interesting in the light of his ecumenical work. His thesis states that formal and perfect membership is enjoyed by those baptized, recognized by the Church and in sanctifying grace; formal but imperfect membership is held by those baptized, recognized by the Church but lacking sanctifying grace.[50]

Father Weigel then dealt with how God saves those not in the visible Church. God has indeed founded a Church through which salvation is offered to all. However, God can work outside this ordinary order. "He can therefore give the fruits of Christ and the Church to souls without the social mediacy of the Church where such mediacy is impossible because of the limited nature of the Church."[51] Weigel held that God would only act in this extraordinary way if his chosen instrument was not at hand and functioning adequately. Even when God takes this extraordinary means, it is still ecclesiological grace that is offered "because the virtue proper to the Church was being used in favor of an individual and applied immediately by the source of the Church's virtue, God . . . The salvation granted to the individual puts him in some relationship to the Church."[52]

Thus, though not belonging juridically to the Church, those who receive salvation extraordinarily share in the mystical, graced foundation of the Church. Weigel railed against those who consider the Church primarily juridical in this instance. His more mystical and interior understanding of the Church helped him in this regard.

> Any attempt to reduce the Church into a Procrustean bed of a legalistic philosophy must fail, and no theologian knowing the fuller nature of the Church will be led to make so small-minded an attempt. How God works with the individual soul, that ineffable mystery, is something we do not know. Nor need we try to give God a scheme which he must follow, for he is far above "the human lore, of man's nicely calculated less or more."[53]

Nevertheless, Weigel did attempt some sort of schematization for "members" in the Church. First, he stated that all people, in virtue of their humanity, are potential members of the Church. Secondly, those baptized by the Church and recognized as members of the Church are formal members whether they are in grace or in sin. Thirdly, those baptized by the Church but not recognized because of excommunication, are members *radicaliter*. They have graced roots in the Church, though juridically declared out of the society of the Church. Fourthly, Weigel said that those not recognized as members of the Church but upon whom God has exercised his extraordinary saving action and who remain in sanctifying grace, are members *virtualiter*.[54]

Weigel concluded his discussion of the axiom, "Extra Ecclesiam, nulla salus," by providing an opening for ecumencial work. This became his own personal approach to the ecumenism which consumed the last years of his life. He said that no one knows from revelation whether God actually does work with "outsiders" in the way above suggested, though revelation certainly shows its possibility and probability.

> Knowing God's mercy and salvific will, we can piously suppose that God actually does use this manner of sanctifying and saving souls. . . . In converse with non-Catholics, and even in the apostolate, it is advantageous to suppose that God is doing so

159

with the people with whom we deal. In this way, they are already virtually in the Church and we are striving to render the virtuality formal. Such a supposition has absolutely no guarantee of validity, but it is a sign of Christian love of the neighbor and a high esteem of God who works in wondrous ways with men, his children. It is justified pragmatically because it makes contact and apostolate with non-Catholics easier. It is the supposition of love which makes much of possibility and needs not probability, and much less, certainty, as a condition for action.[55]

Following Canon 87 of the Code of Canon Law, Weigel said that non-Catholic Christians are material heretics and, even though they may be in good faith, are presumed to be formal heretics. Good faith does not change the non-Catholics' excommunicated status. Juridically, Weigel said, this is perfectly clear.

His initial Baptism joined him to the Church and his bad will, juridically presumed, makes him fall under the ban of excommunication. In Catholic theory there is only one Christian Church, the Roman Catholic Church. Jews and Moslems belong to another religion, but never a baptized person. In fact, of course, we recognize the existence of other Christian churches, but never in theory.[56]

In Weigel's entire discussion of membership in the Church, it is the model of the Church as society which predominates, rather than the Church as *Qahal* or as *Soma*. Though he acknowledges the Church as a community founded in mystery, his treatment of membership nevertheless stems from a juridical sense of society.

A supplement to *Summula Ecclesiologica* treats the relations between Church and State. It states that the Church is a supernatural society distinct from and superior to civil society. Each has its areas of autonomy. However, in matters which fall under the dominion of both, the authority of the State is subordinate to that of the Church.[57] This resembles the position that had been elaborated by John Courtney Murray. To achieve harmony between the two sources of authority in "mixed matters," Weigel thought, the

Catholic principle is that the State may not legislate contrary to the Church. This seems to imply some sort of contrariety between the two powers. He spoke of the two collaborating, not opposing. Since the true ruler in a democracy is the people, the Church exercises her influence on the State indirectly, through direct influence on the people, the true rulers, who will manifest their will in the government.[58] This, Weigel felt, would handle the objections of Protestants who suspect that a Catholic majority in a society would suppress their freedom of religion.

During the 1960 presidential campaign, as John F. Kennedy was being questioned about his ability to hold the highest office in this land, Gustave Weigel had an opportunity to apply this Church-State doctrine. Part of the Protestant fear discussed by Weigel in *An American Dialogue* involved an unreasonable horror that Catholics would take over this country politically, especially through having a Catholic in the White House. The presidency is the symbol of our nation. If a Catholic were elected, all would know that this was not a Protestant land.[59] In 1958, Father Weigel publicly expressed that this fear may well become visible should Kennedy become a candidate for the presidency.[60] Personally, Weigel hoped that Kennedy would not be a candidate because he abhorred the possibility of another 1928 anti-Catholic campaign when all the bugaboos would be raised again and also because he was not personally attracted to Kennedy.[61] After Kennedy was nominated in August, 1960, the two popular ecumenists, Robert McAfee Brown and Gustave Weigel, took to the air to discuss the religious issue intelligently. Six radio dialogues were broadcast around the time of the November election.[62]

Weigel's chief contribution to the candidacy of Kennedy and the religious issue raised was a speech given on September 27, at the Church of the Blessed Sacrament in Washington, D.C. In the speech he hoped to clarify the Church-State issue without appearing to favor any candidate.[63] As a matter of fact, Weigel was not in favor of Kennedy's election. He did not vote for him.[64]

161

In his widely publicized and reprinted address, Father Weigel said, first of all, that the problem lay in the relationship between the sacred and the secular orders. Catholic theology teaches, as a first principle, and most do hold, that the sacred order is superior to the secular. Secondly, the state, though it can take many forms freely chosen by men, is necessary for human survival and progress. Man is subject to both: to the sacred, absolutely; to the secular, relatively. The third principle is that the two orders should exist in an ideal concord. This ideal, in practice, could frighten Protestant Americans. Many were asking: Could Catholics impose their moral and theological positions on others, should they be a majority or rule the land? Weigel replied: "The American Catholic as a matter of fact is not conscious of any desire to suppress all religions other than his own. He finds such an idea shocking and grotesque." Yet Protestant fears persisted. The histories of other lands where Catholicism has ruled were too well remembered. Would not Catholics impose their own peculiar moral positions on others, such as birth control? Weigel's answer was very clear cut:

> Once more we are faced with a confusion. The function of civil law is not to teach theology or even the moral views of the legislator. In conscience, be he Catholic, Protestant, or Jew, it would be immoral for him to impose on the community what he thinks immoral. He would have to disassociate himself from such an action. However, the toleration of immorality, if such toleration is demanded by the common good, is good law, and in accord with the morality of political action. This usually is the task facing the statesman. He is not a moral philosopher nor a moral teacher. . . . The obligation of civil law is not of the same nature and scope as the obligations of the moral law. I do not say that law can prescind from morality, but I do say that the attempt to impose one more theory or another is not the function of the statesman. Here he takes his lead from the consensus of the community.

In conclusion, Weigel assured his listeners that nothing in Catholic theology would prevent a Catholic from holding public office on any level "according to the spirit and letter of our American law." Then he gave the following advice:

> To all non-Catholics I would suggest that they keep in mind the difference of the order of law which is the political concern and the order of religion and ethics which is the believer's concern. The two are not the same nor do they produce conflicts *per se*. The morality of divorce, birth control, liquor traffic and the like are one thing. Civil legislation about them is quite another. Morality is categorical and obliges by inner consent. Legislation is conditioned and works by some kind of external coercion.[65]

The address won the praise of many, including Democratic candidate Kennedy, who wrote a letter of thanks to Weigel for his efforts.[66] Protestant thinker, Reinhold Niebuhr, also wrote a lengthy and generally favorable comment in the *New Republic*.[67]

Others were not as favorably impressed. Jaroslav Pelikan, who had written his book, *The Riddle of Roman Catholicism*, partly to lay to rest Protestant fears of Catholics, said that he doubted that Weigel's presentation represented a truly well-thought-out position. It was an "ad-hoc effort."[68] Avery Dulles thought the distinction Weigel made between the two orders was overly simplistic.[69] An editorial in *Christian Century*, based largely upon the critique of Weigel's address which had been made by H. A. Obermann of Harvard University, claimed that Weigel's separation of law and morality is both interesting and disturbing. It claimed that Weigel's presentation seemed "dangerous and uncommunicative of reality or truth."

> Father Weigel's separation of law and morality, his concept of a President living "a double life," first in one and then in the other realm, carries Jesuit scholasticism to terrifying lengths. If a President were to take it seriously it would cripple him, would rob the nation's highest official and the head of one of the most powerful states in the world of nobility of character and capacity for right judgment.[70]

163

It is my judgment that Weigel's position merited the criticism offered. It is, indeed, simplistic. A person's moral position must influence his official actions in some way. Sad would be the nation headed by a morally neutral leader. Yet, as Weigel correctly stated, it would be immoral for a leader to impose his particular moral judgments on the nation without consensus. The difficulty comes in balancing the moral good for all people with legislation regarding that good. Weigel's division between law and morality is clear in theory but not at all clear in practice. The issue continues to haunt our nation in the controversy surrounding abortion.

Gustave Weigel's near-fatal illness in 1954 coincided with the completion of the final edition of his *Summula Ecclesiologica.* He had intended and been encouraged to write a full treatment on the Church in later years but never did so. Though he did write monographs on ecclesiology and spoke periodically on the subject between 1954 and his death, Weigel's post-illness interests were in ecumenism more than ecclesiology. His basic vision of the Church remained unchanged though certain minor expansions can be detected in later writings and speeches.

Weigel became more and more enamoured with the notion of the Church as symbol and sacrament toward the end of the 1950s. This was a more intensive emphasizing of his roots in the de la Taille and Casel mold. God deals with humans through symbols which are, as Tillich has said, signs which share in the power and being of the things signified. The reality signified is really present in the symbol. Such symbols come to be, not by nature, but by intention. God chose Christ as a symbol of salvation and Christ established the Church as a salvific symbol, sharing salvation through symbolic, sacramental actions. For Weigel, "symbolism is the key to good theology. It takes revelation seriously without debasing it."[71]

As the preparatory work for Vatican II was in progress, Weigel began to move away from his super-hierarchical view of the Church. In an address in 1960, he spoke of the role of the laity in the

Church. He said the Church is the laity; all in the Church, including the hierarchs, are the *laos tou theou*. These members differ only in function, not in any kind of subordination of membership. The people must initiate the life and action of the Church which the hierarchy should coordinate. Yet, Weigel complained that too little autonomy and authority is given to the laity who, today, are so well-prepared and educated to assume an active role in the Church. He urged laymen to be unafraid to take initiatives, though holding firmly to the principle of functional subordination to the hierarchy. "His initiative, even if it should meet with the repression of hierarchy may yet exercise the prophetic function in the Church."[72] Thus, as Weigel began to experience the expanding ecclesiology of Vatican II, he appeared to be moving away from such a heavily hierarchical view of the Church.

During 1963, he prepared three papers which compared canonist ecclesiology with current views of the Church. Here too Weigel's experiences at Vatican II must have made him more aware of the limitations of the older, juridical approaches to ecclesiology and the soundness of his own basic, long-held intuitions about the vital mystery of the Body of Christ. He showed that the ecclesiological view of medieval theologians was based upon a juridical model of the Church which existed in medieval Europe. In making this ecclesiastical model normative, theologians and the Church have absolutized a relative thing. This was especially true of the first tract on the Church, written in 1448–1449 by Juan de Torquemada, O.P.[73] Father Weigel moved more toward a relativizing of the Mystical Body image of the Church as well.

> There is no need of making the Body image do the main work
> in explaining the Mystery of the Church. It does not seem to
> be privileged, even though St. Paul makes it central in his own
> thought. Should some other image be more appealing to our
> time, by all means let our time use it. The function of an anal-
> ogy is to communicate an ineffable truth effectively. That image
> which is more effective should be the image analyzed. The effi-

165

cacy of a symbol lies not in itself but rather in the concrete social environment where the Gospel is being preached. Not all images speak persuasively to all periods. Each era and each generation of an era must choose the analogies which it finds stimulating. What is not permitted is the employment of categories which carry no excitement for those who hear the proclamation of the Gospel.[74]

Gustave Weigel's ecclesiology represents an advance in that it is more vital then juridical and in that it does not attempt to prove the unprovable as had an older apologetic. The Church for Weigel is essentially a mystery, lived in faith. Its beauty, cogency, and depth must be seen in this context. He does, however, underestimate the existence of division and dissent in the Church and he does not adequately acknowledge sin and scandal within the Church itself.

Perhaps the most profound ecclesiological insight uttered by Weigel was a story he frequently told. He would say that there are many churches. There is that of the Woodstock canonist, Joseph Gallen. There is that of the dogmatic theologian, Gustave Weigel. And there is that of the pastor of St. Alphonsus Church at the foot of the hill at Woodstock, Peter McBride. "And you know," Weigel would say, "the *real* Church is Pete McBride's Church."[75]

Endnotes

1. Weigel's ecclesiology in Chile, as mentioned in Chapter VI, focused upon the model of the Mystical Body and upon the episcopal college as the foundation of the Church.

2. Between 1949 and 1954, Weigel wrote the two mimeographed texts for his courses at Woodstock, a 58-page survey of Protestant theology and an 11-page pamphlet on reunion with the Eastern Rites, "Thy Will Be Done." Nine contributions were written for larger works. Sixteen periodical articles were published.

3. Gustave Weigel, S.J., *Summula Ecclesiologica*, 2nd edition, for private use. Woodstock, 1954. Hereafter this is referred to as *SE*.

4. *SE*, pp. 6–7. Weigel described the way in which the treatise *De Ecclesia* developed over the centuries in several writings: *"Modern Orientations in Ecclesiology,"* unpublished and undated (WCA II F 303.17s); "The Present Status of Catholic

Ecclesiology," *Proceedings of the Society of Catholic College Teachers of Sacred Doctrine,* 7:21-31; *Catholic Theology in Dialogue,* chapter entitled "Catholic Ecclesiology in our Time," (New York: Harper and Bros., 1961); "Foreward" to *The Church: Readings in Theology* (New York: F. Kennedy and Sons, 1963), pp. ix-xii.

5. *SE,* p. 3.
6. *Ibid.,* pp. 3-4 and 14.
7. *Ibid.,* p. 6.
8. Robert Bellarmine, *De Controversiis,* Tom. II, Libs III et IV; *SE,* p. 7.
9. "The Church by itself, with its marvelous extension, its eminent holiness and its inexhaustible fruitfulness in every good thing, with its Catholic unity and its invincible stability, is a great and perpetual motive of credibility and an irrefutable witness of its own divine mission." *Dei Filius,* Chapter 3, quoted from Cuthbert Butler, *The Vatican Council* (London: Longmans, Green and Co., 1930), v. II, p. 261.
10. *SE,* p. 8.
11. Other theologians listed by Weigel who used the analytic argument were St. Thomas (Contra Gentiles, I, c. 6); St. Robert Bellarmine (Conciones and Controversiae); in the 19th century, Fenelon, Bossuet, Pascal, De Maistre, Chateaubriand, Lamennais, Lacordaire, Newman, Möhler and Dechamps; in the 20th century, Olle-Laprune, Brunettiere, DePaulpiquet, Blondel, Schell, de Guibert and Kosters. (*SE,* pp. 56-58.)
12. *SE,* pp. 8-11.
13. *SE,* p. 17.
14. Interviews with Avery Dulles, S.J., Donald Moore, S.J., and James Hennesey, S.J. Weigel found the moral argument further developed in Joseph de Guibert, S.J., *De Christi Ecclesia* (Rome: 1928), Th. 3, pp. 25ff and in Ludwig Kösters, S.J., *Die Kirche unseres Glaubens* (Freiburg i.B., 1935), pp. 33ff.
15. *SE,* pp. 17-20.
16. *Ibid.,* pp. 24-26. Weigel said: "It is not our purpose to show in this thesis that these claims are true but we do wish to show by the citations that they are claimed." (*SE,* p. 22.)
17. *Ibid.,* pp. 24-26.
18. *Ibid.,* p. 27.
19. *Ibid.,* pp. 32-35.
20. *Ibid.,* pp. 35-38.
21. *Ibid.,* pp. 38-46.
22. *Ibid.,* pp. 46-47.
23. *Ibid.,* pp. 48-55.
24. *SE,* 31, pp. 48-55.
25. Interview with Donald Moore, S.J.
26. *Ibid.,* pp. 91-92. A further development of the relationship between the Kingdom and the Church can be found in *SE,* pp. 102-106.
27. *SE,* pp. 95-06.
28. *Ibid.,* p. 117.
29. *Ibid.,* p. 132. Weigel wrote several other published works on the Mystical Body: "Mystici Corporis," *Catholic Encyclopedia,* Supplement II (New York: The Gilmary Society, 1950); "The Body of Christ and the City of God," *Social Order,* V. June, 1955, pp. 271-275; "The Inwardness of the Living Body of Christ," *Catholic World,* 193: 352-359, September, 1961.

30. Interview with George Glanzman, S.J. Glanzman stated that despite Weigel's willingness to use several images of the Church, he did not take seriously the strong Pauline theme of the Church as the New Israel which Glanzman urged upon him.

31. *SE*, p. 140.

32. *Ibid.*, p. 121.

33. *Ibid.*, p. 124.

34. *Ibid.*, pp. 140–141. Weigel stated that the *anima* of the Body of Christ is the Holy Spirit. It is both the formal and efficient cause of the unity of the Body. In a rare explicit borrowing from Aristotle, he wrote that the term *anima* is used analogically in the Aristotelian sense to indicate the formal and efficient cause of the Body. He deliberately rejected the tripart Platonic view of the person as *nous, psyche* and *soma* in his attempt to explain his point. (*SE*, pp. 135–137) Weigel drew this notion from John C. Gruden, *The Mystical Christ*, (St. Louis: Herder, 1936), pp. 180ff.

35. *Ibid.*, p. 141.

36. *Ibid.*, p. 142.

37. *SE*, pp. 143–145; pp. 151–152.

38. *Ibid.*, p. 148.

39. Augustine, *In I Ep. Joan.*, cap. 2, i, PL 35, 1940.

40. Chrysostom, *In Eph. V hom*, 20, e et 5, PG 62, 140.

41. *SE*, p. 149.

42. *Ibid.*, p. 156. This is analyzed and explained in *SE*, pp. 156–158. Weigel said the definition is apologetically a probable opinion, but, dogmatically, all its elements are the authentic doctrine of the Church (*SE*, pp. 158–159).

43. *Ibid.*, pp. 161–162.

44. *Ibid.*, p. 165. This theological understanding of the episcopal college was also being discussed by Karl Rahner during the 1950s. Weigel's position and Rahner's appear to be basically similar. Cf., Karl Rahner, "On the Divine Right of the Episcopate," *Episcopate and Primacy* (London: Nelson, 1962). This was first published in German in *Catholica*, Vol. 13 (1959), pp. 260–277. Cf. also Karl Rahner, *Theological Investigations* (Baltimore: Helicon, 1969), pp. 313–360, especially pp. 317–325 which state Rahner's post-conciliar development of this notion.

45. *Ibid.*, p. 168.

46. *Ibid.*, p. 221.

47. *Ibid.*, pp. 237–239.

48. Interview with Donald Moore, S.J.

49. *Ibid.*, p. 262.

50. *SE*, p. 259. The doctrine of "Extra Ecclesiam Nulla Salus" was first used by Cyprian and then by Augustine, Weigel's two favorite theologians. After Augustine, the principle is proposed by all theologians in almost identical terms. It is evident in the Athanasian Symbol of the fifth century.

51. *Ibid.*, p. 263.

52. *Ibid.*, p. 263.

53. *Ibid.*, p. 264.

54. *Ibid.*, pp. 264–266.

55. *SE*, p. 269.

56. *Ibid.*, p. 274.

57. *Ibid.*, p. 283.

58. *Ibid.*, p. 298. "Consequently in a *democratic* state in our *time*, which accord-

ing to 'many' is the form of government dictated by reason, whether the majority is Catholic or non-Catholic, free opinion, free assembly and free speech, are not only rights which the democratic government should respect in all its citizens, but it should foster these rights so that they become greater. Only one limit is placed on such rights: the end of the State, namely the common good."

59. Robert McAfee Brown and Gustave Weigel, *An American Dialogue* (New York: Doubleday, 1960), pp. 166–167.

60. Gustave Weigel, "The Temper of Protestantism Today," *National Conference on Convert Work Proceedings* (Washington, D.C.: St. Paul's College, 1958), p. 77; "American Roman Catholicism and Ecumenism," *Lutheran World*, V, June 1958, p. 32.

61. Interviews with Mrs. Frank Otenasek, Robert McAfee Brown, Paul Cassidy, S.J., and Carlos Eyzaguirre to Patrick Collins, Salt Lake City.

62. Interview with Robert McAfee Brown, *The Catholic Review* (Baltimore), November 4, 1060.

63. Gustave Weigel "Church State Relations: A Theological Consideration," *Catholic Theology in Dialogue,* p. 101; Carrol J. Bourg, S.J., to Sister Aquinas Neft, Baltimore, July 24, 1967 (Files of Sister Neft); *New York Times,* September 28, 1960, contained a lengthy article on the address with generous excerpts, pp. 1 and 28. Weigel also wrote an article in *Ave Maria,* May-June, 1960, entitled "Bishop Pike and a Catholic President." Weigel, who never liked Pike at all (Interview with Dr. Richard Ferguson, October 21, 1971), pointed out the lack of logic in giving special scrutiny to Catholic candidates and notes that Bishop Pike's theological questions were irrelevant to political questions.

64. Interview with Paul Cassidy, S.J.

65. *Catholic Theology in Dialogue,* pp. 103–117.

66. Interview with Robert McNally, S.J. This letter which McNally claimed Kennedy sent to Weigel was not in the Weigel papers.

67. Reinhold Niebuhr, "Catholics and the State," *New Republic,* CXLIII (October 17, 1960), pp. 13–15; Cf. also *Catholic Messenger,* September 29, 1960, p. 1; *Tidings* (Los Angeles), September 30, 1960, pp. 1 and 3; and *Time,* LXXVI (October 10, 1960), p. 27.

68. Interview with Jaroslav Pelikan.

69. Interview with Avery Dulles, S.J.

70. *Christian Century,* LXXVII (November 2, 1960), pp. 1267–1268.

71. Gustave Weigel, "Sacrament and Symbol," *Catholic Theology in Dialogue,* pp. 49–60, especially p. 66. He also discussed this in a radio address on WBAL in Baltimore in 1959 which was entitled "The Church and the Sacraments." (WCA II F 303.19y.)

72. Gustave Weigel, "The Role of the Laity," CFM Chaplains Meeting, Denver, July 28, 1960. (WCA II F 303.20a.) This was published in *Act,* January, 1961, vol. 14, no. 5, pp. 3 and 6. Also on this topic is a set of notes for a speech entitled "The Laity in the Church," undated, WCA II F 303.21b. This would appear to be from the early 1960s.

73. Gustave Weigel, "Reflections on Juan Torquemada's Methodology," unpublished and undated paper though it is probably from 1963. WCA II F 303.20a.

74. Gustave Weigel, "Current Ecclesiology and Canonist Ecclesiology Compared," unpublished, 1963. WCA II F 303.20a.

75. Interview with Joseph Doty. This church has been destroyed by fire.

CHAPTER NINE

An Uncompromising Ecumenist

"It would be easier for me to become an atheist than a Protestant."[1] Gustave Weigel spoke these words to Frank Otenasek shortly after his return from Chile in 1948. Strange words, indeed, coming from the man who was soon to become the leading Catholic ecumenist in the United States.

Weigel's entire background had been Roman Catholic, from his beginnings in Buffalo through his exclusively Jesuit education and academic activities in Santiago. In Chile, however, he had been close to the English-speaking colony which was largely Protestant. He had been impressed by them and was, himself, impressive to them, especially in his human warmth and openness. His friendships with non-Catholics in Chile, as has been seen, led to his being invited to speak at two non-Catholic memorial services for President Roosevelt, for which he was criticized by Church authorities.

Intellectually and religiously Weigel felt distant from Protestants, though he could be open to understanding their positions. His humanity sensed and expressed a closeness that was infectious. This combination of favorable personal factors prompted John Murray in 1948 to invite Weigel, lost and confused in his early days back in the States, to become the specialist in Protestant thought for *Theological Studies.*[2] Weigel willingly accepted. He published two articles in 1950 which earned him instant attention as an ecumenist: "Contemporaneous Protestantism and Paul Tillich,"[3] and "Protestant Theological Positions Today."[4] Weigel's reading of Tillich convinced him that this was a serious and in many ways acceptable

170

form of theologizing.[5] A personal encounter with Tillich before 1950 supported his judgment.[6]

Prior to 1950, ecumenism in the United States had been practically non-existent. Little interest was shown by the hierarchy, the clergy, or the laity.[7] It had been largely a European phenomenon which had been put under suspicion by the Holy Office *monitum* of 1948 and the restrictive *Instructio Ecclesia Catholica* of 1949. The latter document had asked that each diocese establish an ecumenical commission but none were formed in this country.[8] American Catholics were generally nervous about the whole matter.[9]

The encyclical, *Humani Generis,* 1950, cast a dark spell over the ecumenical movement too. It was condemnatory and suspicious of theological tendencies in Catholic circles which, in actuality, reflected basic Protestant approaches. Later the same year, *Munificentissimus Deus* proclaimed the dogma of the Assumption of Mary, a doctrine hardly calculated to please non-Catholics. It seemed that the Roman Catholic Church was not willing to acknowledge the fellowship that had come about as a result of ecumenism. The disappointment caused by this definition caused promising contacts to be broken. Many Protestants saw their negative picture of Catholicism confirmed and, increasingly, Catholicism was charged with lacking any real interest at all in unity.[10]

Until 1900, the United States was considered a Protestant land, operating from a basically Calvinistic vision of religion. The Catholics were always a minority, never in possession as in Europe. American Catholics were largely urban, eastern, and lower middle-class, with no aristocratic backbone as in Europe. Because they had no "golden age" to recapture, American Catholics could be more forward looking and accommodating to the national scene.

Some Catholics, in this foreign and often hostile land, lost their faith. But others "developed a stubborn and warm attachment to their church." As Weigel said,

> These were the Catholics who imparted their spirit to American Catholicism. American Catholics are very conscious of their faith

171

and, by and large, strict in their observances. The strongest characteristic of American Catholicism is its strong sense of loyalty which makes for conservatism rather than for a tendency toward change. One manifestation of this spirit is the high veneration of American Catholics for the pope, perhaps more visible than in some European churches.[11]

The general hostility of Protestant Americans toward the immigrant Catholics caused a tendency to insular solidarity, in Weigel's judgment. The Irish alone merged with American society, winning political power in eastern seaboard cities, as well as in the Church's hierarchy. Germans and other non-English speaking Catholics tended to build Catholic ghettos to preserve their faith and their culture. The overall compactness of Catholicism and the educational system it built impressed, yet frightened Protestants, increasing their hostility.

Catholics, though considering theirs the true religion, did accept Protestants. They generally felt some religion was better than none, wrote Weigel. Yet American Catholics, except for participation in some non-religious programs, remained aloof from ecumenical projects. Their only ecumenical efforts centered around the Chair of Unity Octave.[12]

Weigel said there were three reasons why American Catholics were so little interested in ecumenism. First, Catholics knew little about Protestants and were not allowed to attend their worship services nor were they inclined to discuss religion with them. Secondly, historical animosities were still alive and divisive. Thirdly, for Catholics, reunion must mean a return to the Catholic Church. Either one was a Protestant or a Catholic. The two could not become one without one absorbing the other.[13] "American Catholic ecumenism simply boils down to a cordial but general invitation to non-Catholics to become Catholics."[14] They make Protestants welcome, at best, "but they have not gone out to meet the non-Catholic on his native heath."[15]

Since 1900, Weigel noted, the situation had changed. Protestants had come to realize they were not inviolable in their positions and power. They were aware of an increase in Catholic membership and decrease in their own hold upon their people. This anxiety engendered humility.[16]

Catholics, for their part, had gained a new sense of security in this land. They had become transformed from an immigrant and poor people to true Americans, coming to share in the power and wealth of their country. Intellectually, too, they were coming into their own through the growth of universities and schools.[17]

Catholics and Protestants alike were anxious about the attacks upon religion made by naturalism, pragmatism, and secularism. They consequently felt the necessity to join arms to do battle with these common enemies of faith.[18] They also were coming to share the fruits of the scriptural, liturgical, and ecumenical movements that were being brought to this country from Europe.[19]

Weigel listed six results of these changes in Catholic and Protestant mentalities and positions: 1) Both groups shared in more common projects, even in some theological discussions; 2) Anti-Catholic and anti-Protestant literature had decreased; 3) Theological schools were attempting to be more fair and accurate in presenting the positions of other faiths; 4) Catholics and Protestants were studying together in universities and even some Protestant seminarians were attending Catholic theologates; 5) At least six doctoral dissertations were being done on Paul Tillich by Catholics at Catholic universities; 6) Both groups had become more united around the scriptures. "The retreat of Protestantism from its dissolving analysis of the Bible and the advance of Catholic biblical scholarship in its scientific exposition of Sacred Scripture have brought both camps much nearer to each other."[20]

Weigel's interest in ecumenism grew rapidly during the early years at Woodstock. Though primarily concerned with building his course in ecclesiology between 1949 and 1954, he also studied and wrote in the ecumenical field. In addition to the two important contributions in 1950 previously mentioned, Weigel delivered

173

an address at the eighth annual convention of The Catholic Theological Society of America in 1953 entitled "A Survey of Protestant Theology in Our Day."[21] In the same year, he published "Recent Protestant Theology," a survey of literature from the early 1950s, especially the writings of Tillich.[22] For the Great Book series, Weigel did an analysis of Calvin's *Institutes of the Christian Religion*.[23] He also continued his interest in oriental Churches through an address at the Fourteenth Annual Fordham Conference on Eastern Rites and Liturgies in 1952,[24] and a short sketch of the non-Latin rites of the Roman Catholic Church.[25] And it should be noted that from 1949 to 1961, Father Weigel was in charge of Woodstock's annual Oriental Days when an oriental rite liturgy was celebrated.[26]

During his tour of Europe for the State Department in 1953, Father Weigel had spoken about ecumenism to the German Reformation scholar, Father Joseph Lortz. Lortz told Weigel that it was a "disgrace and a sin" that Christians were not working for unity in the United States. He asked Weigel, "Why don't you do something?"

> I saw his point and I felt the first thing that had to be done was to understand. Unless we understand each other, we cannot possibly achieve real unity. In this country our situation is objectively and antecedently quite favorable. We live in a pluralistic society. Any civil community in this country with rare exceptions is made up of every kind of human being; Catholics and Protestants and Jews and other groups are mixed up. We are antecedently favored in coming together on a basis of friendship, on a basis of Christian charity with our non-Catholic Protestant friends. Now, to make this possible we have followed a tactic up to the present that may not have been the wisest one. We used the American trick which is the ostrich technique. We refused to talk about religion when we are in a group that is of mixed faith. The result was that both sides of the Catholic-Protestant division have remained totally ignorant of what the other fellow believes. This is wrong!. . . . If you understand,

you will not be shocked, you will not be annoyed. Understanding makes for clarification; and clarification is precisely the air in which good, if not fellowship at least cameraderie, shall flourish.[27]

Thus, early on in the ecumenical movement in this country, Gustave Weigel set the tone for his participation in that movement. His role was to be one of searching for mutual understanding, based upon mutual respect and friendship between the differing parties. It was a role for which his life had prepared him beautifully. His natural openness, human warmth and acceptance of differences, native intelligence, facility in expression and spontaneous wit and humor made him an excellent bearer of the ecumenical standard in those early days of dialogue.

Eugene Burke, C.S.P., of St. Paul's College, Washington, D.C., was a very close friend of Gustave Weigel's especially in ecumenical encounters. He said Weigel was able to open ecumenical doors that others could not because "he was in its richest Christian sense a man of tradition, a man shaped and permeated by the Christian experience and open to God's Word as He speaks it today."

> In all this Father Weigel was the very embodiment of Hemingway's "grace under pressure." Enabling him to do this was a combination of many things that were constitutive of his personality. He had a deep desire to understand the real mind of the person he was dealing with, and an almost intuitive acuity in putting his finger on the personal question at issue. Along with this was the strongly conveyed sense of seeking out the answer together or at least realizing together what the real question was. Also notable was a flexible, modern vocabulary that allowed him to be precise yet effective in explaining his position and understanding the other. Finally when the chips were down he had a bluntness that could be singularly gracious and resolved the issue without closing the door.[28]

Weigel's cancer surgery in May of 1954 interrupted his writings and activities for the remainder of that year. Once recuperated, he became a man possessed with the need and the desire to be at the disposal of all who called upon him, especially in the field of ecumenism. He then wrote and traveled widely to speak the message of Christian unity, seeing the finger of God in every invitation.

Ecumenism for Weigel was always conversation between differing brothers and sisters. In this exchange, there was no attempt at debate where one wins and the other loses.[29] In these conversations across denominational lines, Weigel felt that ignorance of the partner's confession could be eliminated and a mutual understanding of shared faith, though differing, could be achieved.[30] This was the first step that had to be taken and he felt eminently qualified to lead the way.[31]

In a 1962 dialogue with Angus Dun, bishop of the Episcopal Diocese of Washington, D.C., Father Weigel spelled out his definition of ecumenism:

> I would call ecumenical, any aspiration, any action, any institution whose purpose is to bring together the separated churches which bear the name of Christ, through representatives, in order to teach and learn, in the hope that God will use this conversation as an instrument to bring about the greatest unity possible among the churches which bear the name of Christ.

The hope of unity was something secondary to the actual coming together.[32] Through these friendly conversations, in which neither party tries to outwit the other, both learn from the other and inform the other. "This is a new thing in inter-church relations and it is pleasant," said Weigel. "Above all, the first efforts must be made by men who know both their own faith and the faith of others. Good will cannot substitute for knowledge. Knowledge and good will make a sound partnership. On such a foundation our conversations will be worthwhile."[33] As Weigel once said regarding conversation:

> The dialogue does not want polemically prepared people. The preparation that's required is a psychological preparation, a readiness and a willingness and a friendliness to be with the other

and to speak sincerely. Above all, we don't want 'techniques' or Madison Avenue tricks.[34]

Knowledge was one of Weigel's fortes. His own broad and deep grasp of the Catholic tradition plus his ability to express simply and clearly made him well-respected among the Protestant theologians and people. They were always sure that he was giving the Catholic position, without compromise and stating it with love and respect for others' positions. His integrity was beyond doubt. He was the first American priest to be willing to do this freely and widely and the Protestants fell in love with his large Christian humanness.[35] As his close friend Robert McAfee Brown put it, "That must be the way he is remembered—as a great, open-hearted man, who by the genuineness of his personal concern for others broke through barriers between Catholics and Protestants, Catholics and Jews, Catholics and secularists."[36] Personal friendship and respectful listening were the heart of his ecumenical practice.[37] With his strong feeling for unity in diversity and his radical respect for the human person, he was able to transcend ideological differences. He met the person and accepted him, though he might not agree with his ideas.[38]

Richard Cardinal Cushing recalled Weigel's speaking with him about the ecumenical needs of the country. Weigel told him:

> In this matter of ecumenism, I live from day to day, not worrying about or planning for tomorrow but living with the given and the now. I must practice friendship now without ulterior motive, not only with all men, but especially with the members of the household of faith. There must be talk, much talk and more talk while each side learns how the other understands the Gospel of Christ. We must move into the union of dialogue before we can think seriously about any other kind of union. The Holy Spirit will do the rest.[39]

Father Weigel was deeply convinced that the work of Christian unity was, in actuality, God's work. The coming together is man's work but the final union and the way it will be achieved is God's work.[40] God's grace alone can accomplish the final breaking of the barriers between Christians. And how this is to be done, Weigel could not see. He merely knew what he had to do at that moment to work toward the divine unifying action—talk and talk and talk to his Christian brothers and sisters. Christian unity and the appearance of but one visible Church was not in the foreseeable future, said Weigel from the beginning.[41]

This was because union, as Weigel saw it, could only mean one thing. Protestants would have to become Roman Catholic. He stated this clearly in a 1956 letter to his fellow ecumenist, George Tavard.

> I agree with you entirely that we must try to understand the psychology of the Protestant. We must know his history. We must recognize the sincerity and fervor of his piety. We must never forget his dedication to God, to Christ and the Word. We must not forget our own errors and our own lack of charity. Yet we must keep one thing clear always. We are humbly asking him to become a Catholic and that means he will be a Protestant no longer. In sincerity and truth we can tell him that he will lose none of the religious values so dear to him. Yet the total structure of his values will be changed, by enrichment we insist, but very definitely changed. I do not think that this message will please the Protestant. He is willing to become a Catholic provided he be permitted to retain his structure.[42]

Weigel's ecclesiological vision forced him to be strict on ecclesial structures. He was uncompromising in his ecclesiological notions.

Frequently Weigel mentioned three solutions to unity. *Compromise* is the way of give and take, in which a common basis is finally decided upon. No one wants this. "One cannot compromise with the will of God." *Comprehension* is the way of acceptance of certain principles of faith, polity and worship but allowing variety in the understanding of the accepted principles. Weigel pointed out that the Protestants would accept this approach but Catholics and Orthodox would not. The third approach is that of *Conver-*

sion. All the churches would disband and join one remaining Church. Catholics and Orthodox would agree to this but Protestants believe they are already the Church of Christ and aren't "coming back."[43] In his later dialogue with Angus Dun, Weigel specified a fourth way which must be the way for that day: *Convergence,* in which the churches, gathered in conversation, move closer and closer to one another.[44]

Father Weigel often warned his readers and listeners against adopting a utopian and euphoric attitude to Christian unity. He believed that grace can make all one within the Catholic Church but he did not see grace working in that way.

> Protestant and Catholic must live side by side throughout the foreseeable future. . . .
>
> The Lord wanted all those who believe in His name to be one. They will be one in God's time, not necessarily in ours. Until that time comes we must be patient. Until that time comes, we must live together, work together and even marry one another. For this necessity we need friendship. Anything honorable to promote and strengthen it is good. Catholics are for the friendship and Protestants need not be afraid. Catholics on principle will ask for only one thing, namely the recognition that the friendship exists in spite of religious differences and not as a means to dissolve the Catholic difference.[45]

To foster this ecumenical spirit Weigel encouraged the Catholic Press to explain the movement to its readers.[46] He also urged the Catholic laity to enter into friendly and sincere conversations with their fellow Christians on topics of religion.[47] By such active charity the churches will remain distinct but not really separate for love will have achieved a kind of unity.[48]

The ecumenical movement had been spawned in Europe, especially in response to the need for sharing and support as a result of the two great wars that devastated the continent. It was largely a Protestant movement, however. Faith and Order, inspired by the speech of Bishop Charles Brent at an ecumenical gathering in Edinburgh in 1910, was concerned chiefly with doctrinal unity. Life and Work stressed unity through life and action. Both were founded in the early part of this century. These two groups joined at a meeting in Amsterdam in 1948 to form the World Council of Churches. In this country, the Federal Council of Churches and the National Council of Churches were formed.

On the Catholic side of the ecumenical movement, there was the German-founded *Una Sancta* movement of Max Metzger; the *Istina Centre* of Father Christophe Dumont, O.S.B., and the work of the Benedictine monasteries at Chevetogne, Belgium, and Niederaltaich, Netherlands. Finally there was the work done by Abbé Paul Couturier of Lyon who urged prayer for unity: "Pray for the unity of the Church of Jesus Christ as He wills and when He wills." In Rome, Charles Boyer, S.J., who had been involved as a reader on Weigel's doctoral dissertation, was publishing the journal, *Unitas,* which spread to this country through the Friars of the Atonement at Graymoor, New York.[49]

Weigel was very much aware of the history of the movement in Europe. Yet he judged that American ecumenism had to be different. Despite the fact that there had been a dearth of American theologians, he felt the time was at hand to develop a truly American theology and enough good thinkers were available to do so.

He had no sympathy for the approach of Boyer's *Unitas*; and he mistrusted the overly "eirenic" approach of the French and the Belgians who seemed to be compromising too much for the sake of instant unity. He felt the need for eirenicism but of a more "hardcore" nature than the "soft-cored variety of some of our Gallic brethren." He saw the Germans, Irish, English and Americans as holding the doctrinal line more closely in ecumenical work.[50]

These sentiments Weigel expressed in a published introduction to an originally French book on ecumenism.

> A word of warning must be uttered. The English-speaking lands are not France. History has shaped us differently. The ecumenical

dialogue in the British Isles or in North America will have to be distinct from that on the Continent. We cannot simply import the European Way. We must produce our own way for better or for worse. The motives for acting in our lands will be the same as elsewhere. The basic structure of the enterprise will not be different, but the modalities of our conversations will be distinct. It would be quite useless to ask which way is better. . . . Chairs are good things and tables are good things but there it little sense in attempting to find out which is better. The only reasonable question would be to demand which is better for what. Good chairs make bad tables and good tables make bad chairs.[51]

Despite his "hard-core" approach to ecumenism, Weigel was not a fixist. He did not insist on retaining non-essential, historical accretions. He saw the need to "correct any angularities which derive from our historical conditioning." Modes and manners which stem not from belief but from environments of the past need not be retained. "We do not all want to drop the characteristic marks of our faith, but there is no need to hang on to model quirks and kinks which might make us stand out as an unpleasant people."[52]

It was in areas of dogma that he insisted on no compromise. He said the Catholic position reflected that of the Faith and Order organization, namely, doctrinal unity must precede actual union.[53] This was especially true in his own specialty, ecclesiology. He felt the greatest problem facing the ecumenical dialogue was the nature of the Church. This question had to be answered before any significant progress could be made.

The question has excruciating consequences. It comes down to this: must the Protestant admit that the Protestant Reform was a huge mistake with the consequence that it and all its specific fruits must be abandoned, or must the Catholic admit at long last that the Protestant Reform was substantially God-inspired and right in its intentions and aims.

Neither of these two questions will today be answered affirmatively by the group to which it is relevant.

181

Undoubtedly complicated realities cannot be adequately formulated in two such simple questions. Catholics and Protestant
thinkers must study the problem in the light of distinctions. Then
perhaps questions can be proposed to the partners in conversation which will not be so absolutely shocking to their sensitivi-
ties.[54]

Weigel's own ecclesiology, typical of all Catholic theological
works of that day, was antithetical to Protestants. Although he
allowed they were virtually in the Church, he was not willing to
give much credit to their ecclesial realities.[55] As one reads through
Weigel's *Summula Ecclesiologica,* finalized in 1954, it is hard to imagine that the author was America's first and best-known Catholic
ecumenist. Every reference to Protestantism is negative.

Despite this theological thought which seemed unfavorable to
Protestantism, Weigel's personality allowed him to transcend his
own thought patterns and relate with acceptance, understanding
and love to his non-Catholic colleagues. Jaroslav Pelikan stated that
Weigel did not revise his ecclesiology but merely adjusted his ecumenical practice.[56] As Warren Quanbeck, the Minneapolis Lutheran
theologian, put it, Weigel was more open as a person than as a
thinker. His theology seemed to be one of confrontation, but his
ecumenical practice was quite open to dialogue.[57] There were those
who felt that Weigel's openness was dangerous and that he was
not always quite honest in his dialogues with Protestants. The Graymoor ecumenist, Edward F. Hanahoe, S.A., said Weigel would
say one thing at a public meeting and another thing in private.[58]

The World Council of Churches presented a major dogmatic
and ecclesiological problem to Father Weigel. The Council, established in 1948, "is a fellowship of Churches which accept our Lord
Jesus Christ as God and Saviour."[59] The organization is not able
to define doctrine or impose policy on member churches. According to Weigel, "It wishes only to provide opportunity for discus-

sion and common contribution to the solution of questions. It also formulates and distributes the findings of such conversations."[60]

> The World Council is like the evangelical concept of a sacrament. It does not produce a given grace, but it is the stimulating occasion in which the churches can elicit acts under grace given immediately by God.[61]

Any church can join the council if it accepts the basis of the organization and is willing to cooperate on that basis. Unity of belief and a clear definition of the Church are neither presupposed nor prescribed.[62] The solid core of membership is the middle-of-the-stream Protestant churches, which among themselves lack homogeneity.[63]

Writing in 1955, Gustave Weigel first rejoiced in the formation of the World Council of Churches. Better to have some unity than none was his position. Such union, though imperfect, was the fruit of charity.[64] Then he explained why Catholics could not participate in the council. The confederation of churches shares no understanding of the Church. At the Evanston, Illinois, meeting of the council in 1954, an act of contrition was made for "the sinning Church." This presupposed a Protestant approach to ecclesiology, one in which the Church can sin. For Catholics and Orthodox, Christians can sin but not the Church. "A holy church by definition does not sin. . . ."[65] This is one position Weigel revised during Vatican II:

> The Evanston message makes sense only on the postulate of Protestant ecclesiologies, for all Protestants and even the Anglo-Catholics with some reservations will willingly, if not insistently, admit that the visible Church or churches as such are guilty of sin. They admit perhaps that the invisible Church is sinless, but this admission is possible because the invisible Church is the unrealizable ideal of the churches, or a mystical union unconsciously formed by the sinless saints.[66]

Catholics cannot accept a presupposition that the *Una Sancta* is still to be formed. Because of her divine constitution, she cannot be reestablished without becoming something else. A Catholic would find himself most uncomfortable in an organization which did not hold this ecclesiological position.[67] For the Catholic Church to join the World Council would be an admission that it is not what it claims to be. It would cease to be the Catholic Church.

> The Catholic insists that man dare not judge God and His word, and the word of God is spoken by the Catholic Church only, for the divinely inspired Scriptures and the ecclesiastical tradition are merely two means whereby the Church infallibly communicates her message. The moment a Catholic drops this point of view, he automatically ceases to be a Catholic. He implicitly drops his conviction when he is willing to drop any proposition taught by the Church as the genuine word of God, or if he seriously enters into a conversation where the silently operating postulate is such a willingness.
>
> When this is clearly recognized by both parties, it seems that neither Catholic nor Protestant could want the Catholic Church as a member of the World Council of Churches. The Protestant need only reflect that the Catholics could not take seriously the rationale of the World Council debates which are organized to construct or reconstruct, eliminate or adapt, or merely criticize the traditional dogmas.[68]

Father Weigel insisted that he wanted Protestant-Catholic dialogue. However, he did not think the World Council was the proper place for it, given its ecclesiological presuppositions. Individual and small group discussions are of great value and should be entered into, he thought, but the larger meetings would produce little fruit.[69] Weigel revealed his constant bias against working in large groups. He felt that informal observers from the Catholic Church might be sent to meetings of the World Council but no formal delegate could be sent "for his presence would be a silent protest to all that was going on. . . . A formal Catholic delegate would be an official alien critic of the sessions and such a concept is logically weird."[70] Weigel's opinion changed later as he himself would become an official delegate to meetings of the World Council.

In 1957, Father Weigel expanded his explanation of his difficulties with the council. He said that, although the council claimed to take no dogmatic stands, the very fact that dogmatic variety, especially ecclesiological variety, was allowed to co-exist in the confederation of churches was a dogmatic position, the position of the anti-dogmatic group which favored formal unity before dogmatic unity. Because it is a fellowship of churches, an ecclesiology is implied. "This ecclesiology could be described as methodic indifferentism in order to overcome indifferentism. It is difficult to see how Catholics are wrong when they find that indifferentism is the great danger of present non-Catholic ecumenism."[71]

Weigel claimed that the World Council was basically indifferent to the question which urged him on throughout his lifetime, the question of truth.[72] It was the non-dogmatic churches that were setting the tone for the Council and he was certain that their influence would increase.

> By ignoring the supposition of those who believe that unity of belief is the first task, the Council, practically though not by formal theory, is accepting the ecclesiology of the anti-ecclesiologist.
>
> If this analysis is correct, the Council of the future is going to grow more and more activist. The question of truth will recede more and more from the minds of those engaged in its work. Anglo-Saxon pragmatism will be the melting force fusing the elements together. Those elements which resist this force will naturally be left outside of the fusion.
>
> In other words, if the truth-first defenders are not converted, they will eventually have to withdraw. If they do, the World Council will have failed in its hope, though it will have united a great segment of the Protestant Churches of the world. It will be a partial union reducing the manifold of churches into fewer groups, but the remainder will be more irreducible than ever. I do hope that no one will see hostility in this sober and calm opinion.[73]

Weigel's basic attitude to the ecumenical movement was typically realistic: "Christian pessimism."[74] Weigel counseled patience.

> There is an impatience in our action. We think things can be changed from night to morning. They can't. This is a problem which faces a generation. One generation brings it to a certain point. The next generation takes it a bit farther. We must always think in terms of generations. I consider myself a member of the middle generation. The older men before me, the generation on its way out, certainly did not have the same point of view that my generation has. But, consolingly enough, they are not hostile to what's happening, though they are reserved. In my generation, yes, we began to go out more, to meet the non-Catholic. It was kind of pioneer work. But in the next generation what we did will be taken so for granted that they again will go farther. This much we can prophesy without fear.[75]

Father Weigel saw the need for much serious discussion on the theological notions of Revelation and the Church. The emotionally charged words must be removed from the dialogue. In these theological discussions, clarifications of positions and ultimate differences must be made. This will demand the transposition of themes from one terminology to another. "This is no easy task, because the dynamism of much of any man's thought is found in unrecognized assumptions. To get these assumptions out into the open requires cool analysis and kindly objectivity."[76] Here, too, Weigel urged patience.

> We are in God's hands and it is His will which we seek and not our own. We see the necessity of working for reunion, because such is His will and that is reason enough for doing it. Success is not the proper goal of human effort. . . .
>
> The danger which must be avoided is the mere exuberance of the heart. That organ may well have its reasons which reason does not know, but without the resonance of the heart with reason informed by knowledge, action can degenerate into sheer sound and fury, signifying nothing.[77]

186

During the 1950s, Gustave Weigel became increasingly popular as *the* American Roman Catholic ecumenist. His facility for friendship endeared him to many leading Protestant and Jewish theologians and ecumenists: Robert McAfee Brown, Paul Minear, Jaroslav Pelikan, George Lindbeck, Robert Calhoun, Warren Quanbeck, Albert Outler, Douglas Horton, Fred Corson, Eugene Carson Blake, Abraham Heschel, Will Herberg, Alexander Schmemann, Angus Dun, John Coleman Bennett, Paul Tillich and both Reinhold and H. Richard Niebuhr, to name only some of the more prominent ones. Late into the night he would wax eloquently on every conceivable topic, enchanting his friends of other faiths with his own deeply graced yet earthy humanity.

Gustave Weigel also participated in many formal ecumenical activities. In August 1957, Weigel and John B. Sheerin, C.S.P., editor of the *Catholic World,* were invited to be the first Catholic informal observers at the North American Faith and Order Study Conference in Oberlin, Ohio. The invitation came through Dr. Samuel McCrea Cavert, Executive Secretary in the United States for the World Council of Churches.[78] This was arranged through Bishop John Wright of Worcester, Massachusetts, a personal friend of Cavert's.[79] They were to be present not representing anyone or anything but simply as interested Catholic theologians.[80]

Between September 3 and 10, representatives of forty member churches from the United States and Canada met, together with consultants and observers from some thirty other churches. About five hundred persons were present. The theme of the study conference was "The Nature of the Unity We Seek." Three groups were formed: I, The Nature of the Unity We Seek in Faithfulness to the Eternal Gospel; II, The Nature of the Unity We Seek in Terms of Organizational Structures; III, The Nature of the Unity We Seek in View of Cultural Pressures. Both Sheerin and Weigel attended sub-committee sessions of the first group. Weigel's subgroup discussed doctrinal consensus and conflicts.[81]

To Weigel's displeasure but not to his surprise, the desire of

187

the conference was not for uniformity in doctrine and polity. But much to his pleasure there was a deep concern for the visible nature of the Church. "This is tremendous progress," said Father Weigel; "progess *to what,* I don't know. It is progess *from.*"[82] Weigel summarized these encouraging ecclesiological assumptions which he saw operative at Oberlin, acknowledging valid ecclesial realities in Protestantism:

> The Church is more than an invisible spiritual fellowship. It has its visible and experimental unity as well. Unfortunately, owing to human sinfulness, the external unity is not as perfect as it should be; the multiplicity of differing churches is an evident sign of disunion.
>
> However, the fact should not be considered in isolation. *De facto* there is a visible unity binding the churches together. In faith all accept Jesus Christ as God and Saviour. They all in some way use Christian sacraments. All to some degree rely on the Bible. Hence there is a common faith in all Christians; a common sacramental life; a common credal criterion recognized by all.
>
> More important than these things, Christ Himself made all ontologically one by His saving work. All are ontolly in Christ, and it is this one Christ who gives Christians a unity which cannot be lost, nor need it be constructed by me. It is God's gracious gift to the Church. The work, then, of the divided churches is to manifest ever more visibly this basic unity which is there.[83]

Weigel's and Sheerin's report on the conference mentioned "a strong activist mood" reflected there. This disturbed Weigel.

> The discussants were not so much interested in doctrine as such but in doctrine as a help to unified work and as a means to closer union of the churches. The Church was considered to be an institution of service. Its real unity was Christ at work in Christians. Doctrinal formulas were not considered to be very significant and were unobjectionable in great variety as long as they fostered witness and service.[84]

This "strongly voluntaristic unconcern for doctrine" convinced Weigel even more that Catholics could not take an active part in the World Council.[85] Can there be unity when there is no shared faith in something like the meaning of baptism? One party must be right and the other wrong by any logic, wrote Weigel. A unity of such diverging groups is one achieved by "a common will toward unity," without the support of intelligence and truth. "Truth was measured by practical consequences, and no other criterion seemed necessary or even in place."[86] For Weigel, true unity must involve doctrinal unity first. "The Truth," "The Real," demands this.

A sermon delivered by Bishop Johannes Lilje, the Lutheran bishop of Hanover, Germany, disturbed the Catholic observers as well as some of the non-Catholic participants, especially the Orthodox. Lilje stated that return to the Roman Catholic Church could not be the purpose of the ecumenical movement and that the Apostolic Succession of Bishops is an outdated doctrine. The latter remark drew complaints from Father Georges Florovsky, an Orthodox delegate. And the former comment offended not only the Catholics but the conference officials as well since the theory of the World Council excludes no possible future development, even return to Rome. It was obvious to the Catholic observers, however, that no one there seriously considered such a return.[87]

The two Catholic observers found the delegates most genial and accepting of them. The first day or so was rather stiff and formal, Sheerin recalled, but after that things loosened up between the Catholics and non-Catholics. Weigel and Sheerin then became "part of the gang" and though instructed by Wright not to participate in the discussions unless questioned, they did enter into the debates with some frequency and were welcomed into the discussions by the delegates.[88]

The openness and humanity of both Sheerin and Weigel was most appealing to the delegates. The leading figures of the meeting gave a private dinner for them, something that was done for no others at Oberlin. Included among the hosts were Bishop Angus Dun, the chairman of the meeting; Eugene Carson Blake, Presbyterian and vice-chairman; Paul S. Minear, Congregationalist of Harvard University and secretary of the conference; Dr. Willem Visser t'Hooft, general secretary of the World Council of Churches; Dr. Hans Harms, associate director of the Studies Division of the Council; Dr. J. Robert Nelson, dean of the Divinity School at Vanderbilt University; Dr. Robert L. Calhoun of the Yale Divinity School and Dr. Douglas Horton of the Harvard Divinity School.[89]

Though the atmosphere at the meetings was warm, the debates were heavy. After what Sheerin described as "long, interminable theological discussions," he and Weigel would repair to Sacred Heart rectory in Oberlin where the pastor, Father Martin Engelhardt, extended "Catholic hospitality" in the form of drinks. Weigel had a chance to relax with his scotch in milk and discuss the events of the day. Two things always irked him about these Protestant meetings. One was the lack of alcoholic refreshments and the other was the long, spontaneous prayers offered by the Protestants.[90] "He felt that these improvised prayers were a bit too theatrical for his taste and he commented that they make one realize the beauty and dignity of liturgical prayer."[91]

It was at the Oberlin meeting that Weigel first met Warren Quanbeck. He recalled Weigel's friendliness, humor and intelligence. However, he remembered being surprised that his knowledge of Luther and the Lutheran tradition was so "old hat" and filled with clichés. Toward Calvin and his interpretation of the Last Supper, Quanbeck said Weigel seemed more sympathetic but toward Luther he appeared "emotionally negative."[92]

Several Protestant theologians, like Quanbeck, have stated that Weigel's understanding of Protestantism and Protestant theology was at times inadequate. Pelikan felt that Weigel improvised rather than studied his way through the ecumenical movement. Yet Gustave Weigel was deeply admired and loved by these men as the first American Catholic priest to take their churches and their theology seriously.[93] Albert Outler, who first met Weigel at the Oberlin meeting, said that the Jesuit was "remarkably easy to get to know, wonderfully interesting to talk to."

190

> Oberlin was Weigel's first prolonged exposure to Protestant churchmen assembled and he was frankly baffled by their ease with themselves in the absence of any common or visible *magisterium*. But he had the rare gift for listening—really listening! Dialogue was no parlor sport for him but rather a vital business in which speaking the truth in love was the only rule that mattered.[94]

In their evaluation of the Oberlin meeting, Sheerin and Weigel listed their favorable reactions. First, Catholic presence prevented remarks unkind to the Church. Secondly, conversations between official sessions corrected errors in good faith by the non-Catholics. Thirdly, meetings of this kind enabled Catholics to secure first-hand information on the moods, doctrines and tendencies in the non-Catholic churches. Finally, such unofficial representation made it easy for Catholics and other Christians to meet and discuss. They wrote: "It also pleases them that we are willing and anxious to deal with them in love and courtesy even though we cannot join with them in the fellowship they have set up."[95]

In his *America* commentary on the conference, Weigel gave his personal theological evaluation of the progress made at Oberlin. First, he appreciated the recognition that the Church is visible and ontologically prior to the members. Secondly, Christian unity was not a matter of indifference to the participants. Thirdly, sacraments were seen as a cause and a sign of unity. Finally, there was an appreciation of the value of tradition as "somehow directive of belief." Weigel saw these as "consoling developments." However, with characteristic pessimistic realism, he judged the advances to be unsubstantial.

> The advances are imbued with the genius of Protestantism, the spirit of free construction. There is nothing in historical Protestantism which logically rejects these new positions. The Protestant of any epoch could consistently and on principle accept the doctrines enunciated. He often did so implicitly. In the past and in the present they are justified by the Protestant principle of the freedom of construction.

191

If this principle itself is not subjected to criticism, there is no substantial advance. Oberlin gave no sign that Protestant ecumenism is at all willing to question the principle.[96]

In an address on the Faith and Order conference to the students at St. Mary's Seminary in Baltimore, Father Weigel also spoke of the progress made among Protestant ecumenists. But, for him, the saddening anguish was that, though they have been able to get together, they have not found unequivocal unity on matters of substance.[97]

The Oberlin meeting was only the first such for the Jesuit and the Paulist. They were appointed official Vatican observers to a meeting of the Central Committee of the World Council of Churches in Rochester, New York, in August, 1963.[98] Weigel's earlier recommendation that no official Catholic observers be sent to these meetings had changed over the years.

Earlier in February, 1961, Weigel was informed by Monsignor Jan Willebrands, informally, that he would probably be one of the official Vatican observers at the World Council Assembly in New Delhi later that year. However, due to the Holy Office's decision that no one involved in preparing for Vatican II be appointed as observers, Weigel, Jerome Hamer and Willebrands were cut from the list of observers. The "disillusionment and embarrassment," Willebrands wrote, was compensated for by the fact that at least five Roman Catholic observers would attend the Assembly for the first time.[99]

Gustave Weigel not only met with Protestants in dialogue. He also wrote about their churches. At the request of a nun-catechist,[100] he wrote a series of articles on the churches in the United States for *Hi-Time* between September 1960 and May 1961.[101] Later these descriptions of thirty American religious groups were published in book form by Weigel's friend, David L. McManus of Helicon Press. The volume was entitled *Churches in North America*.[102] Many of the chapters were further published during 1962 and 1963 in *The Catholic Review* in Baltimore.[103] Weigel confessed that these were mere sketches of very complex religious beliefs but he hoped that such elementary and essential facts would be helpful to understand the religious beliefs of "our neighbors" at least partially.

> It is true that the fear, distrust and suspicion which for so long characterized relations between Christians of various confessions have, in recent times, greatly abated—at least on the theologian's level. But a sympathetic knowledge and understanding among *all* Christians is the first requisite of any ecumenic endeavor—namely, the endeavor to unite the churches to whatever degree is possible at a given moment. It is to develop an ecumenical atmosphere—an environment not inimical to friendly and reasonable intercourse and discussion. There is a good deal to be done on this para- or pre-ecumenical level. It is to foster this developing action in the current scene that I have written this book.[104]

Unfortunately Weigel's characteristic impatience with details, especially historical details, caused him to make some errors in his text. Five letters addressed to Weigel from clergy of Protestant, Orthodox and Jewish faiths made minor corrections in his statement of the facts of their faiths.[105]

From the very beginning of his ecumenical involvements, Gustave Weigel sought to understand the bases of Protestantism as a religious system. As a man who thought categorically, it was important to understand Protestant thought systematically. He asked to know their basis for religious truth. How do they come to know God and the Revelation He offers through His Son?

Here he discovered a deep disparity between the Protestant and the Catholic position. He realized early on in his study of their thought that epistemological differences were at the root of ecumenical dialogue. "Both parties know the same facts and both show the same dedication of Christianity but it means fundamentally different things to the two groups. At the bottom of the diversity lie different conceptions of religious truth."[106]

In another place he spelled out what he meant by these two incompatible approaches to religious truth.

193

The basic difference between the Catholic and non-Catholic approach to religious truth is that the non-Catholic *constructs* it in the light of his own experience and needs, while the Catholic receives it so that no reconstruction is called for or is even in place.[107]

But Weigel realized that Protestants cannot overcome the impulse toward "church building" since their principle of protest cannot admit that the Mystical Body of Christ already exists with its indestructible structure and infallible teaching power. "This Protestant situation derives from Protestant theology's inability to answer Pilate's question: What is truth?"[108]

Weigel outlined the different approach to faith of Protestants and Catholics, as these were understood in the light of Vatican I. Vatican II would see these not as contradictory but complementary approaches.

To the Protestant, faith means a trusting self-surrender of the complete man to the revealing God. For a Catholic, however, this act of cordial surrender is called faith, hope and charity. To a Catholic, the word "faith" conveys the notion of an intellectual assent to the content of Revelation as true because of the witnessing authority of God the Revealer.

Consequently the Catholic understands faith intellectually and supernaturally. Faith is the Catholic's response to an intellectual message communicated by God. For the Catholic, God reveals Himself through the medium of the teaching of the living holy community called the Church. . . . A Christian of the Reform tradition believes that God makes Himself and His truth known through a collection of books called the Bible. This book is the teacher and all other teaching is commentary, good or bad. The divine message itself is restricted to the Book.[109]

Through the use of philosophy and literary analysis and the personal inspiration of the Holy Spirit, Protestants feel they can gain access to the true revelation of God by reading the Bible, Weigel said. This principle of personal judgment characterizes Protestantism and makes it constantly flexible. The Protestant personally tests doctrine by the Bible to see if he judges it to be true. "Before he accepts it, he weighs the doctrine in the balance of his own experience, of his own understanding of the Scriptures, of his own postulate concerning what God should be and say."

> This is just the reverse of the Catholic's approach to belief. As the Catholic sees it, he must accept God on God's terms and not his own. It is not for him to "judge" the divine message but only to receive it. Since he receives it from a living teaching organ, he does not have to puzzle over the meaning of the revelation because the ever-present living magisterium can tell him exactly what the doctrine intends.[110]

Weigel was initially frustrated in his attempts to find a consistent system of Protestant thought. Each theologian differed from the next. Denominations varied and within each denomination there was often inconsistency of belief and practice. He was vexed in attempting to synthesize Protestant thinking into a whole. He once asked a prominent Protestant theologian to tell him the unifying principle in Protestantism. The man suggested that Weigel stop wasting his time. There is none, he said.

Father Weigel refused to accept this. After much study of Protestant theology and polity, he felt he had achieved a two-principle synthesis which could embrace Protestantism. He expressed this in an address in 1958. The first principle is that God is known to the Protestant immediately through experience. "The whole man, his feelings, his emotions, his will, his intelligence all go into the act of surrender which is the faith experience." The second is the principle of free construction. "All forms of Protestantism feel that the man that has so met God has the freedom in God to explain the significance of that experience, according to the categories and according to schemes that he finds adequate."[111] The Protestant has a quasi-mystical warming and inspiring experience of the ultimate through an encounter with Christ in the Scriptures and in the Liturgy. This non-conceptual, experienced message is communicated through concepts and words freely chosen. The only test of truth is the Bible.[112] Since the Protestant is always free to construct his own doctrine from his religious experience, there is no clear consistency in Protestant faith. This is not an embarrassment to Protestants as it would be to Catholics since truth comes from varying unique and ineffable experiences.[113]

Weigel spoke of the "Protestant Principle" in a conversation with Donald McDonald, published in 1960, in a way that expanded his earlier notion somewhat:

> It can be said that the Protestant principle consists of three interrelated propositions. It is an affirmation that God must be experienced immediately in an experience which is non-conceptual and whose whole intellectual content is not central, not specific. Because it is primary it is self-standing and self-justifying. The second proposition states that the conceptual expression of the vague intellectual content which will necessarily follow on the experience is a task which the believer must perform in freedom. This freedom is not absolute. Hence, the third proposition, which declares that there is a check and that that check is the Biblical text. The conceptual expression of the epistemological content of this experience must be expressed in Biblical terms.[114]

In 1958, in an address to the National Conference on Convert Work, sponsored by the Paulist Fathers in Washington, D.C., Gustave Weigel described American Protestantism as he saw it. His synthesis and understanding was always of American, not European, Protestantism.[115] This speech was later printed in a French journal[116] and a Chilean journal.[117]

He first pointed out that Protestants, although they base their beliefs upon Scripture, do not agree on scriptural interpretations. Fundamentalists hold to literal interpretation. More liberal Protestant spokesmen see the Bible, not as revelation itself, but as a record of a revelation event. The Book merely puts people in contact with the ones who received the revelation experientially. The Bible is indeed a privileged book to them but inerrancy is an outmoded notion. "The book is indeed inspired but this is not something supernatural in the older sense of the word." Between these two extremes is every possible compromise position. This means the Bible as an authority is dubious and a vague test for a theological proposition.[118]

Weigel classed American Protestants into five groups, according to the five kinds of limitations they placed upon the principle of free construction.

> The Fundamentalist, who tests his construction by the Bible, usually with a high degree of literalism; The Activist, who tests his creed and his cult by its power for witness and service; The Holiness Protestant, who wants his doctrine to foment and make deeper a life of Christian simplicity; The Charismatic Groups, who want their doctrine to lead them to an experience of God, sensible; and lastly, The Adaptive Protestants, who will construct their doctrine so that it will meet effectively the people at the moment which they are in.[119]

In a 1963 address, Father Weigel classified Protestant groups according to their "mind." There were the *Catholicising* ones who were loyal to the tradition without making it ecclesiastically functional. These would include the Anglo-Catholics. Then there are *Evangelical* ones, some of whom kept the traditions of Luther and Calvin, like the Missouri Synod Lutherans and the United Lutheran churches, while others, such as Bultmann, Reinhold Niebuhr and Tillich, are naturalists and do not believe in the supernatural, holding that the Bible and Christ are mere myths or existential symbols. Others of an evangelical mind-set would be the old-fashioned liberals, such as the Unitarians and Universalists, and finally the neo-orthodox, such as Barth. The next type of Protestant mind is the *Moralist*. They affirm an experience of salvation but are not anxious to define it. Brotherhood and service rather than doctrine are the primary concerns. Such would be the Holiness groups, Amish, Mennonites, Southern Baptists and Brethren. Others who would not be quite so conservative in their moralism would be the Quakers, Presbyterians and Congregationalists. Fourth are the *Bibli-*

cal Free Churches who use the principle of *sola scriptura*. Such would be the Mormons and Christian Scientists, Jehovah's Witnesses and Seventh Day Adventists. The final group would be the *Ecstatic Worshippers* who emphasize heavy emotion and have no concern for doctrine. In a toned-down fashion, this is Methodism. The more extreme groups include revivalists and Pentecostals.[120]

One characteristic common to American Protestants is social activism in the sense of "felt fellowship" in their congregations. Service, in the sense of the Suffering Servant, is the test of true doctrine. This is the witness to the Gospel that is most important. This type of pragmatism leaves little room for deep concern for doctrine.[121]

The next characteristic of American Protestantism is its "nervousness." Realizing that it is losing its numerical, moral and political power in this country, Weigel said, Protestants see Catholics growing in numbers and influence, making them nervous and anxious for success in the ecumenical movement. They fear that Catholics are working against their traditional liberties. "All Protestant fears of Catholicism come to life when there is a recognition of the possibility that a Catholic could be president." Yet there is a growing openness, one group toward the other. Respect increases and fear decreases due to friendly conversations and due to the ecumenical and liturgical movements.

Father Weigel regretted the fact that American Catholics were slow to enter into dialogue. "This interest is still timorous and restricted to a small sector of the Catholics." With regard to the future of Protestant-Catholic relations, Weigel said, "To make prognostication for the future when the present is so fluid would be rashness and folly."[122] In a response to a question from his audience regarding how long he thought Protestantism could survive by neglecting dogma and abandoning traditional moral principles, Weigel recalled the Nestorians who lasted about 1,000 years but did not completely disappear for 1,500 years. In this regard, he feared the appearance of a completely undogmatic Christian Church, as Toynbee advocated syncretistically. "The great danger would be a new religion which would not even pretend to be Christian."[123]

In 1960, at the instigation of Will Herberg, Gustave Weigel authored a book, together with his good friend, Robert McAfee Brown: *An American Dialogue: A Protestant Looks at Catholicism and a Catholic Looks at Protestantism.*[124] It was immensely popular. The book is unfortunately titled, however. It is not a dialogue at all but rather two monologues. The authors never saw each other during its composition and only corresponded once about an insignificant matter. Matters were exchanged and each discovered that, though the scope and style were somewhat different, it was similar enough to go ahead for publication.[125] Archbishop Lawrence Shehan of Baltimore, though fully approving of the work, did not wish to give it his official approval, nor was an *Imprimi Potest* issued by the Jesuits. The socius to the Provincial simply wrote to Weigel: "*SCRIPTUM EDI POSSE.*"[126]

An American Dialogue, though it broke fresh ground, was very much a period piece, rapidly out-dated. It was an early effort to confront each other in a public and friendly way. Weigel's positions were especially hard-nosed and reflected peripheral issues that had been raised historically in this country, such as bingo, liquor, papacy and power. By 1963, both Weigel and Brown discussed writing a follow-up to the book giving a report on the state of ecumenical affairs. They agreed that they should each have an initial chapter called *Retractiones,* indicating where they had changed their minds about certain things. Weigel freely admitted that "what he had written in 1960 was no longer an adequate index of what he thought in 1963." He was not sure where he stood in the ecumenical situation after the Council but he knew it was not where he had stood in 1960.[127]

Father Weigel opened the "dialogue" by expressing his initial puzzlement with Protestantism. How can such variety, often contradictory variety, go under a common name? As a young man, Protestantism had been merely something there but irrelevant to

Weigel's existence. Later, after much study, he was able to see the Protestant principle which was outlined above. Yet he admitted that someone outside a tradition cannot truly explain it as an insider can.[128]

His second chapter deals with Protestant piety. It appeared to him as a paradox. It is an effort to achieve mysticism by the experiential and personal approach to religious truth, yet it explicitly rejects the validity of mystical prayer.

> It has the aspect of great simplicity but actually is quite complicated. It is ambiguous about the use of sacraments because it does not want the reality of God mediated by things material. Its efforts are directed valiantly to the purity of the God-encounter, ignoring the fact that the encounter must take place in a material situation. As an effort one must recognize its nobility and valor but one cannot help but feel that this superhuman effort is involved in distressing frustrations.[129]

On the positive side, Weigel admired the Protestants devotion to the Bible and the "manly and stern piety manifested" in their worship.[130] However, he was most uncomfortable with the Pentecostal "lack of control" in worship and also disliked spontaneous prayer which he had experienced negatively at Oberlin. "Spontaneous it may be, but it is not the spontaneity of our daily existence but a labored attempt to achieve a studied biblical language expression." He was uncomfortable too with the personal witness to grace approach of some Protestants. The subjective theological and psychological interpretations made Weigel "squirm."[131]

In the chapter on Protestant morality, Weigel mentioned that, though "American moral principles are to a high degree homogeneous," Protestants and Catholics have different styles of morality. On the surface, the difference appears to be that the Protestants are more concerned with gambling, drinking, smoking and dancing whereas the Catholic appears to be nervous about sex. The real difference lies much deeper, Weigel claimed. It is in different concepts of virtue.

> The Protestant esteems the natural virtues while the Catholic makes more of the supernatural virtues. The Protestant thinks highly of truthfulness, sobriety, reliability and industriousness. The Catholic most esteems humility, mortification, penance, chastity, poverty and abnegation. Both admire charity, but Catholic charity is warmer and more personal, while Protestant charity is more efficient and better organized.[132]

This makes Protestants more reserved, stiff and grave, he said, in contrast to Catholics' tendency toward spontaneity, Baroque display, and even Rabelaisian earthiness.[133]

Father Weigel felt the Protestants lacked any authority to deal with moral issues which leads to "a complete anarchy in moral judgment." They have no sense of the natural law. They operate, most certainly, out of sincerity in making up their own minds but "we all know that great mistakes are made in all sincerity."[134]

> To put it briefly, a Catholic sees a distinctive Protestant morality but he cannot discover a working norm in Protestantism. There is indeed a fluid unity of Protestant moral views but there seems to be no moral authority capable of justifying the unity in fact.[135]

Weigel was at his insightful best in the chapter on the Protestant Stance. He said the American Protestant combines a "confident audacity" with a "generous tolerance." The audacity comes from his general unconcern for tradition and the tolerance from his appreciation of formal variety. Weigel commented, "It is tolerant of diversity but irritated by the theory of conformity." Therefore Protestants have difficulty appreciating the absolute conformity demanded by Catholicism.[136]

In his remarks about Protestant intellectuality, Weigel's whole intellectual background came to the fore to criticize their Kantian voluntarism. Their approach produces scholarship, but, without any authority to guide, scholarship leads to skepticism which is only overcome by voluntarism. Practical reason is the faculty that makes the act of faith in a meaning or a power that is not understood.

Here is the heart of the Protestant-Catholic problem: radically opposed epistemologies. "A meeting of Catholics and Protestants is not so much the confrontation of Peter and Paul but rather of Kant and Aquinas."[137] This volitional approach to certitude frightens the Catholic. He fears Protestantism will lose the substance of Christian doctrine. Yet,

> as long as the *vestigia ecclesiae* are in Protestantism, we are not altogether divided. There is ground for an ecumenical hope. However, should the skepticism and voluntarism of Protestant thought continue to grow, will these vestiges remain vital? Can we even talk to each other meaningfully if our epistemologies are so different?[138]

Finally, the Protestant Stance is characterized by an "abiding Modernity." He usually accepts whichever way the cultural wind is blowing. Weigel said this has certain advantages. But, though he may envy Protestant modernity at times, he realized this "can be a luxury at once too costly and quite unnecessary."[139]

Catholics are willing to accept modernity but with caution.

> The whole action of ecclesiastical authority is always a brake on modernism. . . . Changes will indeed come and there is evolution in dogma but novelty must not be revolutionary nor reckless. To the man who is thoroughly modern this attitude is necessarily treasonable. The Protestant easily escapes his ire, but the Catholic will be its certain object. The Catholic has the consolation that modernity is shifting and uncritical; what is wisdom in one modernity is folly in another. This consolation, however, does not eliminate the malaise produced by being left behind as the band-wagon moves away. We all like to get on the band-wagon, even when it is not wise to do so.[140]

Weigel listed three elements necessary to a good vision of reality. 1) It must be coherent with the data of experience. 2) It must be logically consistent. 3) There must be an economical harmony of the parts. Weigel's philosophical model, Plato, did not trust experience. For him and for Weigel, "consistence and beauty discipline experience so that experience does not have the last word."[141]

The Protestant's concern for modernity leads him to be more concerned for experience than for metaphysics. Empiricism is timely whereas metaphysics is timeless. Here the Protestants are simply following the general Anglo-Saxon intellectual bent toward the primacy of experience.

> Some wag has defined basic epistemological positions in terms of a baseball umpire—calling balls and strikes. The Scholastic umpire calls them as they are. The Existentialist umpire insists that they are what he calls them. The Protestant by and large is a subjectivist with a strong leaning toward existentialism.[142]

Weigel reaffirmed his "Greek" metaphysical approach as superior for understanding reality. He wondered if Protestant complacency in modernity is not a sign of resentment against pure intelligence.[143] The way of intelligence is harder, Weigel conceded, but, for him, definitely better. "This is a burden of which so many of my Protestant friends seem to be free. But I personally feel no great envy. After all I have found the yoke is sweet and the burden light."[144]

The ideas in the chapter on the Protestant Fear have been dealt with previously in this study. Weigel summarized the fear by saying that it is twofold: 1) the fear of the death of Protestantism and 2) the fear of the possible loss of political and cultural dominance. The second is less significant than the first but Weigel judged that in America it can be the more visible and the more urgent. They fear Catholic solidarity over against Protestant divisions.[145]

The chapter on the Protestant Principle does not add anything significantly new to the notion as treated previously in this study. Weigel simply stated the three interrelated propositions of the principle.[146]

In his "Envoi," Father Weigel expressed the possibilities and the limitations of the ecumenical movement. The main task is to overcome fears and ignorance by dialogue leading to respect and understanding. Since one Church can only come about if Protestants convert to Catholicism, the one Church is not near. But hope for unity must not be the immediate goal of the endeavor. Watering down differences to achieve instant unity must be avoided.

His Christian pessimistic realism was revealed when he saw little hope for real ecumenical encounter, given the incompatible positions of the two Christian groups. True ecumenical encounter will demand a change of the rules and this he did not see coming soon.[147] Ecumenism at that time could only be para-ecumenical, i.e., "action along side of but not identical with the current ecumenical enterprise." This would reduce hostilities but not eliminate essential differences.[148]

> Difference is always an occasion for tension. There are tensions between the male and the female, between the young and the old, between Catholics and Protestants. Tension is not altogether bad. It makes the steel spring move the clock. We can live with our tensions and get some good of them. But in God's name let us not needlessly exacerbate our frictions.[149]

The reviews of *An American Dialogue* were generally quite favorable. However, one writer took issue with Father Weigel's basic approach to dialogue. Para-ecumenical action which leads Protestants to understand Catholics as Catholics and Catholics to understand Protestants as Protestants seemed to be a defeatist attitude toward proselytism and convert making, according to Leslie Rumble, an Australian convert priest. He said, "It is difficult to see how the 'imperative of faith' operating in Catholics at least will be content to restrict itself to that." Polemics must be done kindly, but never dropped, he said.[150] Rumble was not the only one complaining about what appeared to many American Catholics as an overly irenical approach to Protestantism. Ecumenism was still slow to seep into the life of American Catholics in 1960.

In addition to his study of Protestant denominations, the Protestant mind and problems peculiar to Protestant-Catholic relations in this country, Weigel was particularly interested in Protestant theology. He found this initially as confusing as his early encounters with Protestantism. He sought but was unable to find "a synthetic but authentic expression of the Protestant mind." One thing he was sure of. Protestant theologians did not feel bound to support the positions of the Reformers. Whatever did not fit the modern positions was cast aside with impunity.[151]

One thing that frustrated Weigel in his study of Protestant theology was its lack of a clear systematic. Barth, Brunner and Tillich appealed to him most because they were analytical and, to an extent, systematic in their presentations, but Weigel readily admitted that these were not widely accepted scholars within the Protestant community, especially in the United States.[152]

> One gets the feeling that the Protestant either has not the patience or the courage to bring all of his theological thinking together into one disciplined synthesis. One reason for such a situation is that any system made has a de facto value only. It represents the views of the author and his followers, and even they may reject it altogether at some later date. The only possible extrinsic norm that Protestantism has is the Bible, and each Protestant is free to construct and interpret it as best he can. Under these circumstances to call the Bible a norm is to use words in a Pickwickian sense.[153]

Weigel claimed that Protestant theologians were unable to systematize their thought because their chief interest was epistemology, not metaphysics. Ironically, epistemology had also been Weigel's chief interest since his student days. He felt that, inspired by current philosophies, they tend to replace systematic theology with attempts to outline a valid method of dogmatic theology. Yet they always protest against the intrusion of philosophy into theology.

> This paradoxical position brings many advantages with it. First, the Protestant theologian is not faced with the task of constructing a philosophy slowly over the years and centuries; he plunges *in medias res theologicas*. Second, there is always a timeliness to his

205

thinking, because it is embedded in the philosophy of the moment. Third, it gives Protestant theology its fluidity and flexibility, because the philosophy which the Protestant uses as the matrix of his thought is not something that he has to cling to. He is not 'stuck with it,' for he got it by being sensitive to the prevailing winds of thought and when those winds change, so does he.[154]

Gustave Weigel, with his penchant for order and synthesis, grouped Protestant theologians into three camps which he labeled: Left, Right and Center.

Those on the Left are further subdivided. First are the Liberals. Adolf von Harnack, the liberal historian of the nineteenth century, typified Protestant theology until World War I. His spirit, Weigel affirmed, is alive in the works of Rudolf Bultmann, "a metamorphosed Harnack, but the change is very great."[155] Weigel observed that Bultmann only slightly affected American Protestantism since existential philosophy, from which it arises, is not congenial to America.[156] For Bultmann, Weigel had a mixture of praise and complaint. Positively, Bultmann's thought was a theology, not just a philological exercise reminiscent of nineteenth century Protestant thought. Theology was given in terms of Jesus' teaching and its modifications and expansions by the Church and Paul.[157] But insofar as it reflects Harnack's faulty historicism, Bultmann is dangerous and weakens the faith of Christians by his de-mythologizing.[158]

The second group of the Left is the Neo-Liberal faction. These thinkers dropped the Kantian and Hegelian philosophical bases but retained their empirical method. This happened more in America than elsewhere and the result was a streamlined liberalism, "which dropped all Victorian gingerbread subjectivism." John Dewey and Alfred North Whitehead were the mainstays of this approach.[159]

One group of Neo-Liberals Weigel called Neo-Naturalists, centering around the University of Chicago. Henry Wieman and Bernard Meland were the leaders in this group.

> The Neo-Naturalist theologians are far from being atheists and far from selling religion short. They are merely overawed by the

empirical method of philosophizing which has made a deep impression on them. They have not dropped God or piety because of this awe, but the genuine religiosity has forced them to accept the titanic challenge of expressing their faith in the very language and categories of naturalism.

Whether they have succeeded is another question. As has been pointed out by other Protestant theologians, the Neo-Naturalist formula is not true to the common conception of God and religion, nor does it make agnostic or atheistic philosophers look more kindly on the Christian message. The Neo-Naturalists have fallen between two chairs. As fireworks, theological Neo-Naturalism is fascinating, but it has made little or no impression on the mass of believing Christians, and even the Protestant theological brotherhood as a whole is not moved by it.[160]

Father Weigel referred to the other group of Neo-Liberals as Personalists. This group of empiricist thinkers centered around Boston University and included Albert Knudson, Borden Parker Bowne, Edgar Brightman, and Peter Bertocci. They try to preserve the more characteristic features of Christian theology by means of empiricism. For them there is no supernatural revelation; Christ is divine only in an accommodated sense and God is finite. Religion is given in experience and is considered to be a quest for values.[161]

On the Right, Weigel listed the Pentecostals, Jehovah's Witnesses, Seventh Day Adventists and the Christian Scientists. All of these, he said, have clear beliefs, founded upon fundamentalist views of Scripture and are zealous in propagandizing and exclusive in their membership.[162]

The Center represents a return to the supernatural and Weigel divided them into five sub-groupings. The first is Anglo-Catholic, whose representative for Weigel was W. Norman Pittenger. Though these appeal to tradition, they still assume that the real meaning of Scripture can be found only through naturalistic philosophy. Tradition tends to be restricted to the first seven Councils and the theologian can individualistically choose what he accepts as true tradition.

It is my personal opinion that the Anglo-Catholic with the exception of those few who simply accept everything that the Roman Catholics do, including their method of theologizing, are anxious to *use* the consecrated formulas of the abiding Church, but give them a meaning foreign to their genuine intent in order to harmonize the Catholic propositions with the contemporary moods and movements.[163]

Weigel, who usually was very mild in his printed criticisms of non-Catholics, rather harshly said the term "Anglo-Catholic" is "double talk. . . .whereby the speaker can be understood simultaneously both as a Catholic and as a naturalist. There is no insincerity in this position, but there is a voluntary ambiguity deriving from an indeliberate theological schizophrenia."[164]

Next in the Center ring are the Neo-Orthodox theologians, whose representatives are Karl Barth, Emil Brunner and Reinhold Niebuhr. They advocate the return to the Bible as the Word of God and the transcendence of God. The dialectical character of this theology, especially in Barth, is quite paradoxical. It constantly affirms the poles of God and man. God is God and man is man and the two can never be subsumptions one of the other.

The paradoxical character of such thought is bewildering because the constant linking of "Yes" and "No," with no possibility of bringing them into some kind of unified synthesis, leaves the student dizzy.[165]

Father Weigel praised Barth for recovering the reality of the absolute otherness of God, on a plane above nature and outside of human consciousness. However, because of his emphasis on man's sinfulness and consequent pessimism, his thought was not influential in this country.[166] Barth, like Luther, stressed that man meets God in an existential encounter. But, according to Weigel, men are not satisfied with this since it is not meaningful until it is made intelligible by a concept. And conceptualization is what the Neo-Orthodox avoid. "I simply do not know what Barth means when he speaks of God and His Christ. I personally believe that I have 'met' Christ but I sincerely do not know whether Barth and I have met the same Christ.''[167]

Emil Brunner's approach to theology resembles Barth's, except that he emphasized Calvin, who was influenced by Augustine and who built a systematic theology reflecting sixteenth century Protestantism. For Brunner, the encounter between God and man is expressed in the I-Thou terminology of Martin Buber. This appealed to Weigel. Brunner's lack of metaphysics, however, drew criticism from the Jesuit. Weigel insisted that the theologian must be more than a witness to faith, in the Brunnerian sense. He must also be a scientist using metaphysical speculation.[168]

Father Weigel's final criticism of these two Neo-Orthodox thinkers is predictable, given his concern for certain knowledge.

> God is unknowable to man's intellect as a faculty of conceptualization. . . .
> If God is not grasped in terms of metaphysics, He is not grasped meaningfully at all. . . . God must be met in existence and only there can we find Him, but it is an existence illuminated by metaphysics. Without it, existence and its resulting experiences are meaningless.[169]

Activist Evangelicalism is the next group considered by Weigel. This is the most typical American Protestant position. John A. MacKay of Princeton University, Winfred E. Garrison of the University of Chicago, and *The Christian Century* exemplify this stance. They sound like but are not fundamentalist. The Bible is the sole vehicle of revelation but it is not inerrant. They stress faith and *agape*. Faith is the surrender of man to the God of the Bible and *agape* is the urge to witness to Christ. Dogma is not important to the Activist Evangelicals. What matters most is "the active rendering of ethical and kerygmatic witness to society in order that all men may know that there is salvation from sin through faith in the atonement of Christ Jesus, the risen Saviour.''[170]

Paul Tillich alone represents the fourth type of Center theology for Weigel. Weigel found it hard to locate Tillich. He is probably in the Center but definitely not Neo-Orthodox, Weigel judged. This is an opinion that most scholars do not share today. "One thing can be said safely: he is the most impressive figure on the American Protestant theological scene, by reason of the vigor, clarity and amplitude of his doctrine."[171]

In four published articles, between 1950 and 1956, Gustave Weigel had synthesized and commented upon the theology of Paul Tillich. Each time he seems to have come to understand Tillich more fully and, at the same time, to have become slightly more uncomfortable with his theological bases. His depth of appreciation for Tillich's systematic and ontological approach to theology never diminished, however. He always judged that Tillich gave everything in the Protestant tradition a place in his system.[172]

His first article, in 1950, which was based largely upon Weigel's reading of *The Protestant Era,* published in 1948,[173] noted that Tillich's work was "a high-point in current theology." Why? Because of "the rational coherence that he gives to a phenomenon that seems to be indifferent to coherence."[174] In a letter to Weigel, after having read the manuscript of this article, Tillich praised the Jesuit's analysis.

> I have told everybody with whom I spoke that this is the best analysis of my thought I ever have seen. It is incisive, clear and benevolent at the same time.[175]

Gustave Weigel praised Tillich for taking ontology seriously, even though it was an ontology influenced by existentialism.[176] It showed the influence of Weigel's heroes, Plato and Augustine, both of whom were admired by Tillich.[177]

The Tillichian method of correlation was responsible for what Weigel approvingly called Tillich's coherence. This method demanded that

> the theological answer must cohere with the theological source data; it must cohere logically with the other elements of the system; it must cohere with the totality of man's experience of God and human life.[178]

210

This manifested Tillich's great theological virtue: a mature balance which achieved freshness of thought while still respecting the thought of others in the past and present.[179]

In the 1950 article, Weigel expressed enthusiastic admiration for Tillich's theological brilliance though he was frightened "at the thorough reduction of all accepted formulas to existentialist symbolisms."

> A Catholic theologian cannot but wish that the others would follow in the path of Tillich. A Catholic theologian, trained to orderly procedure and conceptual precision, can read his book and in spite of its non-Catholic emphasis and positions find himself at home because of its method, whereas much Protestant theology strikes the Catholic reader as in large part meaningless and quite irrelevant. He misses in so much Protestant writing the intellectualization which is the first thing that Catholic theology seeks.[180]

By 1953, Weigel was more reserved in his praise. "For the theological tyro the encounter with this theology must be overwhelming in both senses of that word: excitingly awesome and awfully confusing."[181] And in the final article in 1956, Weigel cautioned: "The brilliance of the Tillichian synthesis cannot soothe the disturbance caused by his theology."[182]

What were the causes of Weigel's growing disturbance with Tillich's thought? Weigel had never been comfortable with existentialist thought, though in Tillich he felt what was good in existentialism was displayed.[183] Yet he feared that it eliminated objectivity and took the content out of man's knowing. He judged that Tillich's existential ontology was not really the formal guide in his theology. Rather it was his suspicious epistemology.[184] He intimated this in the 1950 article when he observed that Tillich "recognized no literal truth in the old formulas, which for him are only symbols of existentialist thought." Faith is not, as it is for the Catholic, an assent to propositions revealed by God. There is nothing absolute in the content of revelation.[185]

211

Revelation, then, "is possible wherever we have man reflecting ecstatically on the ultimate ground of his threatened being." Weigel, therefore, surmised that Tillich must hold that anyone who accepts this personal, immediate revelation through reflection is saved and is Christian, even a Buddhist. "The upshot of Tillich's doctrine is that he is a Christian who is saved, and salvation comes from faith alone."[186]

This approach would appear to eliminate the necessity of a Church in the Tillichian synthesis. But this is not true, as Weigel noted. The social union of Christians is needed to pass along the Gospel. However, for Tillich, the form of the Church was not important. Given the clear necessity for a hierarchical Church in Weigel's ecclesiology, this, too, made Weigel uncomfortable. He was consoled, however, when Tillich said he felt the Catholic Church preserved the religious substance of Christianity more than Protestant churches.[187]

Gustave Weigel also found difficulty with Tillich's Christology. For the Protestant thinker, the historical person of Jesus was not the Son of God. It was Jesus as Christ-symbol that was God-man. In 1950, Weigel called this a Nestorian Christology, reflecting an Antiochene Christology.[188] In reply, Tillich agreed with Weigel regarding his Antiochene tendencies.[189] Weigel was convinced that this symbolic approach to Jesus, the Christ, could not be squared with the dogmatic demands of Chalcedon.[190]

It was in this notion of symbol that Tillich and Weigel found their deepest disagreement, a disagreement that was rooted in epistemological differences. The Jesuit held to the analogical knowledge of St. Thomas Aquinas. Tillich claimed that his use of symbol was basically the same as Thomas' use of analogy. Tillich felt, however, that no natural theology could be based on such analogical knowledge.[191]

Weigel claimed that this coincidence with Thomas was superficial. Tillich's concept of Thomistic Analogy was inadequate.

> Analogy for Tillich is essentially symbolism. A distinction is made between being-itself, the logical ens ut sic, and the unconditioned

ground of being, which latter cannot be expressed properly but only symbolically in logical discourse. The ground of being is not conceived; it is existentially intuited. Although this intuition must be expressed conceptually, the concept is not a definition, but by affirming and negating itself becomes a pointer.[192]

Weigel felt that symbol for Tillich meant merely an extrinsic proportionality whereas for Thomas it was an intrinsic proportionality. In a letter commenting on Weigel's article which was to be published in 1956, Tillich thanked Weigel for forcing him to clarify his thought on the notion of symbol.

One of the things I always forbid my students to say is "*Only* a symbol." This bad phrase is rooted in the confusion of sign and symbol. Signs point to something different in which they do not participate at all. Symbols participate in the power of what they symbolize. . . . Every symbol. . . . says something positively true about God. He is not the 'ineffable' simply and unconditionally; but on the basis of his ineffability much can and must be said about him. It is not true that in the proportion finite-infinite there is no difference between the kinds of the finite which enter this proportion. There is a profound difference between the proportions; stone—the infinite and man—the infinite. This difference is the basis of the possibility that God is manifest in his innermost nature in a man but not in a stone. I am grateful to you that your incisive criticism enables me to clarify my doctrine of the symbolic knowledge of God.[193]

Tillich said Weigel was right in saying that his understanding of analogy is more negative-protesting than positive-affirming. "I am more worried about the idolatric character of traditional theology and popular beliefs about God than you are. But I am glad and very grateful that such a conversation between Catholicism and Protestantism has been made possible by your kindness."[194]

Gustave Weigel profited greatly by his personal friendship with and knowledge of the thought of Paul Tillich. His writings and speeches to the end of his days reflected much of the existentially oriented thought and terminology of the German-born Protestant thinker, though Weigel was always fearful of existentialism and its possible deteriorating influence on religious knowledge and faith.

Did Weigel interpret Tillich correctly? For the most part, Tillich seemed to think so, though in the questions of ontology and epistemology, he felt Weigel misunderstood his framework. Weigel, by his own admission, interpreted Tillich against his own intellectual background which was eclectic and Thomistic. This, it would seem, did not allow Weigel truly to understand Tillich's position. Existential ontology and epistemology appeared as too much of a threat to Weigel for him to grasp appreciatively this new approach to "The Real."[185]

Following Tillich in the Center group, is the Lund School of Sweden. Nels Ferre of Vanderbilt University brought to the attention of American theologians the works of Anders Nygren and Bishop Gustaf Aulen. These Lutheran thinkers are deeply imbued with the knowledge and spirit of St. Paul. "There is a serious meditation of the Catholic substance in Lutheranism," Weigel wrote. In Nygren's *This is the Church,* Weigel found an explanation of ecclesiology which was quite pleasing to him.

> Here we find the truly modern note of contemporaneous Protestantism: a recognition of the Church as an objective, structured fellowship with the supernatural dimensions of the Body of Christ. It is not merely spiritual but quite manifest in the world. The Catholic notion is not dominant in the studies, but elements of the Catholic notion which were formerly despised are once again considered and adopted.[196]

In the conclusion of his 1953 paper, "A Survey of Protestant Theology in Our Day," Father Weigel pointed out that these theologies are shared in various ways by the various churches. However,

> Active Evangelism is the predominant tone of American Protestantism, numerically superior to a stubborn fundamentalist mass numbering millions. All other theologies, brilliantly conceived or expressed do not touch the generality of Protestants, and only lightly touch the average minister or preacher.[197]

Weigel analyzed the writings of many other non-Catholic theologians, too many to analyze in detail here: Reinhold Niebuhr,[198] Carl Henry,[199] Martin Buber,[200] and H. Richard Niebuhr.[201] In 1955, he wrote an article in *Theological Studies* entitled "Protestantism as a Catholic Concern." He discussed the works of three rather weak and unrepresentative Protestant theologians, Clarence Tucker Craig, Kenneth A. Holmes and Norman Vincent Peale.[202] Protestants were irritated by his choice and criticized him for this in print.[203]

Weigel's critique of Peale, because of its unreservedly and unusually critical nature, bears quotation. Usually Weigel attempted to emphasize the positive aspects of Protestant thinkers, only later and somewhat reluctantly offering criticism. With Peale, he abandoned his usual pattern. In commenting on Peale's *The Power of Positive Thinking,* Weigel wrote:

> After reading this book the Catholic theologian gasps and goes limp . . . It has all the aspects of modern high-pressure advertising for some potent medicine which cures every ill known to man. . . .
>
> Dr. Peale has reduced God to the status of an unlimited stockpile of free atomic energy. . . .
>
> God is something of which man can naturally avail himself. . . .
>
> Paul preached Christ and Him crucified. Peale preaches Christ successful like the innumerable business executives, well-known actors, popular football coaches and radio impressarios who figure on almost every page of Dr. Peale's book. St. John of the Cross spoke movingly of the Dark Night of the Soul. Unfortunately for him, he never had the chance of reading Dr. Peale, who would have explained to him that by positive thinking he could have blown the darkness away. . . .
>
> We need not lose our temper at the sight of this witch's broth, but we have the right and duty to protest bitterly when it is labeled as Christianity. . . .
>
> The reader of Dr. Peale's book cannot possibly avoid the impression that he is listening to a pitchman, who uses every form

of mass appeal to induce his hearers to acquire his wares. This is not the climate in which religious truth is either taught or learned.[204]

In a question and answer period following a 1953 address, Father Weigel was asked, "Where does Norman Vincent Peale stand?"

> As far as I am concerned, he doesn't stand at all. He, then, is just a horrid caricature of religion, and don't think that I am alone in that. Many of my Protestant friends think exactly the same way. They are more ashamed of him than I am, and they ought to be—he belongs to them.[205]

For Billy Graham, Weigel had kinder words. He acknowledged that Graham's revivalistic religion is based on his own personal experience, which does not make it necessarily true, or valid for others. Despite the fact that Weigel distrusted Graham's lack of rational justification for his brand of religion, he admitted that he had helped many with his Bible-oriented approach to conversion. Though "the search is not for the truth, but only for the felt good," men do come to him and "even a defective version of the perennial gospel, so long as it keeps at least some of the fundamentals, will command the attention of modern man."

> Faced with the vast popularity and substantial shortcoming of Graham's crusade, we can only sigh and reflect that we, like him, are also Adam's children, defective and half-blind. Unlike him, we have been favored, through God's love and mercy, with the sure guidance and infallible teachings of Christ's one, true Church. It would ill become us to be harsh or cynical toward a man whose zeal and sincerity, even in a misguided cause, might shame many a lukewarm Catholic. Rather let us hope and pray that God may lead him to the One Faith that is worthy of all man's dedication.[206]

Gustave Weigel appreciated the theologies of the various Protestant thinkers. But he was persistently distressed that the solid Protestant systematic theology did not have much influence in Protestant seminaries. In 1958, Weigel deplored the fact that semi-

216

naries and ministers were not interested in this kind of theology. They talk religion, not theology, said Weigel. In their discussions, however, theological positions are latent. Because of this, fruitful dialogue is difficult.

> These men take certain positions for granted, assuming that you hold these positions as well. They are usually not put in explicit form, the major premise is not usually stated. That is why they sometimes arrive at an entirely different conclusion from your own. Their training is completely different from ours.
>
> In most of their seminaries, systems will be treated but the average students prefer Bible studies, key texts and their contexts, and homiletics. There are not too many Protestant theological centers where theology is pursued scientifically.[207]

Later, however, Father Weigel noticed an improvement in Protestant seminary training. There was an increasing concern for systematics. In an address to the faculty and students at Wesley Seminary in Washington, D.C., in 1961, he mentioned the need for formal theology in the training for the ministry. To the embarrassment of the faculty, the students agreed. Weigel remarked:

> I would venture to say that the present day Protestant seminarian is not at all content with an exclusively philological analysis of the Scriptures or with a rapid survey of the history of dogma. He wants to investigate dogma itself and find a genuinely objective dogmatic system for his faith.

Systematic dogmatics, Weigel said, must be the central concern of every theologian. Piety is theology's by-product, not its goal. Piety always overrules theology in Protestantism, Weigel thought. He was pleased to see Protestant theology "taking kindly to conceptualization." As an example, he mentioned Gerhard Kittel's *Theologisches Wörterbuch zum Neuen Testament*.[208]

In the same 1961 address, Weigel pointed to other recent developments in Protestant theolgy. In reaction against the quest for the historical Jesus, theologians were beginning to refuse to consider religious data as historical. In trying to deal rationally with the religious object as it is found in history, the subjective and phenomenological methods were being adopted in a potentially dangerous allegorizing. Weigel feared this approach could lead to a new gnosticism, making "existentialist interpretation of scriptural myth and symbol the only valid way to interpret biblical affirmations."[209]

The two trends mentioned above—conceptualizing and allegorizing—must not lead to an abandonment of concepts, symbols and myths, he said. Realizing that scientific philology of the Bible would not give normative facts for faith, certain current Protestant theologians were looking toward tradition. Such were Jaroslav Pelikan and Albert Outler, both personal friends of Gustave Weigel.

> Protestants are only now beginning to see the dynamism in tradition. They have not yet moved far. . . . Tradition is an ecclesiological dimension and can be utilized through the theological disciplines. This is beginning to be seen by not a few Protestant theologians and it is going to be most interesting to follow the future of this new theology of traditions. One grateful thing will inevitably result. The conflict between Scripture and Tradition will finally evanesce. It will not be one versus the other. They will both be simultaneously affirmed and in that affirmation Scripture will support the tradition and tradition will buttress the Scripture. They will be one after too long a separation.[210]

Thus in his late writings and speeches, Father Gustave Weigel saw these three trends in contemporary Protestant theology: 1) a movement toward conceptualization and systematization; 2) a sloughing off of an out-dated historicism; 3) a renewed concern for tradition.

He saw Catholic theology moving in similar directions, with slightly different modalities. Catholic theology has always favored conceptualization. However, contemporary Catholic thinkers were no longer spinning their thoughts out of "a foggy Aristotelian past" but were using the sources of Scripture and tradition. Secondly,

Catholic theologians, too, were more aware of the value and the limits of the historical method for theologizing. They were attempting to set up some viable canons whereby they could validly do theological history rather than write a mere history of dogma. They were also examining devices held for a long time such as the concept of analogy and the notion of the evolution of dogma. The third parallel movement was the notion of tradition: "the Catholics are bringing the Scripture into the tradition while the Protestants are bringing the tradition into the Scriptures."[211]

Weigel rejoiced in these theological convergences. "As a result," he said, "for the first time in hundreds of years Catholic theology is relevant to the Protestant theology and also the other way around."[212] He ended his lecture on a hopeful note:

> Can we be blamed if we feel thrilled with the present buoyancy
> of theology which seems to promise an even more vibrant and
> vigorous action in the future just around the corner?[213]

Gustave Weigel's life, following his 1954 surgery, was directed chiefly toward interpersonal ecumenical encounters, public and private. His study of Protestant theology decreased as he met face to face with his non-Catholic brethren. According to his epistemological position, this was "The Truth" arrived at and affirmed. In conversations, the intuitions of "The Real" were substantiated and clarified.

He went anywhere and everywhere to live out his approach to the ecumenical movement: understanding through dialogue. He brought Yale Divinity School students to Woodstock and took Woodstock students to New Haven for dialogues.[214] He spoke at an ecumenical colloquium at Harvard Divinity School.[215] He served on committees and commissions in Baltimore and nationally.[216] He gave immensely popular retreats to Protestant clergymen at Loyola-on-Potomac Jesuit retreat house in Faulkner, Maryland.[217] He was involved in the 1960 ecumenical meetings at St. John's Abbey in Collegeville, Minnesota.[218]

In conclusion, what can be said about Gustave Weigel, the uncompromising ecumenist? Despite the rather closed, traditional ecclesiology and theology out of which he operated, his warm humanity was able to transcend his intellectual limits and he welcomed his Protestant friends as brothers and sisters in Christ. This was his role as a member of the "middle generation" of ecumenists. As his critiques of Protestantism and Protestant theological thought indicated, he was disturbed by their lack of authority; he was frightened by the lack of content and their lack of ontological and epistemological coherence. Yet, through existential encounters, he came to love them as sisters and brothers.

Did his ecumenical thought and practice develop between 1949 and his death in 1964? Yes and no. The stage for ecumenical performance had grown wider and deeper, largely as a result of Weigel's personal efforts. His understanding of Protestantism and Protestant theology did not actually change, however, except insofar as he increased his knowledge of it. His appreciation and basic judgments remained the same. Yet in his personal existential life, there was a noticeable development.

Toward the end of his life, Gustave Weigel told his intimate colleague, Robert McAfee Brown, that he had come to assume that his non-Catholic brethren were somehow in the Church, even though it was difficult to explain theologically how this was so.[219] This personal acceptance of Christians who differed with his thought came across during a visit Weigel had with Carl Henry. They were attending an ecumenical meeting, frankly expressing their dogmatic differences. Henry wrote:

> Then suddenly, Dr. Weigel reached a hand across a table and clasped mine. Calling me by name, he said, "I love you."

Henry stated that he had met scores of Protestant theologians and philosophers who shared many different points of view. "No one ever demonstrated as effectively as Gustave Weigel that the pursuit of truth must never be disengaged from the practice of love."[220]

Nowhere was this more obvious than at the Second Vatican Council.

Endnotes

1. Interview with Francis J. Otenasek, June 9, 1967 (Neft).

2. *One of a Kind,* p. 16.

3. Gustave Weigel, "Contemporaneous Protestantism and Paul Tillich," *Theological Studies,* June, 1950, pp. 177–202.

4. Gustave Weigel, "Protestant Theological Positions Today," *Theological Studies,* December, 1950, pp. 547–566.

5. Donald McDonald, *Catholics in Conversation* (New York: Lippincott and Co., 1960), p. 54.

6. "About Books and Authors," *Baltimore Sunday Sun,* Section A, April 6, 1963, p. 5. WCA II F 303.12i.

7. *One of a Kind,* pp. 17 and 89.

8. Interview with John B. Sheerin, C.S.P., September 16, 1971. *Acta Apostolicae Sedis,* 1949.

9. McDonald, *op. cit.,* p. 57; Gustave Weigel, "Forward," *The Catholic-Protestant Dialogue* (Baltimore: Helicon, 1960), pp. vii–ix.

10. Harold E. Fey, ed., *A History of the Ecumenical Movement, 1948–1968,* volume 2 (Philadelphia: Westminster Press, 1970), pp. 316–18.

11. Gustave Weigel, "American Roman Catholicism and Ecumenism," *Lutheran World* V, June, 1958, p. 30.

12. *Ibid.,* pp. 31–33.

13. *Ibid.,* pp. 34–35.

14. *Ibid.,* p. 36.

15. *Ibid.,* p. 37.

16. Gustave Weigel, "Catholic and Protestant: End of a War?", *Thought,* 33:130, Autumn, 1958, p. 385.

17. *Ibid.,* p. 388.

18. *Ibid.,* p. 389.

19. McDonald, *op. cit.,* pp. 60–61.

20. "Catholic and Protestant: End of a War?," *op. cit.,* pp. 390–393.

21. Gustave Weigel, "A Survey of Protestant Theology in Our Day," *Proceedings of the Eighth Annual Convention of the Catholic Theological Society of America* (Baltimore: 1953), pp. 43–76. Hereafter referred to as "Survey."

22. Gustave Weigel, "Recent Protestant Theology," *Theological Studies,* December, 1953, pp. 568–594.

23. Gustave Weigel, "Calvin: Institutes of the Christian Religion, Selections," *The Great Books: A Christian Appraisal; A Symposium on the Third Year's Program of the Great Books Foundation* (New York: Devin-Adair, Co., 1951), pp. 69–79.

24. Gustave Weigel, "Thy Will Be Done," *Road to Reunion* (New York: Catholic Near East Welfare Association, 1952), Address given at the Fourteenth Annual Ford-

ham Conference on Eastern Rites and Liturgies, March 28, 1952, commemorating the Fifteenth Centenary of the Council of Chalcedon. This talk discussed Orthodox churches.

25. Gustave Weigel, "The Other Masses: A Glimpse into the Oriental Liturgy," *Jesuit Seminary News* (New York Province, XXVII, April, 1952), pp. 14–16.

26. WCA II F 303.27h.

27. Gustave Weigel, "Belief of Your Non-Catholic Neighbors," undated, WCA II F 303.21c.

28. *One of a Kind,* p. 86. Donald Campion, S.J., said that John Courtney Murray became interested in ecumenism through the influence of John LaFarge, S.J., and Wilfred Parsons, S.J., who had been interested in intercredal co-operation during the 1930s and 1940s. Murray became slightly involved in the Protestant and Jewish groups which LaFarge attended. It was a kind of social ecumenism which was touchy due to the fearful attitude of Rome. Campion said that Weigel was able to be more congenial about the ambiguities and evolving situations that came up in such ecumenical relations than was Murray. Weigel was "a breath of fresh air" in the movement. He was relaxed, not in the typical Catholic clerical mold, and was able to express Catholic theology in a very personal way. Murray was slower to move in this area because of his more shy personality and his strict Thomistic system. Weigel's eclecticism was more amenable to Protestant thought. (Interview with Donald Campion, S.J., November 9, 1971).

29. "Expert Says Catholic Press Played Substantial Role in Developing Ecumenical Spirit," NCWC News Service, February 4, 1963. WCA II F 303.30a.

30. Gustave Weigel, "Preface" to Max Lackmann, *The Augsburg Confession and Catholic Unity* (New York: Herder and Herder, 1963), p. vii.

31. Interview with Robert McAfee Brown, October 13, 1971.

32. *Protestant and Catholic* (Silver Spring, Md.: Forward Movement Publications, 1962), p. 6. Dialogue between Angus Dun and Gustave Weigel, February 11, 1962.

33. *The Catholic Protestant Dialogue,* "Forward," p. 2.

34. McDonald, *op. cit.,* p. 66.

35. Interviews with George Lindbeck, Warren Quanbeck, Jaroslav Pelikan, George Glanzman, S.J., Donald Campion, S.J., Robert McAfee Brown; Albert Outler, "An Uncommon Ecumenist," *One of a Kind,* pp. 43–49; Holt M. Kenkins, "Unstuckness," *One of a Kind,* pp. 77–82; Douglas Horton, "A Living Epistle of Christ," *One of a Kind,* pp. 51–59; Interviews with Francis McCool, S.J., Paul Cassidy, S.J., and Alexander Schmemann.

36. *One of a Kind,* p. 88.

37. Interview with Eugene Burke, C.S.P., November 21, 1971.

38. Interviews with Eugene Burke, C.S.P., November 21, 1971; Thomas Stransky, C.S.P., September 23, 1971; Sister Cleophas Costello, R.S.M., November 22, 1971.

39. Cushing as quoted in John A. O'Brien, *Steps to Christian Unity* (New York: Doubleday, 1964), p. 187.

40. Gustave Weigel, "Ecumenism and the Roman Catholic Church," *Catholic Theology in Dialogue,* pp. 69–70; *Protestant and Catholic,* p. 15.

41. "Jesuit Cites European Protestant Unity Quest," *Catholic Review* (Baltimore), February 3, 1963, p. 2; Gustave Weigel, "In Our Love is Our Hope," *Catholic Mind,* LVII, May-June, 1962, p. 223.

42. Weigel to George Tavard, Woodstock, January 18, 1956. (Files of George Tavard).

43. "In Our Love is Our Hope," pp. 224–26.

44. *Protestant and Catholic,* p. 13.

45. "Catholics and Protestants: End of a War?" p. 396.

46. NCWC News Service, February 4, 1963.

47. "Laymen Can Help Unity," *Catholic Review,* May 10, 1963.

48. "In Our Love is Our Hope," pp. 227–28.

49. Fey, *op. cit.,* pp. 320–21. The American Protestant position in ecumenism during the 1950s involved a belief directly contrary to the Catholic position which Weigel emphasized. Winthrop Hudson, in *Great Tradition in American Churches* (New York: Harper and Bros., 1953), p. 258, stated that "the true Church of Christ composed of all those in whom Christ lives and works and reigns can never be fully represented by a single ecclesiastical structure."

50. Weigel to George Tavard, Woodstock, Jan. 18, 1956.

51. *The Catholic Protestant Dialogue,* "Forward," p. 3.

52. Gustave Weigel, "A Catholic Postscript," in Philip Scharper, ed., *American Catholics: A Protestant-Jewish View* (New York: Sheed and Ward, 1959), p. 232.

53. *Protestant and Catholic,* pp. 29–30.

54. "Jesuit Cites European Protestant Unity Quest," *Catholic Review,* February 3, 1963, p. 2.

55. Gustave Weigel, *Summula Ecclesiologica,* p. 269.

56. Interview with Jaroslav Pelikan, September 27, 1971.

57. Interview with Warren Quanbeck, September 25, 1971.

58. Interview with Edward Hanahoe, O.S.A., September 15, 1971.

59. Gustave Weigel, *A Catholic Primer on the Ecumenical Movement* (Westminster: Newman, 1959), p. 3. This first appeared in *The Thomist Reader,* I, 1957, pp. 18–70. Hereafter referred to as *Primer*.

60. *Ibid.,* p. 5.

61. *Ibid.,* p. 7.

62. *Ibid.,* p. 9.

63. *Ibid.,* p. 12.

64. Gustave Weigel, "Ecumenism and the Catholic," *Faith and Understanding in America,* (New York: Macmillan, 1959), pp. 156–157. First appeared in *Thought,* XXX, 16, 1955, pp. 248 ff.

65. *Ibid.,* p. 162.

66. *Ibid.,* p. 162.

67. *Ibid.,* p. 163.

68. *Ibid.,* pp. 165–66.

69. *Ibid.,* pp. 167 and 169–70. "Besides, many small groups widely spread over the world can be more efficient in the production of reunion than one large association with headquarters far away even for those who live in its shadow. We must go to the grassroots, for the nearer the ecumenical movement comes to the soil of the commonality of believers the greater are its prospects of achieving its high goal" (p. 170).

70. *Ibid.,* pp. 167–68.

71. *Primer,* p. 57.

72. *Ibid.,* pp. 55–57.

73. *Ibid.,* pp. 27–8. In a speech given at Yale University in 1960 and later pub-

lished as "Ecumenism and the Roman Catholic Church," *Catholic Theology in Dialogue,* pp. 69–82, Weigel reiterated this position regarding the World Council of Churches.

74. L'Heureux, *op. cit.,* p. 31.

75. McDonald, *op. cit.,* p. 58.

76. *Primer,* p. 68.

77. *Ibid.,* pp. 67–8.

78. Report of Rev. John B. Sheerin, C.S.P., and Rev. Gustave Weigel, S.J., to Most Rev. John J. Krol, Vicar General of the Diocese of Cleveland, concerning the Oberlin Conference on Faith and Order, September 3-10, 1957. WCA II F 303.26B, p. 1. Hereafter referred to as Krol Report.

79. Interview with John B. Sheerin, C.S.P., September 16, 1971.

80. John Wright to John B. Sheerin, C.S.P., Worchester, Massachusetts, August 13, 1957 (Sheerin Files).

81. Krol Report, p. 2.

82. "Faith and Order—Significance of Oberlin Conference," *Voice,* St. Mary's Seminary, Baltimore, Maryland, XXXV, January, 1958, pp. 11 and 25; Gustave Weigel, "Faith and Order at Oberlin," *America,* October 9, 1957, p. 68.

83. Gustave Weigel, "Faith and Order at Oberlin," *op. cit.,* pp. 68–9.

84. Krol Report, p. 4.

85. *Ibid.,* p. 6.

86. Gustave Weigel, "Faith and Order at Oberlin," *op. cit.,* pp. 68–9.

87. Krol Report, p. 5; the address of Bishop Lilje is attached to the report, pp. 1–13.

88. John Wright to John B. Sheerin, C.S.P., Worcester, Massachusetts, August 13, 1957; Interview with John B. Sheerin, C.S.P., September 16, 1971. According to the report made to Krol, however, "we had neither the privilege of the floor nor the privilege of the vote and consequently our presence was completely passive." (Krol Report, p. 2).

89. *Ibid.,* pp. 5–6. Interview with John B. Sheerin, C.S.P., September 16, 1971. Those who most impressed the Catholic observers according to the report were Dr. Albert Outler who explained the role of tradition; Dr. Robert Calhoun who spoke on the theology of the Church; Dr. Douglas Horton, Rev. Georges Florovsky and Rev. Alexander Schmemann. Calhoun, Horton, Florovsky and Schmemann were termed most "approachable." The latter two met regularly with Weigel and other Catholic and Orthodox priests in warm and intimate dialogue at Fordham University during the 1950s. Weigel seldom missed these encounters and was at his best after drinks and dinner. (Interview with Rev. Alexander Schmemann, September 30, 1971).

90. Interview with John B. Sheerin, C.S.P., September 16, 1971.

91. *One of a Kind,* p. 63.

92. Interview with Warren Quanbeck, September 25, 1971.

93. Interviews with Jaroslav Pelikan, September 27, 1971; Robert McAfee Brown, October 13, 1971; George Lindbeck, September 25, 1971.

94. *One of a Kind,* p. 44.

95. Krol Report, pp. 6–7.

96. Gustave Weigel, "Faith and Order at Oberlin," *op. cit.,* p. 71.

97. "Faith and Order—Significance of Oberlin Conference," *op. cit.,* p. 28. At the conclusion of this address, Weigel urged his audience to stress the positive

things the Church of Christ demands of its members. Once he knows that, the Protestant will see that the Roman Catholic Church is the Church of Christ. "At the present he cannot see this and he is not going to see it because we are very wise, or because we handle syllogisms very beautifully or because our rhetoric is superlative. He will see it only because the God of love and mercy gives grace. Therefore, we need ardent prayer to God for our Protestant friends, and that very prayer will engender in us a true love and sympathy for them. Love and sympathy in prayer will do much more than polemics. In fact I wouldn't advise polemics at all." This is a good description of Weigel's own ecumenical methodology. (p. 29).

98. Interview with John B. Sheerin, C.S.P., September 16, 1971.

99. Jan Willebrands to Weigel, Rome, July 26, 1961. WCA II F 303.35jjj; Fey, *op. cit.,* p. 238.

100. Interview with Avery Dulles, S.J., June 21, 1966, (Neft).

101. "What Others Believe," *Hi-Time,* VII, September 1, 1960–May 10, 1961.

102. Gustave Weigel, *Churches in North America: An Introduction* (Baltimore: Helicon, 1961).

103. Gustave Weigel, "Churches in North American," *Catholic Review* (Baltimore), May 18, 1962; May 25, 1962; June 1, 1962; June 8, 1962; June 15, 1962; July 13, 1962; July 20, 1962; August 3, 1962; August 10, 1962; August 17, 1962; August 24, 1962; August 31, 1962; September 7, 1962; September 14, 1962; October 5, 1962; October 19, 1962; November 2, 1962; November 16, 1962; November 23, 1962; December 21, 1962; December 28, 1962; February 1, 1963; February 8, 1963; February 15, 1963; February 22, 1963; and November 29, 1963.

104. *Churches in North American,* p. 146.

105. William Whalen to Weigel, LaFayette, Indiana, December 15, 1961, WCA II F 303.35fff; Rev. W. Francis Forbes, S.S.B., Hialeah, Florida, January 23, 1962, WCA II F 303.34ii; Rev. Manfred Manrodt, Baltimore, July 25, 1962, WCA II F 303.35p; Rabbi Jacob B. Agus, Baltimore, February 22, 1963, WCA II F 303.34a; Rabbi Samuel Glasner, Baltimore, December 10, 1963, WCA II F 303.34mm.

106. "Protestant Theological Positions Today," *op. cit.,* p. 103.

107. *Faith and Understanding in American,* p. 13.

108. *Ibid.,* p. 130.

109. *Ibid.,* p. 1. *Dei Verbum* of Vatican II changed this conception of Catholic faith, Cf. # 2–5.

110. *Ibid.,* pp. 12–13.

111. Gustave Weigel, "Modern Protestant Theological Positions," address delivered at Regis College, Denver, November 19, 1958, WCA II F 303.19w, p. 2.

112. Gustave Weigel, "The Protestant Notion of Faith," address delivered at St. Paul's College, Washington, D.C., June 27, 1962, WCA II F 303.20c.

113. Gustave Weigel, "Beliefs of Your Non-Catholic Neighbors," undated, WCA II F 303.21c, pp. 5–7.

114. McDonald, *op. cit.,* p. 62.

115. Weigel to George Tavard, Woodstock, January 18, 1956; George Tavard to Patrick Collins, Delaware, Ohio, October 5, 1971.

116. Gustave Weigel, "Le Protestantisme en Amérique du Nord," *Lumière et Vie,* tome VII 40, December, 1958, pp. 73–90.

117. Gustave Weigel, "El Protestantismo en los EE.UU.," *Mensaje,* no. 95, December, 1960, pp. 527–535. This journal was established in Santiago by Weigel's former colleague, Alberto Hurtado.

118. Gustave Weigel, "The Temper of Protestantism Today," *National Conference on Convert Work Proceedings* (Washington, D.C.: St. Paul's College, 1958), pp. 68–83.

119. *Ibid.,* p. 15.

120. Gustave Weigel, "The Protestant Mind," undated, WCA II F 303.20c.

121. "The Temper of Protestantism Today," pp. 70–73.

122. *Ibid.,* pp. 74–80.

123. *Ibid.,* pp. 81–82.

124. Robert McAfee Brown and Gustave Weigel, S.J., *An American Dialogue: A Protestant Looks at Catholicism and a Catholic Looks at Protestantism* (Garden City, New York: Doubleday, 1960), pp. 125–208. Hereafter referred to as *American Dialogue.*

125. *One of a Kind,* pp. 88–9; Interview with Robert McAfee Brown, October 13, 1971.

126. Thomas A. Brophy, S.J., to Weigel, Baltimore, February 1, 1960. WCA II F 303.34v.

127. *One of a Kind,* p. 94; Interview with Robert McAfee Brown, October 13, 1971; Robert McAfee Brown to Sister Mary Aquinas Neft, Stanford, June 12, 1966, and January 2, 1967. (Neft Files).

128. *American Dialogue,* pp. 127–30.

129. *Ibid.,* p. 138.

130. *Ibid.,* pp. 135 and 137.

131. *Ibid.,* p. 136.

132. *Ibid.,* pp. 141–143.

133. *Ibid.,* p. 144.

134. *Ibid.,* p. 146.

135. *Ibid.,* p. 148.

136. *Ibid.,* p. 150.

137. *Ibid.,* p. 153.

138. *Ibid.,* p. 154.

139. *Ibid.,* p. 155.

140. *Ibid.,* p. 156.

141. *Ibid.,* pp. 156–57.

142. *Ibid.,* p. 157.

143. *Ibid.,* pp. 158–59.

144. *Ibid.,* p. 160.

145. *Ibid.,* pp. 172–173.

146. *Ibid.,* pp. 189–190.

147. *Ibid.,* pp. 195–99.

148. *Ibid.,* p. 200.

149. *Ibid.,* p. 208.

150. *Leslie Rumble,* "Polemics or Dialogue?" *Homiletic and Pastoral Review,* April, 1961, p. 653.

151. "Survey," pp. 5–9.

152. *Ibid.,* p. 9.

153. *Ibid.,* pp. 9–10.

154. *Ibid.,* p. 10. In an article published in 1956 and again in 1959, Weigel outlined and contrasted Protestant and Catholic theologies.

"The Catholic theological tradition is not a series of historically contiguous but different theologies; it is a continuous effort in a uniform line. A twentieth century theologian can go back to the thirteenth or sixteenth century and not be in an unknown, strange world. He is quite at home, because it is the very house he is living in today. Certain necessary remodeling jobs have been done and certain additions have been made, but it is still the same edifice, the old rooms are still lived in.

"The Protestant theological house does not follow such a plan; it is really a rambling complex of buildings. At any moment it obeyed the dictates of the tastes of the time, but one can see in the whole that there were once other structures where present ones now stand. The older parts have been torn down, though elements thereof were employed in the present erections." (Gustave Weigel, "Catholic and Protestant Theologies in Outline," *Faith and Understanding in America;* pp. 91–92). This was first published in *The American Scholar,* XXV, 3, 1956, p. 289.

155. "Survey," p. 14.

156. *Ibid.,* p. 17.

157. "Protestant Theological Positions Today," pp. 109–10.

158. *Ibid.,* p. 111; Gustave Weigel, "Chair of Unity Talk on the Lutherans," St. Patrick's Cathedral, New York City, January 21, 1956. WCA II F 303.19p.

159. "Survey," p. 18.

160. *Ibid.,* pp. 21–22. Cf. Gustave Weigel, "The Paradox of Stable Change," *The Empirical Theology of Henry Nelson Wieman,* edited by Robert W. Bretall (Carbondale: Southern Illinois University, 1963), pp. 343–353.

161. "Survey," pp. 22–24.

162. *Ibid.,* pp. 45–54.

163. *Ibid.,* p. 28. Weigel also discussed Pittenger in "Recent Protestant Theology," *Theological Studies,* December, 1953, pp. 585–89.

164. *Ibid.,* p. 28.

165. *Ibid.,* p. 30.

166. *Ibid.,* pp. 30–31 and 34.

167. "Protestant Theological Positions Today," pp. 117–120.

168. *Ibid.,* pp. 122–123.

169. *Ibid.,* pp. 124–125.

170. "Survey," pp. 36–8.

171. *Ibid.,* p. 40.

172. "Contemporaneous Protestantism and Paul Tillich," *Theological Studies,* June, 1950, pp. 177–202; "Recent Protestant Theology," *Theological Studies,* December, 1953, pp. 573–85; "A Survey of Protestant Theology in Our Day," The Catholic Theological Society of America, *Proceedings of the Eighth Annual Convention* (Baltimore: 1953), pp. 43–76. (This was reprinted as a book under the same title by Westminster, Md.: Newman Press, 1954); "The Theological Significance of Paul Tillich," *Gregorianum,* XXXVII, No. 1, 1956, pp. 34–54. This was reprinted under the same title in *Cross Currents* VI, Spring, 1956, pp. 141–55 and *Theology Digest* VI, Winter, 1958, pp. 45–50; and in Thomas A. O'Meara, O.P., ed., *Paul Tillich in Catholic Thought* (Dubuque: The Priory Press, 1964), Part I, pp. 3–24). Cf. "The Theological Significance of Paul Tillich," p. 47.

173. Paul Tillich, *The Protestant Era* (Chicago: The University of Chicago Press, 1948).

174. "Contemporaneous Protestantism and Paul Tillich," p. 186. ". . . Tillich's synthesis is the only one at hand that includes all the elements of the Protestant phenomenon, and arranges them organically. The system is coherent and it

is rational. So many things in Protestant thought and action which at first sight seem completely unintelligible become logical and consequent in the light of his theory." (p. 196).

175. Paul Tillich to Weigel, New York, March 25, 1960. WCA II F 303.35zz.

176. "Contemporaneous Protestantism and Paul Tillich," pp. 185 and 190.

177. Lorenzo Avial, O.F.M., "Introducing Paul Tillich," *Priestly Studies*, XXXI, Spring, 1965, p. 14.

178. "Recent Protestant Theology," p. 578.

179. *Ibid.*, p. 574.

180. "Contemproaneous Protestantism and Paul Tillich," p. 199.

181. "Recent Protestant Theology," p. 585.

182. "The Theological Significance of Paul Tillich," p. 47.

183. "Recent Protestant Theology," p. 573.

184. "The Theological Significance of Paul Tillich," pp. 48–49. In "Recent Protestant Theology," p. 585, Weigel stated that Tillich "stands or falls on his epistemological positions."

185. "Contemporaneous Protestantism and Paul Tillich," p. 142. Weigel reiterated this critique in "Recent Protestant Theology," p. 581.

186. "Recent Protestant Theology," pp. 581–582.

187. "Contemporaneous Protestantism and Paul Tillich," pp. 194–95.

188. *Ibid.*, pp. 193–194. Cf. also "Recent Protestant Theology," p. 577.

189. Paul Tillich to Weigel, New York, March 25, 1960. WCA II F 303.35zz.

190. "Recent Protestant Theology," p. 576.

191. Paul Tillich to Weigel, New York, March 25, 1960. WCA II F 303.35zz.

192. "Recent Protestant Theology," p. 582. In "The Theological Significance of Paul Tillich," p. 50, Weigel explained why Tillich had an inadequate conception of analogy.

"First of all, he has identified being with existence *sensu negante*. Secondly, he supposes that class-concepts have meaningful content only for extra-personal reality as achieved in ordinary human experience. Beyond such an empirical context class-concepts can only be pointers. Thirdly, he recognizes a form of knowledge which gives dimension but not content. The expression of such knowledge is symbolism. Fourthly, the knowledge which gives dimension is an awareness achieved in the autoperception of existence at the point of its ultimate ground. In consequence, he sees God in his own existence, not because God is identified with the finite subject, but because the finite subject is rooted in an infinite subject, who can be known only as a subject and never as an object. Fifthly, existential awareness is specifically different from the conceptual achievement of empirical objects. This latter knowledge is 'natural,' i.e., it achieves 'nature.' The deepest awareness of existence, since it does not give us 'nature,' can be called supernatural, at least in the sense that it is not 'natural.' Lastly, though reason is inevitable in all thinking, yet true reasoning, or what Aristotle would call the syllogism, can only use univocal terms. An analogous term cannot enter into a syllogism; and when it does, we have a fallacy and not a true reasoning."

193. Paul Tillich to Weigel, New York, July 9, 1956. WCA II F 303.35zz.

194. *Ibid.* It would seem that Weigel did not fully understand the depth dimension of symbol as it was being used by Tillich.

195. Interviews with Warren Quanbeck and George Lindbeck, September 25, 1971.

196. "Survey," p. 44.

197. *Ibid.*, p. 56.

198. Gustave Weigel, "Authority in Theology," in Charles W. Kegley and Robert W. Bretall, eds., *Reinhold Niebuhr: His Religious, Social and Political Thought* (New York: Macmillan, 1961), pp. 368–377.

199. "Recent Protestant Theology," pp. 590–92.

200. Gustave Weigel, "A Voice of Time and Eternity," undated tribute to Martin Buber on his birthday. WCA II F 303.21c.

201. Gustave Weigel, "Reflections on H. Richard Niebuhr's paper, 'The Nature of Faith,' " October 22, 1960, at New York University's Institute of Philosophy. WCA II F 303.20f.

202. Gustave Weigel, "Protestantism as a Catholic Concern," *Theological Studies,* June, 1955, pp. 214–32.

203. Cf. reviews: Robert McAfee Brown, Review of *Faith and Understanding in America* in *World View,* vol. 4, no. 2, April 2, 1959, pp. 10–11; John T. Middaugh, Review of *Faith and Understanding in America* in *Catholic Review,* April 17, 1959, p. 6.

204. "Recent Protestant Theology," pp. 145–53.

205. "Modern Protestant Theological Positions," p. 13.

206. Gustave Weigel, "What to Think of Billy Graham," *America,* May 4, 1957, pp. 161–64.

207. "The Temper of Protestantism Today," pp. 82–3.

208. Gustave Weigel, "When Catholic and Protestant Theologies Meet," Summary of *Proceedings,* Fifteenth Annual Conference, American Theological Library Association, Wesley Theological Seminary, Washington, D.C., June 13–15, 1961. WCA II F 303.10e (1).

209. *Ibid.*, p. 6.

210. *Ibid.*, p. 9. This is precisely the unifying direction taken at Vatican II in *Dei Verbum.*

211. *Ibid.*, pp. 10–11.

212. *Ibid.*, p. 11.

213. *Ibid.*, p. 12.

214. Weigel to Henry O'Brien, Archbishop of Hartford, Woodstock, January 20, 1960; O'Brien to Weigel, Hartford, February 3, 1960. WCA II F 303.35cc. Commenting on the proposed encounter at Yale, O'Brien wrote: "I think you will find this visit an interesting experience—possibly akin to the feeling of St. Paul when addressing the people of Athens at the Areopagus."

215. The colloquium was held March 30, 1963. WCA II F 303.20c.

216. *Catholic Messenger,* November 1, 1962; *Catholic Review,* January 26, 1962.

217. *Catholic Review,* August 10, 1962; Press Release, Loyola-on-Potomac Retreat House, 1963; Egil Grislis, "A Catholic-Protestant Retreat," The Duke Divinity School Bulletin, February, 1963, pp. 39–40.

218. Interview with Vincent Arthur Yzermans, October 8 and 9, 1971; and with Godfrey Diekmann, O.S.B., May 16, 1966 (Neft).

219. *One of a Kind,* p. 94.

220. *Woodstock Letters,* Summer 1968, Volume 97, Number 4, p. 607.

Weigel at Vatican II

On October 9, 1958, Eugenio Pacelli, Pope Pius XII, died at the age of eighty-two. He had been the reigning Roman pontiff since 1939. His pontificate had been marked by high intelligence, ascetical aloofness and diplomatic ingenuity. He spoke often, on almost any topic. His sense of his role demanded that he offer spiritual and scientific reflections on subjects currently affecting mankind: war, medical discoveries, theology, Church-state relations, etc. His many allocutions became the subject for theological speculation in the Catholic academic community. Yet his communication with the Church was largely one way. The pope spoke. Everyone else was to listen. Gustave Weigel, who always had the greatest respect for ecclesiastical authority, was relieved at the death of Pius XII. He felt the pope was too old to effectively lead the Church through those rapidly changing and troubled times. Consequently, he told a friend that he had long prayed for his happy demise.[1]

Weigel was not overjoyed, however, with the choice of Pius' successor.[2] At the time of the conclave, he had said that one person who would not be elected was Roncalli.[3] Yet it *was* the Patriarch of Venice who became the successor of St. Peter on October 28. Angelo Giuseppe Roncalli and Weigel had met on a European train some years previously when Roncalli was an ecclesiastical diplomat. He had not favorably impressed the American Jesuit at the time. He remembered him as a "fat, silly papal diplomat" of whom he would never hear again.[4] After the election, Weigel was pessimistic and distressed. He saw John XXIII as an unintellectual, uncultured, peasant sort who would be merely an interim pope.[5]

The new pope soon made skeptics reconsider their negative view of him. He was a man whose diary indicated the depth of his humanity and his openness to the Holy Spirit.[6] In this he was much like Gus Weigel. Jaroslav Pelikan suggested that Weigel was the theological equivalent of Pope John. Both were able to see through the complexity of things to the basic, simple Christian truths. Roncalli wrote:

> To have been able to accept as simple and capable of being immediately put into effect certain ideas which were not in the least complex in themselves, indeed perfectly simple, but far-reaching in their effects and full of responsibilities for the future. I was immediately successful in this, which goes to show that one must accept the good inspirations that come from the Lord, simply and confidently.

This pious approach to truth resembled Weigel's own more intellectual, yet intuitive approach to "The Truth," "The Real."

From intuition, without any forethought, in January 1959, Pope John suggested to his Secretary of State, Domenico Tardini, the idea of an Ecumenical Council, a Diocesan Synod and the revision of the Code of Canon Law. He admitted later that this was "quite contrary to any previous supposition or idea of my own on this subject. I was the first to be surprised at my proposal, which was entirely my own idea."[7]

Five days later, January 25, 1959, the Holy Father announced his "ideas" to some eighteen cardinals assembled at the Basilica of St. Paul-Outside-the-Walls. The ecumenical council would be assembled not only for the good of the Catholic people but also "for a renewed invitation to the faithful of the separated communities that they also may follow us amiably in this search for unity and grace, to which so many souls aspire in all parts of the earth."[8]

The reaction of the assemblage was silence. The disappointed pope recorded the moment:

> Humanly, we could have expected that the Cardinals after hearing our allocution, might have crowded round to express approval and good wishes. Instead there was a devout and impressive silence. Explanations came on the following days . . .

The true explanation is probably that the prelates were simply shocked and confused. In the next weeks, Vatican advisors began to confront the pope with stiff objections to the idea of a council.[9] Pope John, however, trusted the intuition he had as a breath from the Spirit. There would be a council!

World reaction to the announcement varied from enthusiasm to confusion to disappointment. Gus Weigel tended to be typically pessimistic about the council's prospects. He felt that a good council depended upon a good pope and, as he told John Sheerin, "We have no pope. Pope John is no pope."[10]

Preparations for the world assembly began in Rome in May 1959, under the direction of an antepreparatory commission, headed by Msgr. Pericle Felici, who worked closely with Cardinal Tardini. Their function was to gather, classify and synthesize the recommendations solicited in June from the world's bishops, Catholic universities of the world, superiors-general of men's orders and the Roman curial congregations. Superiors of women religious were not included. The council was prepared by men.

The antepreparatory commission for Vatican II gathered the approximately 2,000 letters and documents into fifteen volumes, totalling 9,520 pages. Three of those volumes contained the *Vota* of ecclesiastical faculties, thirty-seven of which were outside of Rome. The *Extra Urbem* volume of 824 pages included the suggestions of the faculty of Woodstock College. This relatively open approach to conciliar preparation should have been impressive to anyone cognizant of the history of ecumenical councils. Yet the fact that it was presided over by the curialists left many, like Gustave Weigel, pessimistic about the outcome.[11] This consultative method of preparation was a departure from Vatican I, which, itself, had broken with tradition in this matter. Trent had prepared no agenda but left it in the hands of the Fathers once the council began. Vatican I had sought suggestions for its agenda from thirty-five selected conservative European bishops and the agenda was prepared by curia-dominated commissions.

Father Weigel prepared the *Vota Dogmatica* sent to the antepreparatory commission from Woodstock in May 1960.[12] He suggested that two matters be treated: the nature of the Church which he had long felt needed to be clarified if ecumenical dialogues were to progress; and relations between the Church and the temporal order of human life. The *Vota* made two dogmatic points about the nature of the Church. First, the Church should be defined as the Mystical Body of Christ in order to complete the doctrinal work of Vatican I and to clearly enunciate the mystical and spiritual Church's union with the visible and juridical Church. Secondly, it should be affirmed that the Church transcends every historical age and culture. Yet, without compromising its divine constitution and doctrine, it should accommodate itself to the world and seek means of colloquy with non-Catholics to begin preparation for Christian unity.

The Woodstock *Vota* also mentioned five practical ecclesiological points:

1. "Extra Ecclesiam nulla salus" should be reaffirmed but it should be made clear how God works with those who are outside the Church but yet who "pertain" to the Church through divine faith and infused charity.

2. The question of membership in the Church should be clarified.

3. The office of the bishop should be more accurately defined, showing his dual office as teacher of faith with proper jurisdictional authority.

4. Academic freedom should be defended against certain past practices of the Holy Office.

5. There should be an explicit treatment of the laity in the Church.

Chapter II of the *Vota* made suggestions concerning Church-state relations. The first principle is that the Church is free. Secondly, the document affirms the liberty of people and the limits of the power of the state. Thirdly, the principle of concord between Church and state was discussed. Finally, it suggested the ways in which the state should care for religion.[13]

On May 30, 1960, Pope John told a semi-public meeting of cardinals in Rome that he would erect a special secretariat to help the separated brethren follow the work of the council. The *Motu Proprio*, "Superno Dei nutu," issued June 5, formally established The Secretariat for Promoting Christian Unity, along with fourteen other preparatory commissions. The following day he appointed Augustine Cardinal Bea as the president of the secretariat and, on June 24, Monsignor Jan Willebrands was made the secretary. In September, the first group of members and consultors was appointed. Among the consultors were four North Americans: Gregory Baum, O.S.A., from Toronto, Canada; George Tavard, S.S., from Mount Mercy College in Pittsburgh, Pennsylvania; Edward F. Hanahoe, S.A., of the Friars of the Atonement in Graymoor, New York; and Gustave Weigel. A few weeks later, Monsignor John Oesterreicher of Seton Hall University, was added to the consultors. Members alone had voting rights. Those selected to work for the secretariat represented not only many nations but also many diverging viewpoints on ecumenism.[14]

On June 29, 1960, Pope John issued an encyclical, *Ad Petri Cathedram*, in which he announced the purposes of the council. First, it was to bring about a development of the Catholic Faith; secondly, it would revive standards of Christian morality; thirdly, it would seek to bring the Church's discipline into closer accord with the needs of the times; and, fourthly, by a "wonderful manifestation of truth, unity and charity . . ." the separated brethren would experience the council as "a gentle invitation to find that unity for which Jesus Christ prayed so ardently to his heavenly Father."

The work of the Secretariat for Promoting Christian Unity was also outlined: to work with the separated Christians by accepting their suggestions and conveying them to the proper preparatory commission, to guide the commissions in those theological and pastoral matters which would directly or indirectly bear on the problem of Christian unity, and also to come to understand other Christian bodies. These were the purposes of the secretariat to which Gustave Weigel was appointed.[15]

The secretariat assembled with members of other preparatory commissions in the hall of the Biblical Commission in the Vatican Palace on the morning of November 14, 1960, for an audience with Pope John. The remainder of that day and the next day the secretariat had its first general meetings. The agenda was discussed and both members and consultors were assigned to various working sub-commissions.[16] Weigel's work-group was to study the question, "On the priesthood of all the faithful and on the role of the laity in the Church." This included the issues of religious freedom and religious tolerance. Bishop Francis Charrière of Lausanne, Geneva, and Fribourg was the sub-commission's chairman. Other members were Bishop Emile de Smedt of Bruges, Gregory Baum, and Jerome Hamer, O.P., for whom Weigel had great respect.[17]

Sub-commission work proved frustrating. Members lived far apart and communications were poor. Due to the rules of the Central Preparatory Commission, the antepreparatory volumes were to be distributed only to member bishops of the commissions and secretariats. Since there were no North American member-bishops on the secretariat, only one copy of the volumes was made available surreptitiously for the North American consultors by the secretariat.[18] Gregory Baum wrote to Weigel of these difficulties, wondering if they could be solved.[19]

Weigel attended the first sessions of his group in Rome and returned in a pessimistic mood. In addition to his general dislike for working in groups, he felt the conservatives would win the day and the council would be a failure.[20] He said the only person in

Rome who wanted the council was the pope and the conservatives were determined not to let him have it.[21] Sister Cleophas said Weigel saw the Secretariat assignment as an "annoyance." John Murray, who was not invited to the preparatory work, wrote of his friend's "participation" in the secretariat:

> This disposition to think by himself and not with others may explain why it was that in the conciliar period and at the Council itself he took no part and wanted to take no part in the work of the sub-commissions of the Secretariat for the Promotion of Christian Unity, to which he was attached. Not for him was the bruising business of composing a text in collaboration with other minds. I chided him, for instance, for his disinclination to put an American hand to the drawing up of the two pre-conciliar texts on religious freedom. He simply remained disinclined.[21a]

George Tavard recalled, too, that Weigel never became deeply involved in the preparatory work and, consequently, "had much less influence at Vatican II than he ought to have had." He took no active part in the writing of the Decree on Ecumenism, and was not in the small group of consultors that met to do the writing.[22]

Somehow the whole process seemed remote to Weigel. Sheerin and Thomas Stransky, C.S.P., a member of the Secretariat staff, think that Weigel did not feel he was appreciated by the others on the secretariat. His scholarship had slipped over the years and his ecclesiology and ecumenism were quite out-dated by comparison to many of his fellow consultors. Baum mentioned this in a letter to Weigel:

> There are other reasons why I would have liked to talk to you. One of them is that, after reading all of your books, I do not understand your position. This sounds strange; but I do not see what you are driving at. On the one hand you are full of generosity, deep understanding, sympathy for Protestant thought, and on the other your occasional remarks about Catholic theology seem to me so inflexible, so untouched by that wisdom and understanding you acquired by studying dissident thought, yes, so conservative.[23]

Stransky said that, in general, Weigel was silent at the Secretariat meetings. He had a deep love for Cardinal Bea. The Cardinal was almost like a father-figure for him, suggested Stransky. But as for Monsignor Willebrands, Weigel could not stand him.[24] They were very different as personalities. He felt Willebrands did not appreciate him and, at times, did not trust him.[25]

The second meeting of the Secretariat was held in February, 1961, at the Casa Gesu Divini Maestro, a retreat house on the shores of Lake Albano at Castel Gandolfo. Weigel attended. But he was unable to attend the third session held in the same place in mid-April.[26] In March, Willebrands asked Weigel to prepare a paper on American Protestantism. This would form part of a report on "The Ecumenical Movement and the Actual State of Protestantism."[27] Weigel's twelve-page report summarized much of what he had published about the subject over the past years.

Weigel made two formal interventions at the meetings of the secretariat. In them he urged that ecumenical dialogue be distinguished from evangelization and proselytizing. The ecumenical dialogue is a witnessing to the Word of God by believers who intend to impose nothing upon one another. The dialogue, as he had consistently insisted, simply leads to mutual understanding. He felt that the dialogue and its resultant understanding would be harmed if the Protestant ecclesiastical communities would not be referred to as such. Their ecclesial realities must be taken seriously, he said; here he seems to have advanced over his previous stand on Protestant churches as expressed in his *Summula Ecclesiologica*.

The sub-commission to which he was appointed asked Father Weigel to prepare a short paper on the priesthood of the laity and on tolerance of error. Weigel favored discussion of the priesthood of the laity at the council. He saw a difficulty, however, in that it was not clear what rights the laity have to initiate and maturely carry out action in the Church. Concerning the tolerance of error, Weigel simply reiterated his position on Church-state relations found in his 1954 *Summula Ecclesiologica*.[28]

Weigel attended the fourth meeting of the secretariat in Bühl, Germany, in August, 1961, and was appointed to serve on a subcommission to study the permanency of the secretariat. He crossed the Atlantic for the fifth session at Lake Albano in November and for the sixth and last session in Rome in March 1962.[29]

The secretariat had prepared four chapters in a schema for discussion by the Central Commission: 1) On the necessity of prayer for Christian unity, especially in our times; 2) On the Word of God; 3) On religious liberty; 4) On Catholic ecumenism. Weigel battled successfully to have the title of chapter four changed to "Catholic Principles of Ecumenism" indicating that there was no special ecumenism for Catholics but merely a Catholic way to go about the joint Christian search for unity.[30] Robert McAfee Brown recalled Weigel saying that talking about "Catholic Ecumenism" is like talking about "Catholic weather."[31]

In addition to these projects in preparation for the council, the secretariat invited Weigel to be their official representative at two Central Committee meetings of the World Council of Churches, one in Paris in August 1962, and the other at Rochester, New York, in August 1963.[32] He could not attend the Paris meeting and, at his suggestion, Sheerin was invited as observer instead. He did attend the Rochester meeting. John Sheerin recalls that he and Gus were invited to lunch with Archbishop Nikodim and Archpriest Borovoy. The two Catholic priests prepared theological points for discussion but much to their surprise, the luncheon did not include theological dialogue. The archbishop, with Borovoy as interpreter, simply amused his guests with humorous stories. Naturally, Gus Weigel, at home in this medium, drew from his vast storehouse of jokes to entertain his host.[33]

As interest in the council grew, Father Weigel was frequently called upon to explain the meaning of this event to people across the United States. In November, 1961, he stated that four areas would definitely be considered at the council: clarification of episcopal power, the role of the laity, Church-state relations and ecumenism. In regard to episcopal power, he said the decree of Vatican I on primacy might well be modified by Vatican II, but not cancelled out. The doctrine will simply be put in a fuller context, he said. Weigel insisted that the Church needs an active laity: "In the laity, Church and world meet. We must understand the rights, obligations and powers of the layman, powers that are charismatic and not from the sacrament of orders." He failed to see their powers rooted in baptism. He also mentioned the need for clergy-laity united action in the liturgy. "They can't very well do this if one speaks a language the others don't understand. So the question of vernacular in the liturgy will definitely come up." He hoped, also, that the bishops would clarify the Church's thought on the relation of the Church to secular society and what the Church thinks about religious freedom. In regard to Christian unity, Weigel looked for the relaxation of certain canons which inhibited relations between Christians. Such would include making exceptions for converted non-Catholic clergymen to continue their ministry and remain married. He also looked for a married diaconate. Weigel concluded his remarks by saying the council would be neither a revolution nor a restoration. It would be "a vital approach of the Church to the world in which the Church lives."[34]

One month before the opening of the council, Weigel outlined three mentalities which he expected to be reflected in the workings of the assembly. First, the "fixist" mentality which would want little or no change. Secondly, the drastic adjustment mentality which would seek to reformulate doctrines, decentralize administration, recognize the secular order as pluralistic and favor progressive ecumenism. Finally, the moderate adjustment mentality which was shared by most of the bishops. The latter was also Weigel's mind.

He further spelled out some of the subjects which might be treated. First was the definition of episcopal power which involved decentralization, questions of exempt religious and more local autonomy. Secondly, the laity should be involved in the Church's life even in administrative and doctrinal matters. They should be consultors of the bishops. Thirdly, in the Church's confrontation with culture, Church-state relations had to be clarified, the ecumenical dialogue had to be considered, the Index needed to be eliminated or modified, clerical training needed to be changed to reflect the new findings of science, the questions of married deacons and priests needed to be opened up, outmoded Latin needed to be dropped, and the sacred-secular tension clarified. Fourthly, certain isolated questions would be discussed: Mary as Mediatrix, Co-redemptrix and Queen of Heaven; the language of the liturgy; moral theology, especially birth control and the whole area of sexuality.[35]

Gustave Weigel's natural pessimism was often exacerbated by his physical and psychic condition. As the council's opening approached, he was very tired. He knew that some of his theology had become outdated and that for some time, he had been merely repetitious in his speeches and writings. Just as he had been bored with his teaching in the mid-1950s and sought an outlet in ecumenical activities, so now he had become bored with the repetitious role he found himself playing in American ecumenism. He was, therefore, relieved to be invited to the council as a new stage for the activities he so needed to keep alive and alert.[36]

At the opening sesssion on October 11, Pope John set a progressive, positive and pastoral tone in his opening address. Gustave Weigel was present as a theologian-interpreter for the delegated observers and guests of the secretariat.[37] He heard what could only have pleased him as the elderly pontiff read his Latin address. John XXIII served to reflect Weigel's own mind in questions of religious truth and ecumenism.

> In the present order of things, Divine Providence is leading us to a new order of human relations which, by men's own efforts and even beyond their very expectations, are directed toward the fulfillment of God's superior and inscrutable designs. And everything, even human differences, leads to the greater good of the Church . . .

. . . it is necessary first of all that the Church should never depart from the sacred patrimony of truth received from the Fathers. But at the same time she must ever look to the present, to the new conditions and new forms of life introduced into the modern world which have opened new avenues to the Catholic apostolate.

For this reason the Church has not watched inertly the marvelous progress of the discoveries of human genius and has not been backward in evaluating them rightly . . .

The salient point of the council is not, therefore, a discussion of one article or another of the fundamental doctrine of the Church which has repeatedly been taught by the Fathers and by ancient and modern theologians and which is presumed to be well-known and familiar to all . . . The substance of the ancient doctrine of the Deposit of Faith is one thing, and the way in which it is presented is another. And it is the latter that must be taken into great consideration with patience if necessary, everything being measured in the forms and proportions of a magisterium which is predominantly pastoral in character . . .

The Church has always opposed . . . errors. Frequently she has condemned them with the greatest severity. Nowadays, however, the spouse of Christ prefers to make use of the medicine of mercy rather than that of severity. She considers that she meets the needs of the present day by demonstrating the validity of her teaching rather than by condemnations.[38]

This pastoral, progressive and ecumenically oriented address gave Weigel a new vision of the "fat, silly diplomat" which he had not had so clearly before. Here was a man of his own kind: a warm human being who lived his faith close to life and who wanted to enter into dialogue with the world to bring about the unity of the Church and of all mankind. Weigel began to let hope modify his pessimism. He came to know that John was indeed "a true pope."[39] Sheerin noted in his diary (October 17) that Gus said: "We have a fighting chance but we must not relax."

Weigel's enthusiasm for Pope John increased during the first session of the council. John's intervention favoring the progressive groups encouraged Weigel.[40] He also saw John's personality breaking through ecumenical barriers that he himself had sought to melt.[41] The Pope was, to Weigel, a "little man with a vision" who resolved the impasse of the ecumenical movement. By his favoring of ecumenism, suspicion of the movement was destroyed. Pope John insisted that all Christians must give witness to all people, Father Weigel said, thus breaking down the barriers of separateness.[42] When the seriousness of John's illness became widely known in the early spring of 1963, Weigel urged prayer for the pontiff, saying that, if he lives to the conclusion of the council, "results far beyond our hope may develop."[43]

But God's ways are not man's ways, as Weigel so constantly affirmed from his Augustinian background. John XXIII died of cancer on June 3, 1963. Weigel's new appreciation of John was clearly seen in the eulogy he prepared at that time. The paean of praise penned by the Jesuit could well have been a eulogy for himself. His words were written facing "a mirror."

> Precisely here is the point: he did not see foes; only friends and brothers. In him the Catholic Church took a new look. It ceased to be a mere protesting voice, mainly demanding its own rights of a cool world with words of pain and anger. Under John, it encouraged men of good will everywhere and recognized the good which they were doing. In the voice of John, the Catholic Church went out to meet in friendly fashion groups which were not of its own communion . . .
>
> During the days of John, ecumenism became a vibrant surge among all Catholics. Isolation and tenacity for older forms of expression and action began to lose their stiffness and gradually turned into a universalism with a flexible adjustment to our world's reality . . . John could do all this without accepting it as a strategy for proselytising . . . He was one with all Christians, and for a good dogmatic principle which teaches that baptism does unite us all ontologically. He felt anything but alienated from non-Christians, even those who professed no religion whatsoever, because he agreed with old Tertullian that the good-willed man was a soul "naturally Christian."[44]

At Session I, Gustave Weigel continued as a member of the conciliar secretariat for unity.[45] But his contributions to their meetings were minimal.[46] His chief contribution at both this session and Session II was his work with the delegated observers. He literally spent himself in the two sessions to help the English-speaking observers understand the workings of the council and interpret the various documents and speeches.

His day began about five o'clock in the morning when he would rise to go to a nearby church to celebrate his private Mass, something which he seldom missed.[47] He usually returned about seven o'clock to the *pensione* where he lived with a number of observers, *Hotel Pensione Castello,* on the Piazza Adriana, near Castel Sant'Angelo. After breakfast with some of the observers, he would meet in the lounge to translate for those who had difficulty with Latin the *schemata* to be discussed that morning in the general session. This was an extra service which Weigel willingly volunteered. It was called "Weigel's Workshop."

From nine until about twelve-thirty o'clock, Father Weigel was with the observers in the St. Longinus tribune, immediately to the left of the Bernini altar in the Basilica of St. Peter, where the general sessions were held. It was his task to translate instantly for the observers all of the speeches as they were given in Latin by the Council Fathers, "one of the most exhausting intellectual exercises ever devised by man." He was able not only to translate the words but give innuendos and interpretations which were immensely valuable to his hearers and often quite amusing.[48] He was completely delightful and made himself very much available to the observers in all their needs, personal as well as theological. His gift for terse, colorful expression, clarity of thought and his wry, witty comments made him beloved by all.[49] George Lindbeck said: "For us Americans . . . Weigel is the name for us . . . Father Weigel has no hesitation to say in the course of his translation, 'This speaker does not know his theology at all.' "

The translation task was terribly trying and tiring for Father

Weigel. At times an old inner-ear problem would bother him during the general sessions. He would become dizzy, suffering terrible headaches. Someone would signal to Weigel's friend, Monsignor Vincent A. Yzermans, who occupied the press tribune directly opposite that of the observers. Yzermans, who had an automobile, would help Weigel out of the hall, wobbling as though he were drunk, and take him to his hotel to rest. This was very embarrassing to Weigel, but he complained little. He was a Stoic.[50]

Daniel O'Hanlon, S.J., who succeeded Weigel as interpreter at Session III, explained the translation problems Weigel faced. Loud speakers on the wall behind the tribune gave out the Latin speech. The translator would have to listen to the speaker while, at the same time, expressing in English what had just been said and continuing to listen to what was then being said by the speaker in Latin. The technical arrangements for translation were, thus, quite primitive. By Session III, ear-phones were provided for the translators but Weigel was no longer there.

Gustave Weigel's second major contribution at Vatican II was as a member of the United States bishops' press panel. At the beginning of the first session, the press corps felt that it did not have adequate access to conciliar information. On September 14, 1962, Thomas Stransky wrote to Weigel: "The Press set-up is still in a miserable state, but there is little we can do about it. Incompetency, lack of experience and imagination are the basic causes."[51] Therefore a committee, headed by Bishop Albert R. Zuroweste of Belleville, Illinois, was established through the Rome office of the National Catholic Welfare Conference to design a program to assist the newsmen.

A nine-member panel of experts was appointed to meet with the press after each general session to answer their questions. Members were: Fathers Francis J. McCool, S.J., John B. Sheerin, C.S.P., Edward L. Heston, C.S.C., William H. Keeler, Frederick R. McManus, Eugene H. Maly, Robert F. Trisco and John P. McCormick, S.S. Their chairman was Mr. William H. Fanning, Jr., of the *Catholic News* of New York.[52] Gustave Weigel felt the press was not treated fairly at Session I, despite the work of this panel.[53]

As the second session opened, the membership of the press panel had been slightly revised and included Gus Weigel. McCool, Keeler, Maly, Sheerin and Trisco remained. New members, in addition to Weigel, were Father Francis J. Connell, C.SS.R., Monsignor George G. Higgins and Monsignor Thomas J. Tobin.[54]

After an exhausting morning of translations and after a lunch and sometimes a brief rest, Father Weigel would go to a basement room in the U.S.O. headquarters on the Via della Conciliazione to appear on the hour-long press panel at three o'clock. Sheerin was the moderator in the second session and recalled that Weigel was "the star of the press panel." He was entertaining, colorful, witty and always put on a great show. It was like a Woodstock classroom "stage" for him. He was in his glory; he was made for this. Each day brought at least one hundred, sometimes as many as three hundred to the briefings.[55] Louis Cassels, the United Press International reporter, who became very fond of Weigel, wrote: "His lucidity and wit and his remarkable ability to get straight to the point of a complex or obfuscated debate made him invaluable . . ."[56]

John Sheerin recalled some of the humorous incidents involving Weigel at the press panels:

> One day a housewife-correspondent, after Father Weigel had explained the teaching on charisms, proclaimed that she was fascinated by the thought that she could experience a charism as she went about her work in the kitchen. There was a hush for a moment after this unexpected comment but Father Weigel broke the silence with his comment: "Yes, I do think that good cooking is a charism." Sometimes, the humor was at his own expense. One day he was explaining to the press some of the devious ways in which books might be brought under the vigilant scrutiny of the Holy Office. Taking a purely suppositious case, he said: "Let us suppose, for instance, that someone in Oshkosh wants to report a book." Father Stransky immediately popped up, "It

just happens that we have someone from Oshkosh here with us, Bishop Grellinger, who lives there at St. Mary's Church." By extraordinary coincidence the Bishop actually was present.

On another occasion, UPI correspondent Lou Cassels asked for an explanation of the difference between a document labelled a Constitution and one classified as a Decree. Father Weigel proceeded to dilate learnedly on various Council documents at great length and he was followed by Father Bernard Haring who also went into scholarly detail in explaining categories of documents. Whereupon Mr. Cassels said that all this reminded him of the story about the little girl who had to write a report on a book on penguins. She said: "This is a book on penguins. This is a very good book on penguins. This tells you a lot about penguins. In fact, this book tells you more than you really need to know about penguins." Another man might have felt deflated but Father Weigel chuckled as much as did the newsmen.[57]

Several correspondents, entertained as well as informed by Weigel's performances on the press panel, described the Jesuit's work behind the green ping-pong table "desk" used by the panel. Monsignor James I. Tucek wrote:

> Father Weigel sits in his place each day with the other panelists, draping his large-boned six-foot frame in such a relaxed attitude as to hide from the uninitiated, the alert and perceptive mind that is constantly at work. One journalist has likened him to a sea turtle snapping at flies.
>
> His manner of speaking is with the slowly paced, precisely enunciated word that gives the impression, merely from his voice, that he is standing at an imaginary blackboard, outlining and underlining.
>
> With plastic face and deep voice, and the peculiar habit of holding his cigarette between the middle finger and ring finger of his right hand, he banters words with the journalists with a masterful timing that would be the envy of any "deadpan" comic.
>
> "Would you tell us in the language of a journalist . . .?" a correspondent once asked. And, before he had gotten the ques-

tion well out, he was hit with the reply, "I wouldn't dream of using the language of a journalist."

"Would you care to elaborate on . . .?" another said. "No, I would not!" came the deathblow reply.[58]

One correspondent wrote a special for the *Buffalo Evening News* on the activities of Buffalo's native son who learned his first debating and public speaking skills in that northwestern New York city.

> Surprisingly enough—for the Holy Spirit and His work are generally regarded as deserving solemn treatment—Father Weigel's blunt, logical, but witty way of making a point frequently calls forth a burst of laughter; in nearly every case not a flicker of expression crosses his face to betray his consciousness of the witticism. As the laugh dies away, for one split second, his deep eyes lighten ever so slightly—not enough to justify the word "flicker"—as he proceeds to the next point.
>
> Father Weigel uses his wit like a rapier. It flashes, it touches here, there, everywhere and it drives back argument without giving opportunity for it to become opposition. In all honesty, it must be said that he is not always above dipping the point of his epee in acid—the kind that stings but leaves no lasting wound. . . .
>
> Not often, but once in a long time, Father Weigel is hoist with his own petard of wit. On those rare occasions when the laugh is at him, rather than with him, he joins readily in the laughter.
>
> One such occasion occurred during the discussion of the absence of women's jurisdiction in the Church. In Catholic terminology an "ordinary" is a cleric with ordinary jurisdiction in the external forum over a specified territory; "the ordinary" generally indicates the bishop of the diocese.
>
> With the utmost gravity Father Weigel remarked: "A woman is never an ordinary" and then joined in the laughter.[59]

Another description of his facility with the press was printed in the *Baltimore Evening Sun* which likened his voice to that of Senator Everett Dirksen of Illinois.[60]

It was, then, as the theologian-interpreter for the non-Catholic delegated observers and as a member of the United States bishops' press panel that Gustave Weigel made his greatest contributions at Vatican II and likewise found the greatest personal satisfaction. He continued to attend the regular meetings of the secretariat, especially the Tuesday afternoon sessions with the observers. He worked on the secretariat subcommittee to rework chapters I and II, section II, during the second session. He frequently attended meetings of *periti* and spoke periodically at gatherings of both the North American and Latin American bishops.[61] No less than thirteen Latin American bishops attending Vatican II had been Weigel's students during his years in Chile.[62] His schedule of activities was inhumanly packed, as had been his entire life. He could not rest; there was too much yet to be said.

Yet Rome was not all work for Gustave Weigel. Socially active always, he was frequently found having tea at the American Bar near the U.S.O. building after the press panel was held. There, though tired, he would relax and his unique brand of humor shone forth.[63] Sunday evenings would find him at soirees in the apartment of the *Time* magazine correspondent, Robert Blair Kaiser. This was a gathering place for American liberals, such as John Courtney Murray, Frederick McManus, Thomas Stransky, Gregory Baum and Vincent Arthur Yzermans. Hans Küng and Archbishop Thomas Roberts, formerly of Bombay, India, were also guests at Kaiser's parties.[64] To get away from the observers, Weigel would also sneak away now and then with Yzermans for a good Italian meal.[65] And, of course, mystery novels provided continuous relaxation for Weigel.[66]

Gus Weigel returned to Woodstock College after the first session of the council, convinced that what he had witnessed in Rome was the beginning of "a whole new Church."[67] He was alive again in a new way. So many of his life's dreams had come to light at Vatican II and his deepest intuitions were substantiated through the dialogical conciliar process. He spoke of Session I as a "refresher course in theology" for himself.[68] The pessimism with which he entered the council had been tempered by the experience of hierarchy and theologians thrashing things out openly for the good of the Church. The bishops had impressed him.[69] He was particularly impressed with the performance of the United States hierarchy. He said they "grew to formidable stature" as the council progressed. Most of them came to Rome as representatives of the "closed door" mentality but gradually changed their views when they experienced the council in action. In one sense they were the real heroes of the first session, according to Weigel. Had it not been for their change of mind-set, the "open-door" mentality would not have come out ahead in the general voting by approximately 60%–40%.[70]

The terms "open-door" and "closed-door" were coined by Father Weigel to express the two mentalities prominent at the council.[71] He used this terminology as he traveled all over the United States after the first session, explaining the council to Catholics and Protestants who flocked to hear him. In Steubenville, Ohio, he explained his terms:

> I don't like the terms "liberal" and "conservative" that are being bandied about relative to the tendencies the Council Fathers have followed. I prefer the terms "open-door" and "closed-door." The former believes that the Church must modify its practices to keep pace with the changing world. The latter says that any and all changes would be treasonable.[72]

Father Weigel insisted that the council was not like a political convention and not like the United States Congress. It is more like the Supreme Court, he explained.

Earlier in a speech in Baltimore, Father Weigel had explained both positions in greater detail: open-door proponents held that formulations of the council should be unifying in their effect; that good relations should be developed between Protestants and Catholics; and that ancient doctrine should be made intelligible to non-Roman Catholics without substantially changing that doctrine. The closed-door minds feared that "if you change formula-

249

tion (of doctrine) you run the risk of making people think you have changed the old doctrine . . ."[73]

In an interview with Monsignor Yzermans, Father Weigel discussed the theological schools represented at the first session.

> If I hear an Italian speak, I am sure that I will get a résumé and an echo of the types of theology which were current some forty years ago. These men know that theology very well, indeed, but it seems that they have never opened up their theological reflections to the newer kind of theology. In contrast, if I hear a German theologian speak and, of course, a French-speaking theologian, I notice, of course, that he has a newer type of theology, well expressed and put in the form of summary, almost synthetically. To understand them it is necessary to know what the newer theologians are saying. Then there comes an entirely different third group. Most theologians, naturally, do their work in terms of categories and schemes which are abstract. But, say, a bishop from the Congo or a bishop from India have an entirely different point of view which they do explain to us and at times even stress. As a result, the older theologians and the newer theologians suddenly realize that there is a new dimension to theology which has been ignored in the past.[74]

One of the chief reasons for Weigel's optimism at the end of Session I was the ecumenical attitude revealed there by the Council Fathers. None spoke against ecumenism.[75] Weigel said that some of the Fathers thought they were being ecumenical by presenting their positions forthrightly, with sincerity and consideration for the other positions. However, they were often unknowingly offensive. They had clarity because of their old theology "but, unfortunately, they represent a view of reality which no longer is relevant to the reality we are living in."[76]

Ecumenism had been advanced as a result of the first session. Weigel felt that there had been generated there "a great, spontaneous friendliness." Protestants and Catholics were beginning to admit valid points on both sides of religious issues. Catholics admitted validity to the notion that faith alone saves. And Protestants were beginning to take seriously the notion of tradition. Vatican II broadened the base of the ecumenical movement, Weigel thought. Acknowledging that the world in which we live is no longer interested in Christ and His message, the council insisted that all Christianity must give effective witness to the doctrine of Jesus Christ in order to survive. Ecumenism was seen as the instrument for this witness.[77]

Father Weigel was particularly aware that he was living in the post-Christian era. His last book, *The Modern God*, is filled with a Weigelian pessimism regarding this matter.[78] He told a gathering in March 1963: "We are not engaged in a search for church but for a union of those who want to save Christendom."[79] From the same address: "We live in a post-Christian world! We must face it. At one time the Church gave witness to the salvation from God. But today there is no culture anywhere in which this is true. Thus the Christian's obligation to profess God as the Supreme Being is much greater than ever before."[80]

Gustave Weigel's personal experiences with the delegated observers at Vatican II had been sources of encouragement and optimism for him. He said the observers were surprised at the warmth shown them. "They were neither proselytized nor patronizingly tolerated. They were helped to see and hear; nor were they in any way hoodwinked."[81] He felt they were extraordinarily happy at the council.[82]

Despite their basic happiness, the observers did have some disappointment and concerns, Weigel said. First, they had hoped for a discussion of the exact relationship between the non-Catholic churches and the Roman Catholic Church. This had not yet happened. Secondly, they were disappointed that there was not more personal ecumenicity among the Fathers, who, however, were frequently making polite and friendly references in the direction of the observers' tribune. Thirdly, some of the Fathers' theological expressions made them unhappy. Finally, the observers would like to have been able to air their views and reactions personally on the

251

council floor. They were able to do so indirectly, however, through the secretariat and the great kindness of Cardinal Bea who quoted the observers in his speeches.[83] Warren Quanbeck said he felt that in this way they were truly influencing the council. Despite these natural disappointments, Weigel was certain that the delegates had taken a friendly and positive message home with them.

Displaying his natural bent to find sincerity in his Christian brothers, he said that not one of the observers had been a bigot. "They were friendly when they came and they will be more friendly when they go." They would carry back a vision of freedom in the Roman Catholic Church which could hardly square with the monolithic structure they had known in the past.[84]

> Weigel summarized the first session in very positive terms. "In terms of decrees made, of constitutions approved, the first session has not been very rich. But the first session has, indeed, shown that different views are possible within the Church, that the ecumenical conversation is real and should be accepted and engaged in; that there are in the Church many, if not the majority, who are willing to give new formulas to the ancient truths which are always respected and defended."[85]

Gustave Weigel's other major interest, ecclesiology, had been a core issue at Session I. His own view of the Church began to expand somewhat under the influence of the conciliar experience.[86] However, his theology was not significantly altered as a result of the council. He was already firmly set in his theological method and vision. Even if he could have changed, there was not enough time.[87] He was too active being a publicist to do the scholarly work necessary. One area in which he was getting a slightly new understanding was the notion of the magisterium. He began to see, after witnessing the bishops in action, that the teaching office of the Church had to include more than the hierarchy. He began to see more clearly that the magisterium is also the theologians, working in conjunction with the bishops.[88] The biblical image of the Church, the People of God, was appealing to Weigel too.[89]

As Session II was about to begin, Father Weigel reflected on the proposed conciliar action in ecclesiology. He was most at home with the notion of the Church as mystery which is depicted variously by the biblical images. He looked for no *definition* of the Church to come from Vatican II, though he had asked for one in his pre-council *Vota*. Indeed, no council has ever defined the Church. He did expect that the role of the bishop in relation to the pope would be clarified, much in the way he had developed the relationship in his *Summula Ecclesiologica*. Episcopal power would be strengthened.[90] Weigel expected that the new vision of the collegial Church would result in more importance for regional and national episcopal conferences. "The council, therefore, will supply us with a device to get more and more answers when and where questions arise."[91]

Gustave Weigel's speeches on Session I were almost innumerable. Two are of special interest because, for quite different reasons, each involved Weigel in controversy. Father Weigel was considered by Protestant theologians to be a very traditional Catholic theologian. Most of his fellow Catholics would have shared this judgment. However, an incident at the Catholic University of America in the early months of 1963 seemed to place Weigel in the ranks of the radicals.

Weigel, John Courtney Murray, Godfrey Diekmann and Hans Küng had been placed on a list of Lenten lecturers submitted to the administration by the Graduate Student Council in January. Though other names were accepted, those four were rejected, with no reasons given.[92] The graduate faculty voted to send a letter of censure to the rector, Monsignor William McDonald, and the undergraduate student council also filed an official protest.[93] In response to the protests, the vice-rector, Monsignor Joseph McAllister, said the ban implied no criticisms of the theologians individually or of their views. The administration had decided not to invite the four because "they represent a very definite point of view, a very definite attitude, in regard to certain ecclesiastical matters now being debated. The University did not want to put itself in the position of championing this position. A number of matters quite controversial ecclesiastically came up at the Ecumenical Council and there are strong views on both sides.'' Since the Catholic University is governed by the United States hierarchy, the administration did not want to embarrass the hierarchy, although the bishops were not consulted on the decision.[94]

The issue of academic freedom was raised, naturally, and the Catholic University incident became a *cause célèbre* for liberty in both the religious and secular press.[95] The graduate faculty and the Graduate Student Council asked that the decision be reviewed and that university policy regarding public lectures be reconsidered.[96] Newspapers in abundance opposed the ban, as did at least two bishops: Victor J. Reed of Oklahoma City and John King Mussio of Steubenville, Ohio. Professors at Duquesne University in Pittsburgh protested the ban.[97] Monsignor John Tracy Ellis was particularly critical of the administration's decision, saying that such suppression had been going on there for nearly ten years.[98] One writer went so far as to lay the blame for the decision at the feet of the conservative apostolic delegate, Egidio Vagnozzi.[99] The supposed involvement of the delegate prompted a clever limerick which amused Weigel:

> Of Murray, Weigel, Diekmann, and Küng
> The praises were everywhere sung.
> The delegate then
> Seemed out-of-date when
> He gave orders to have them all hung.[100]

Non-Catholics too registered dismay at the rejection. Paul Blanshard said that the American bishops could have reversed the ban but "all but a few of them chose to remain silent."[101a]

Archbishop Karl Alter of Cincinnati wrote to Weigel in support: "Just a word of sympathy, or perhaps congratulations (I am not sure which should be in order) as a result of the recent imbroglio at the Catholic University. The results must certainly be in favor of yourself and your associates, who have been treated in very cavalier fashion. There has been much protest to the University authorities, and I think that by this time there is no doubt sincere and profound regret that the situation was ever permitted to develop. I am sure that you must realize that the four priests mentioned have the respect and esteem of the great majority of the Bishops of our country.''[101b]

Gustave Weigel was true to form through the whole incident: he refused to answer his critics. His only public comment was that he felt the matter had been blown out of all proportion and that it was not important enough to warrant so much attention.[102] Privately he thought the whole matter rather humorous and could not have cared less. It threatened him in no way.[103]

Father David Bowman, S.J., professor of religious education at the university, wanted to help the rector out of the embarrassing situation. On February 12, he went to the rector's office to tell him of the seriousness of the situation on the campus. As an alleviating gesture, Bowman suggested that he invite Father Weigel to speak in his class about Church and Reunion. The rector immediately and gladly assented. He suggested that, before the class, Weigel be brought to Curley Hall for lunch with the rector and faculty. McDonald continued to insist that his only objection was to a *public* lecture by the four theologians. A classroom lecture could be permitted. Weigel accepted the invitation the next day and Bowman brought him and Father Walter Burghardt from Woodstock to the university on February 20. The luncheon with the rector was pleasant and, much to the surprise of all, McDonald invited Weigel to give the university's commencement address on June 9. Weigel later had to decline because of a prior commitment.

At the class in McMahon Auditorium, more than seven hundred people had jammed into the five-hundred-seat hall. They sat on the window sills, the floor and in the aisle. Both Weigel and Bowman were cheered by the enthusiastic audience. Later that afternoon he repeated the lecture at the Nursing Auditorium which was filled with nearly three hundred persons. Bowman recalled that the lecture was magnificent but Burghardt said it was "The Talk" which Weigel gave everywhere and was only mediocre.[104]

Gustave Weigel was able to speak in public with great facility. His sharp mind and his tremendous recall made him a man ever-prepared to comment. Usually this served him well. However, at times, his off-the-cuff remarks could get him into deep trouble. This happened during a public appearance between the first and second sessions of Vatican II.

He had addressed the National Jewish Community Relations Advisory Council in Atlantic City, New Jersey, on June 29. In a question-and-answer period afterwards Weigel referred to the statement on anti-Semitism prepared for but not discussed at Session I. Because of concern that such a statement might be construed as an endorsement for the state of Israel and so be construed by the Arab states as presenting a politically pro-Israeli attitude, he predicted, without instruction from anyone and without representing anyone, that the statement would be avoided at Session II. Though it was a statement of moral principle, he judged the Arabs would consider it political in intent.[105] The reactions were quick and sharp. Jewish leaders—Zachariah Schuster, Marc Tanenbaum, Lewis H. Weinstein, to mention only a few—protested and hoped that Weigel's prediction would not prove true.[106]

On July 4, a spokesman for the Secretariat for Promoting Christian Unity issued a statement saying that Weigel had not been authorized to make that remark and "as far as the statements refer to the future, they do not correspond to the actual state of the question involved." In fact, the Arab Information Center in Rome declared they would welcome a statement on anti-Semitism by the council.[107]

Weigel, realizing that he had erred, issued a statement: "Gladly do I accept information from those in a better position who can give a contrary prognosis." Friends recall that the Jesuit was quite embarrassed about the incident. He was tired the night it happened and felt he had fallen into a trap nicely laid out for him by a journalist. "At the same time he felt his remark had stirred things up and would in the end contribute to the passing of the Declaration."[108] Later in the month, Tanenbaum, in a letter to Weigel, suggested that his "disturbing" statement in many ways had become "a blessing in disguise" since it revealed less opposition to the resolution then he had realized.[109]

"L'Affaire Weigel," as it came to be called at the secretariat in Rome, drew a letter of sharp criticism from Willebrands whom Weigel felt never cared for him anyway.

> We have been receiving many reactions to your statement on the fate of the *Decretum de Judaeis* and I am convinced your Guardian Angel was absent on the day you made those declarations.
>
> Your statement was not accurate and we may excuse you because you did not take part in the last sessions of the Secretariat, where we discussed the developments regarding the schema. Nevertheless, you should never have made the statement. It was indiscreet, because you revealed the names of some of the more responsible participants—a point which is *sub secreto* without doubt.
>
> Now we hope that from this unhappy event there may eventually come good results and clarifications; we wish this especially for yourself and your work.[110]

Monsignor John M. Oesterreicher, an expert on Jewish affairs and one of Weigel's fellow consultants on the secretariat, had been one of the authors of the decree on the Jews. He wrote about the Weigel incident in his commentary on the final conciliar decree. At some points, he said, Weigel's statement did not correspond to the facts.

> To take only two: A mere condemnation of hatred of the Jews was never planned; also, Father Weigel was not aware of the most recent state of affairs, as he had not been present at the latest sitting of the Secretariat . . . Father Weigel frequently indicated that he deeply regretted his overhasty and ill-considered reply.

All the same, he could not help seeing the favorable consequences of his "indiscretion" . . . . When he saw how well things were going, he went so far as to take some small credit for it upon himself and whispered in my ear that his thoughtlessness had proved "a blessing in disguise."[111]

Shortly after "L'Affaire Weigel," Gus had a chance to get away from the pressures of the moment. He went to Winona, Minnesota, to give a colloquium for the clergy. He then asked Monsignor Yzermans if he could go to his lake cabin near Richmond, Minnesota, in Stearns County, to "hide out" for a few days. Those days proved a delightful respite to the weary and pressured Weigel. To "justify" his staying in Stearns County, Weigel asked Yzermans to arrange a lecture for him at the Newman Center at St. Cloud State College. It was one of his typical ecumenically oriented talks about the council.[112] Some of his words on that occasion are memorable: "We do not know where God will lead us or when He will effect Christian unity. At the present moment we must allow ourselves to be led where God wills. This imposes on all of us a tremendous act of hope and trust in God."[113]

Gradually this was becoming Weigel's prevailing mood. It was reflected again on a visit in St. Cloud with the author J. F. Powers. Powers asked Weigel what he was planning to do next and the Jesuit replied that now he could say his *Nunc Dimittis* for he had done everything he could. He said he had brought the ecumenical movement as far as he could and now there was to be no more room in it for him.[114]

At the end of September, Gustave Weigel joined the thousands descending on Rome for the second session of Vatican II. Several days earlier he had spoken very optimistically about the imminent meeting: "It is clear that the council by its doctrine and directive is going to rejuvenate the whole Church. We expect great things."[115]

Within one week, Weigel's hopes had been dashed. In a taped message sent to Peter Bartholome, the ailing bishop of St. Cloud, referred to as "Peter Cloud," Weigel said that it was not the same council as last year. There was more tension and division, especially over the *De Ecclesia* schema. He told the Minnesotan that "the rightists" were trying to puncture the fine document. Bookburning, too, was in the wind, he reported, especially against Hans Küng, Robert Blair Kaiser, Karl Rahner and Xavier Rynne. Weigel predicted the session would be "a resistance contest." He feared that the council might drag on to two or three more sessions, saying that "we cannot afford that except for the boys who live here."[116] According to Sheerin, Weigel lamented the men of the curia who represented only *one* school of theology.

When Giovanni Battista Montini, Archbishop of Milan, had been elected to succeed John XXIII, Weigel was not happy. He had never been impressed with Montini. He felt he was a curialist who would bring more of Pius XII to the papacy. He disliked his interferences in the workings of the council. It was to Paul's style of leadership that Weigel attributed the slow pace of the opening of Session II. He felt the conservatives thought they had new papal backing under Paul. Weigel's lack of enthusiasm for Paul increased as the session moved on.[117]

Despite the procedural drags of the first weeks, Weigel was pleased with the revised drafts of the Constitution on the Church and the Decree of Ecumenism. *De Ecclesia* was superior to the first draft and needed little revision. It was truly pastoral, relevant, scriptural and ecumenical, he judged. Theological squabbles were avoided. Weigel especially appreciated that no definition of the Church was attempted, although in his *Vota* in 1960 he had urged that the Church be defined as the Mystical Body of Christ. The use of scriptural images, however, especially the People of God and the Body of Christ, pleased him. Ecumenically, the schema recognized that Orthodox and Protestants are connected with the Church, though he regretted that nothing was said about them as "churches." The collegial nature of the episcopacy and the fact that bishops are successors of the apostles with their power given to them immediately by God was clearly stressed as he always had done in his own teaching of ecclesiology. Weigel was very appreciative of the fact that the Church was presented as an episcopal, not a papal Church. It would be ecumenically useful. He also approved of speaking of episcopal consecration as a sacrament and of the bringing back of an active diaconate.

Certain elements of the new schema did cause him to object. First, though it did say the bishops and the pope bear one and the same divine power in the Church, the document reflects "a nervousness" about it. It is only left to be inferred that papal power is episcopal power and nothing else. Weigel said, "We must avoid putting two powers in the Church; one papal and the other episcopal." He felt that it should be clearly stated that papal doctrine, while being *sine consensu Ecclesiae* according to Vatican I, does involve the consent of the Church.[118]

Weigel's notes on this schema indicated certain openings in his own ecclesiological thought. First of all, he seemed to appreciate the People of God image, though he considered that the Body of Christ image should be given preference. His mention that the Orthodox and the Protestants should be treated as ecclesial communities was an advance over his pre-conciliar thinking. Previously he had not been so kindly disposed to non-Catholic *churches* though he was always so to non-Catholic *people*. In the final constitution, *Lumen Gentium*, non-Catholic Christian ecclesial communities *are* treated, though the way in which they are linked to the Roman Catholic Church is left open to theological speculation.[119]

De Oecumenismo had both good and bad points too, according to Father Weigel. The "modest" schema described and treated non-Catholics with a benevolence never shown by the official Church. They were declared to be in partial union with the Catholic Church. Dialogue and its support by hierarchy, clergy and laity was encouraged. It was recommended that Catholics come to know the non-Catholic mind and that Catholic statements contain nothing offensive to the separated brethren. Catholics, according to the schema, must come to know their tradition. Weigel was especially pleased that "in dialogue, doctrine is to be expressed without a tacit demand that our language and modes of expression be understood by the partners in the conversation, to whom our language is not known nor even intelligible. We must recognize that modes of theologizing are many, not only one."

On the negative side, Weigel suggested that non-Catholics will be quick to notice that the Catholic Church is not as ecumenical as the principles in the schema. Though much of the suspicion is gone, Weigel said, "Yet the absolute identification of the Church of Christ with the Catholic Church, to which non-Catholic Christians are somehow attached as second class citizens, will not please non-Catholics."

> What is lacking in the present schema is a confession of at least partial responsibility for the rupture of the unity of Christendom. The Schema deals with the Church as the ideal entity as Christian faith paints her. The historical Catholic Church made up of historical human beings manifesting original sin in all of its demonic destructiveness looks quite different from the ideal. It is not merely individual Catholics who sinned, but the historical collectivity made up by these individuals falls short of the perfection of the Gospel.[120]

This acknowledgement of the sinful Church was clearly an advance in Weigel's thought. He had said just the opposite in earlier statements.[121]

Weigel's comments on *De Oecumenismo* substantiate, therefore, the comment of Robert McAfee Brown, viz., that Gustave Weigel had opened up ecumenically during the council. Weigel stated that he was pleased that the schema attempted no definition of ecumenism. Later Weigel admitted that some feared that this left the matter too vague. He said that "the beauty about the ecumenical movement was that it remained something fuzzy and ill-defined; it was desirable to keep it that way and not allow it to become petrified if further progress was to be made."[122]

On October 28, Monsignor Yzermans gathered together the four priests who had been rejected as speakers at the Catholic University of America: John Courtney Murray, Hans Küng, Godfrey Diekmann and Gustave Weigel. For about one hour, he taped their "Conversation at the Council." Since *De Ecclesia* was under debate at the general sessions, much of the discussion centered around ecclesiology. Weigel was strong in his praise for the concept of collegiality. "This vision indicates the Church's power and strength is in the indwelling of the Holy Spirit . . . His power, His direction, His holiness is rendered external in the Church by an inbuilt system of power." This power is the entire episcopacy, governing and teaching the universal Church. Weigel saw that the teaching office is not centered just in the bishops though. The whole Church teaches and the episcopacy "directs and authenticates what is the right teaching either from the local church or the Church universal."

Murray said he did not believe that the bishops really believed in collegiality since they had no real consciousness of it. He feared that bishops would go home and the notion would die. Weigel disagreed. Although the bishops had not known exactly what this episcopal unity meant, he did not think the bishops were ever unaware that they were rulers of more than their own little sections. He felt the bishops had only a "latent" sense of collegiality.

All four theologians agreed that the stress upon the Church as a spiritual community rather than a juridical entity was true progress. Weigel felt the ontological emphasis, insisting that the Church is a living body, was of prime importance. He said that it was strange that canon lawyers were able to make "non-being into being" in their juridical approach to the Church.

In discussing the effect of the council upon the ecumenical movement, Father Weigel was still quite optimistic. There had been an interchange of speakers between Protestants and Catholics after the first session. Bishops in the United States had become personally involved in ecumenical dialogue. "It may be a bit shallow," he admitted, "but nevertheless it happened." Father Diekmann said he felt it was incredible that we have thought of Protestant ministers for so long as "stupid or in bad faith." Weigel agreed but insisted that it was only the Catholic *clergy* who had this narrow view. The people did not. "The people," he said, "never supposed, especially in a place like America where we are living with Protestants and Jews, that all these other people were condemned to hell." Theoretically they went along because it was what the Church said. But in their lives they did not believe it, he averred.

A discussion of theological method followed. Father Küng said he thought we had insisted on too much deep theological reflection in the past. We refused to move until we could see all the intellectual implications of a proposed position or action. Consequently, the Swiss theologian said, nobody acted. Gustave Weigel, with his Platonic and Augustinian approach to epistemology, could not have agreed more. Küng said: "There are few theologians who are capable of action. Perhaps I am wrong but I think we do not have to ask for too much reflection. We need the Holy Spirit. Complete understanding of an action inspired by the Spirit is not necessary. Oftentimes understanding comes only later."[123]

Along about the midpoint of Session II, it was clear that things were almost hopelessly bogged down. For five weeks the Fathers had been debating the schema on the Church without a resolution of the tensions which largely centered around the concept of collegiality and how it was to be interpreted and implemented. Sheerin recalls Weigel complaining about "the interminable procession of speakers." On October 11, Weigel told the press that the collegiality debate was in regard to finding proper expressions and the definition of terms in which to couch the teaching, and that it would not be tabled because of these difficulties. But as November came, no one was so sure that the constitution would go through. Despite twenty-three days of debate—half of the debating days allotted for the session—no final document was in sight.[124]

One of the points at issue was the authority of episcopal conferences. Father Weigel summed up the basic points of division on the matter: "The Continental mind holds that you do not have any kind of agreement unless it is written down and spelled out in law. The Anglo-Saxon mind on the other hand believes that the less law there is the better. As much as possible should be left to the moral sphere." One of those who feared the power of episcopal conferences was James Cardinal McIntyre of Los Angeles. He saw the conferences endangering infallibility for one thing. Commenting upon this in one of his famous *bons mots,* Weigel said, "We must remember that Cardinal McIntyre sees much farther than most of us do, if he can be said to see at all."[125]

In early November, as people were chafing at the slow pace, Gus Weigel put out a news release article on the schema on the Church. He said *De Ecclesia* was the keystone of the council, determining the direction and tone of all else the council would do. The Church was being discussed as a mystery and her reality is left to be experienced by the believer in terms of his faith. "Any mystery," he wrote, "is ultimately beyond the comprehension of rational analysis, but much of a mystery can be known and the very mystery excites us to know more about it."[126]

Weigel said the questions of membership in the Body of Christ had shifted to "belonging" to the Church, the People of God. This was an improvement, a better way to approach the question. The question often determines the answer; Weigel had adopted this Tillichian insight. He said: "Questions change their meaning as time goes on. A good answer in 1910 may be an awfully bad answer in 1960. There must be a readiness to accept the question as the question shows up, and not say, 'Ah, that question. That is on page 96 in the book.' No, no, no. It is a living question and must be approached by a living mind."[127]

The Church as the People of God proclaims the equality of all believers, he pointed out. Only then are functions differentiated. Hierarchs are ministers to the whole Church. Collegiality is the way in which this ministry is exercised. And it is the whole Church that bears the mission of Christ. "Administration lays down guidelines, but the work is done by all." Thus the laity, who "make up most of the Church," must be considered most of all.[128]

Asked about the fact that *De Ecclesia* seemed to treat everybody in the Church seriously except the priest, Weigel said, "The priest is not an altar boy of the bishops."[129] However, the priests participate in the administration of the Church under the single directive power of the episcopate. Bishops empower presbyters to assist them but within definite limits. "Episcopal power is shared with them, but not in its fullness. The presbyter can offer the sacrifice of the Mass and he is a priest of the second order forever."[130]

The last two weeks of the second session were devoted to a discussion of the schema on ecumenism which had been prepared by the Secretariat for Promoting Christian Unity. The revised draft in five chapters included a chapter on the Jews and one on religious liberty. These were considered particularly controversial as Weigel was well-aware. Despite the efforts of many, especially among the American hierarchy, they were not brought to a vote and Session II closed without completing the decree on ecumenism, much to Weigel's disappointment.[131]

As has been mentioned earlier, Weigel's ecumensim was not basically altered at Vatican II although there were some openings perceived in his positions. One such opening was in regard to the World Council of Churches. During the 1950s he had seen no way in which the Roman Catholic Church could formally participate in the discussion of this federation of churches. To do so would have been admission that the Catholic Church was not the true and only Church of Christ. He felt that no Catholic could ever be an official observer or delegate to their meetings. Later, as has been pointed out, he himself was such an official observer.

During Vatican II, Weigel changed his uncompromising stand on the World Council. Once Catholics had become aware that joining in the discussion did not demand of the partners that they recognize each other as churches in the fullest sense of the word, there was nothing compromising in coming together.[132] Weigel's loosening-up was also indicated at one of the press conferences in November. Weigel predicted that some form of membership in the World Council may be extended to the Roman Catholic Church in the future. It would not be strict membership but rather a type of honorary membership.[133]

Despite these openings in the debates of Session II, there was much indecision and political manipulation behind the scenes that kept things from really progressing and this irritated Weigel. The tediousness of the debates, the tiring task of translation, the constant companionship he offered to the observers, the significant speeches made before *periti* and bishops outside the council—all of this combined to make him quite moody and pessimistic. Tavard recalled that Weigel appeared bored by the whole thing in the last weeks of the council. "He had little feeling or sympathy for the lobbying and politics involved on all sides. He was much too straight-forward to appreciate the life in Rome during the sessions." Weigel envied Tavard's leaving the council early.[134] Already in October Weigel had written to his student secretary, James Malley, S.J.:

> The Council is not as interesting in this session as in the last. The rhythm is very slow. At this rate it will take years to finish the agenda. The Bishops will not come back that often. Things look very dim . . .
>
> They like meetings over here—and they are always long. I am counting the days to the end which cannot come soon enough for me . . .
>
> I am expecting to leave at once at the close of the Council. If there be a January session, they will have to get along without me. Hard, but not impossible.[135]

Weigel's October report to the rector of Woodstock, Michael Maher, S.J., clearly indicated his feelings. "If the rhythm of the moment follows on, this Council will be longer than Trent."[136]

November found Weigel's pessimism persisting. Although the open- and closed-door parties were numerically indecisive, the open-door advocates were in the majority. Yet the minority was not small. "Hence there is no clear victory for the Open-Door. There is much tension and the Closed-Door is far from giving in." There was some progress on the episcopal nature of the government of the Church but the fate of the ecumenical schema remained uncertain. He wrote: "My health is good—but I am homesick for Woodstock."[137]

The second session closed on December 4. Weigel's comments publicly accentuated the positive. He said the session must be measured not in terms of formulation of doctrine but in a change of outlook. This change, he asserted, had been great, especially in the areas of ecclesiology and ecumenism.[138] Father Weigel contrasted the participation of the observers at the first and second sessions. Session I found them happy but rather silent, just observing. Session II brought them more completely into the act. They spoke more easily to bishops, were more anxious to learn of rumors and intrigues, "got into our secrets," attended more extra lectures on the council and, in general, followed more intelligently and closely. He praised the great witness of Christian sympathy and friendliness which they gave to the Catholics at Session II.

> This is precisely the value of the ecumenical movement. Little by little we get to understand each other, understand our minds, our ways of thinking. No one wants to lose patience. This cannot be accomplished over-night. This kind of meeting that we have had in the Council with representatives of different churches will be of an incalculable benefit both for the other churches and ourselves. We are getting to know each other.

Weigel had high praise for the open-door stance of the American hierarchy at Session II. He complimented them on their vitality and lack of fear. "They did not try to be very high-hat nor use polysyllable words, but they did stand for the right things," he felt.

In response to a question about the great personalities at Session II, Father Weigel gave a glimpse of the disillusionment and pessimism which he publicly concealed but revealed so readily in private. He began by saying that Pope Paul is not Pope John. Pope

John's faith in the Holy Spirit allowed him to rely upon his insights. Paul, felt Weigel, was more cautious and indecisive. According to Carlos Eyzaguirre, Weigel had "a great dislike for Pope Paul, saying that he was always sitting on the fence with both ears to the ground."

Who were the outstanding leaders of the session then? Weigel wrote:

> This was not the session of the individual, scintillating speakers. This was the session where the rank and file spoke their minds and neither eloquence nor splendor impressed the hearers. In this session ideas counted. Really, it was hard to go through, to listen to these speeches. There was no lift from the tedium which was had from time to time in the first session. There was, rather, a greater seriousness and a greater critical sense on the part of the bishops and it is precisely this attitude which will affect the Church. Wonderful speeches and brilliant writings are not going to bowl us over. Our interest must be the people of the world today, ordinary people in ordinary parishes. This is all to the good.[139]

After the closing ceremonies on December 4, Weigel wasted no time returning to his beloved Woodstock.[140] Tired and worn, pessimistic and peeved, he was determined not to return for another session. This was his plan, and in fact, it was God's plan too, for Gustave Weigel was walking his last days on this earth.

Endnotes

1. Interview with Joseph Doty, October 12, 1971.
2. Daigler reflections; interviews with Joseph Doty, Sister Cleophas Costello, R.S.M., Erwin Geismann, David L. McManus, John B. Sheerin, C.S.P., Francis J. Otenasek; Donald Hinfey to Patrick Collins, Syracuse, New York, January 8, 1972.
3. Interview with Joseph Doty.
4. Daigler reflections; interview with Erwin Geismann.

5. Interview with Francis J. Otenasek.

6. Pope John XXIII, *Journal of a Soul* (New York: McGraw, 1965).

7. Meriol Trevor, *Pope John* (Garden City, N.Y.: Doubleday, 1965), p. 261.

8. Floyd Anderson, ed., *Council Daybook: Vatican II* (Washington, D.C.: National Catholic Welfare Conference, 1965), vol. I, p. 262.

9. Xavier Rynne, *Vatican Council II* (New York: Farrar, Straus and Giroux, 1968), p. 4.

10. Interview with John B. Sheerin, C.S.P.

11. *Ibid.*

12. Interview with Robert McNally, S.J.

13. The *Vota* from Woodstock College are contained in WCA II F 303.28g.

14. Willebrands to Weigel, Rome, November 21, 1960. WCA II F 303.35jjj.

15. Secretariat for Promoting Christian Unity, "The Background to the Preparation for the II Vatican Council," September, 1962. WCA, unfiled. Hereafter referred to as "Background."

16. *Ibid.;* Bea to Weigel, Rome, October 3 and 20, 1960, WCA II F 303.391; Willebrands to Weigel, Rome, November 9, 1960, WCA II F 303.35jjj.

17. WCA II F 303.31a. Of Hamer, Weigel wrote: "Father Hamer deserves particular mention because the serenity and sympathetic spirit of his study of Protestantism, his solid knowledge of the field and his perfect control of the Catholic theological method place him high in the light of Catholic ecumenists" (Weigel, *A Catholic Primer on the Ecumenical Movement,* p. 47).

18. Willebrands to Weigel, Rome, November 21, 1960. WCA II F 303.35jjj.

19. Baum to Weigel, Toronto, December 9, 1960. WCA II F 303.34k.

20. Interviews with Donald Moore, S.J., Sister Cleophas Costello, R.S.M., Donald Campion, S.J., John Oesterreicher, Edward Hanahoe, S.A., Francis McCool, S.J., Eugene Burke, C.S.P.; George Tavard to Patrick Collins, Delaware, Ohio, October 5, 1971.

21. Interview with James A. O'Brien, S.J.

21a. *One of a Kind,* pp. 20–21; interviews with John Courtney Murray, S.J., and John Oesterreicher.

22. George Tavard to Patrick Collins, Delaware, Ohio, October 5, 1971.

23. Gregory Baum to Weigel, Toronto, December 19, 1960. WCA II F 303.34k.

24. Interview with John Courtney Murray, S.J.

25. Interviews with Donald Campion, S.J., and Thomas Stransky, C.S.P.

26. "Background"; Willebrands to Weigel, Rome, January 21, 1961, February 18, March 10, March 27, 1961. WCA II F 303.35jjj; Bea to Weigel, Rome, December 21, 1960. WCA II F 303.34e.

27. Willebrands to Weigel, Rome, March 10, 1961. WCA II F 303.35jjj. Others involved in this project were a Dr. Brandenburg of Paderborn, a Father Van de Pol, Father Bernard Leeming, Father Jerome Hamer and Father Gustave Thils.

28. WCA II F 303.28b,d,e.

29. Willebrands to Weigel, Rome, October 19, 1961. WCA II F 303.35jjj; "Background."

30. Interview with John Courtney Murray, S.J.

31. Robert McAfee Brown, *The Ecumenical Revolution: An Interpretation of the Catholic-Protestant Dialogue Based on the William Belden Novel Lectures for 1964–1965* (Garden City, N.Y.: Doubleday, 1967), p. 194.

32. Willebrands to Weigel, Rome, June 16, 1962, April 10, 1963. WCA II F 303.35jjj.

33. Interview with John B. Sheerin, C.S.P.

34. *Catholic Review,* November 26, 1961.

35. Clergy Conference, Waterloo, Iowa. WCA II F 303.20c.

36. Interviews with Joseph Doty and David L. McManus.

37. Bea to Weigel, Rome, October 4, 1962. WCA II F 303.34e.

38. Anderson, *op. cit.,* vol. I, pp. 25–27.

39. Interviews with John B. Sheerin, C.S.P., Sister Cleophas Costello, R.S.M., David L. McManus, John Courtney Murray, S.J., and Francis J. Otenasek.

40. *Steubenville Register,* March 21, 1963.

41. *St. Cloud Visitor,* July 21, 1963.

42. *Catholic Review,* July 19, 1963.

43. *Steuenville Register,* March 21, 1963.

44. WCA II F 303.21c.

45. Members of the conciliar Secretariat for Promoting Christian Unity were: President Augustine Cardinal Bea; Lorenzo Jaeger, Joseph Martin, Francis Charrière, Emile de Smedt, Peter Nierman, Thomas Holland, Gerard Van Vilsen from the pre-conciliar secretariat. New members were Andrew Katkoff (Bishop of Nauplia), Angelo Provetto (Vicar of Apostolic Administration, Loreto), Monsignor Ignazio Mansourati, Archimandrite Theodore Miniscti of the Basilians. Priest members from the pre-conciliar group were Enrico Ewers, Joseph Hoefer, Michael Maccarone, Gustave Thils, Rudolff Leone, Charles Boyer, Gerard Carr, and James Cunningham. These names are listed in Commissioni Conciliari, Tipografia Poliglotta Vaticana, November 30, 1962. WCA II F 303.29a.

46. Interviews with Thomas Stransky, C.S.P., and Edward Hanahoe, S.A.

47. Interviews with Donald Campion, S.J., Thomas Stransky, C.S.P., and Daniel O'Hanlon, S.J.

48. *One of a Kind,* pp. 45–46 and 90–91.

49. Interviews with Warren Quanbeck, Vincent Arthur Yzermans, Robert McAfee Brown, Alexander Schmemann, Godfrey Diekmann, O.S.B.; Douglas Horton, *Vatican Diary, 1962* (Philadelphia: United Church Press, 1964), pp. 83 and 183; Robert McAfee Brown, *Observer in Rome* (Garden City, N.Y.: Doubleday, 1964), p. 96.

50. Interviews with Vincent Arthur Yzermans and John Courtney Murray, S.J.

51. WCA II F 303.35vv. Cf. also Anderson, *op. cit.,* p. 46.

52. Anderson, *op. cit.,* p. 46.

53. Interview with John B. Sheerin, C.S.P.

54. Anderson, *op. cit.,* pp. 153–154.

55. *One of a Kind,* pp. 46–47 and 91; interview with John B. Sheerin, C.S.P.

56. Louis Cassels to Patrick Collins, Aiken, South Carolina, October 25, 1971.

57. *One of a Kind,* pp. 71–72.

58. James I. Tucek, "Father Weigel Press Corps Favorite," NCWC News Service, October 24, 1963.

59. *Buffalo Evening News,* October 26, 1963.

60. *Baltimore Evening Sun,* November 29, 1963.

61. WCA II F 303.31e. Interview with John B. Sheerin, C.S.P.; *One of a Kind,* p. 91.

62. Interview with James A. O'Brien, S.J.; Juan Ochagavia to James Malley,

S.J., Santiago, Chile, February 1, 1964 (Neft files).

63. Interview with John B. Sheerin, C.S.P.

64. Interview with Vincent Arthur Yzermans; *One of a Kind*, p. 70.

65. Interview with Vincent Arthur Yzermans.

66. Interview with Robert McAfee Brown.

67. Sister Jeremy Daigler, R.S.M., to Patrick Collins, Baltimore, October 24, 1971.

68. Vincent A. Yzermans, *A New Pentecost* (Westminster: Newman, 1963), p. 304.

69. Interview with David L. McManus.

70. *Steubenville Register,* March 21, 1963; *Catholic Messenger,* March 21, 1963.

71. *One of a Kind,* p. 93.

72. *Steubenville Register,* March 21, 1963.

73. *Baltimore Evening Sun,* March 2, 1963.

74. *St. Cloud Visitor,* July 7, 1963; interview with Vincent Arthur Yzermans.

75. Gustave Weigel, "Preface" to Max Lackmann, *The Augsburg Confession and Catholic Unity* (New York: Herder and Herder, 1963), p. vii.

76. *St. Cloud Visitor,* July 7, 1963.

77. "A Greater Spontaneous Friendship," *Catholic Review,* January 11, 1963.

78. Gustave Weigel, *The Modern God* (New York: Macmillan, 1963).

79. *Steubenville Herald Star,* March 13, 1963. This address was published in installments.

80. *Steubenville Register,* March 21, 1963.

81. "Expert Says Catholic Press Played Substantial Role in Developing Ecumenical Spirit," NCWC News Service, February 4, 1963. WCA II F 303.30a.

82. *St. Cloud Visitor,* July 7, 1963.

83. *Ibid.*

84. "A Greater Spontaneous Friendship," *Catholic Review,* January 11, 1963.

85. Yzermans, *A New Pentecost,* p. 318.

86. Interviews with Warren Quanbeck and Robert McAfee Brown.

87. Interviews with Francis McCool, S.J., Robert McNally, S.J., and Walter Burghardt, S.J.

88. Interview with Avery Dulles, S.J.

89. Interview with Warren Quanbeck.

90. "Council in Treating Structure Will Examine Bishops' Place and Function," NCWC News Service, September 23, 1963. WCA II F 303.30a.

91. "Council in Treating Structure Will Examine Bishops' Place and Function," NCWC News Service, September 23, 1963.

92. *The Tower,* Catholic University of America, January 18, 1963.

93. *Catholic Messenger,* February 14, 1963.

94. *Washington Post,* February 17, 1963. Monsignor McDonald's statement issued later was similar (*Catholic Universe Bulletin,* March 1, 1963).

95. *Loyola News,* Chicago, February 21, 1963; *Catholic Messenger,* February 21, 1963; *Catholic Standard,* February 22, 1963; *Time,* February 22 and March 29, 1963; *Washington Post,* February 23, 1963; *The Boston Pilot,* February 23, 1963; *New World,* Chicago, March 8, 1963; *The Visitor,* Providence, R.I., March 1, 1963; *America,* March 9, 1963; and *St. Louis Review,* March 8, 1963.

96. *The Tower,* January 18 and March 1, 1963; *Washington Evening Star,* February 27 and 28 and March 5, 1963.

97. *The Visitor,* March 8, 1963.

98. *Catholic Messenger,* March 14, 1963.

99. *Catholic Universe Bulletin,* March 29, 1963.

100. Michael Novak, *The Open Church: Vatican II, Act II* (New York: Macmillan, 1964), p. 15.

101ª. Paul Blanshard, *Paul Blanshard at Vatican II* (Boston: Beacon Press, 1966), p. 109. Robert McAfee Brown recalled being quite surprised to see Blanshard and Weigel walking and chatting amiably along the Via Della Conciliazione during the council. Cf. also *Christian Century,* March 20 and May 1, 1963.

101ᵇ. Alter to Weigel, Cincinnati, March 8, 1963. WCA II F 303.34c.

102. *Washington Post,* February 18, 1963; *The Pilot,* February 23, 1963.

103. Interviews with Walter Burghardt, S.J., Robert McNally, S.J., and David Bowman, S.J.

104. David Bowman, S.J., to John Connery, S.J., Washington, D.C., February 24, 1963 (Bowman Files); interview with Walter Burghardt, S.J.; *Washington Post,* March 3, 1963.

105. *New York Times,* June 30 and July 1, 1963; *Catholic Review,* July 5, 1963; *Catholic Messenger,* July 11, 1963.

106. *New York Times,* June 20, July 3, July 4, 1963; *St. Cloud Visitor,* July 14, 1963; *America,* July 20, 1963, pp. 70–71; *Newsweek,* July 15, 1963; p. 78.

107. *New York Times,* July 5, 1963.

108. Vincent Arthur Yzermans, *American Participation in the Second Vatican Council* (New York: Sheed and Ward, 1967), p. 570; Interviews with John B. Sheerin, C.S.P.; Abraham Heschel; Donald Hinfey, S.J., to Patrick Collins, Syracuse, New York, January 8, 1972.

109. Marc Tanenbaum to Weigel, New York, July 31, 1963. WCA II F 303.35ww.

110. Willebrands to Weigel, Rome, July 12, 1963. WCA II F 303.35jjj.

111. John M. Oesterreicher, "Declaration on the Relationship of the Church to Non-Christian Religions, Introduction and Commentary," *Commentary on the Documents of Vatican II,* Herbert Vorgrimler, ed., (New York: Herder and Herder, 1969), III, pp. 45–46.

112. Interview with Vincent Arthur Yzermans.

113. Yzermans, *American Participation . . .,* p. 298; *St. Cloud Visitor,* July 21, 1963.

114. Interview with Vincent Arthur Yzermans.

115. "Council in Treating Structure Will Examine Bishops' Place and Function," NCWC News Service, September 23, 1963. WCA II F 303.30a.

116. Tape made by Weigel and Yzermans to be sent to Peter Bartholome, Bishop of St. Cloud, Minnesota, October, 1963, (Yzermans files).

117. Interviews with Joseph Doty, Sister Cleophas Costello, R.S.M.; Daigler reflections; Donald Hinfey, S.J., to Patrick Collins, Syracuse, New York, January 8, 1972; James B. O'Hara to Patrick Collins, Baltimore, November 1, 1971.

118. "De Constitutione Dogmatica De Ecclesia," notes presented by Gustave Weigel to the Most Rev. Lawrence J. Shehan, D.D. WCA II F 303.28f.

119. *Lumen Gentium,* #15.

120. "De Oecumenismo." Notes presented by Gustave Weigel to the Most Rev. Lawrence J. Shehan, D.D. WCA II F 303.28f.

121. Gustave Weigel, "Ecumenism and the Catholic," *Faith and Understanding in America*, p. 162.

122. Rynne, *op. cit.*, p. 246.

123. "Conversation at the Council," *St. Cloud Visitor*, December 22, 1963; "Conversation at the Council" *American Benedictine Review*, September 1964, pp. 341–351; also the tape of the conversation from the files of Vincent Arthur Yzermans.

124. Anderson, *op. cit.*, p. 179; Rynne, *op. cit.*, pp. 206–207.

125. Rynne, *op. cit.*, pp. 196–197.

126. "Describes Importance of Decisions on Church Schema," NCWC News Service, November 8, 1963 (WCA II F 303.30a); Anderson, *op. cit.*, I, pp. 243–245.

127. Quoted in McDonald, *op. cit.*, p. 66.

128. "Describes Importance of Decisions on Church Schema," NCWC News Service, November 8, 1963. WCA II F 303.30a.

129. *Newsweek*, October 21, 1963, p. 101.

130. "Describes Importance of Decisions on Church Schema," NCWC News Service, November 8, 1963. WCA II F 303.30a.

131. Rynne, *op. cit.*, pp. 236–260.

132. Gustave Weigel, "The Ecumenical Movement Is Stronger," *St. Louis Review*, November 2, 1963.

133. Anderson, *op. cit.*, I, p. 314.

134. George Tavard to Patrick Collins, Delaware, Ohio, October 5, 1971.

135. Weigel to James Malley, S.J., Rome, October 21, 1963. WCA II F 303.35o.

136. Weigel to Michael Maher, S.J., Rome, October 15, 1963. WCA II F 303.35m.

137. Weigel to Michael Maher, S.J., Rome, November 11, 1963. WCA II F 303.35m.

138. "Measure Council Success in Change of Outlook," NCWC News Service, December 6, 1963. WCA II F 303.30a. Cf. also Gustave Weigel, "How Is the Council Going?" *America*, December 7, 1963, pp. 730–732.

139. "Bishop Hoch and Father Weigel Review Work of Second Session," *St. Cloud Visitor*, December 22, 1963. Also the tape of their conversation in the files of Vincent Arthur Yzermans.

140. Weigel to Dr. and Mrs. Richard Ferguson, Rome, December 3, 1963. (Ferguson files)

CHAPTER ELEVEN

"The Heavy, High, Dark, Thick, Silent Hangings"

The long, tedious and frustrating days of Vatican II's second session had taken their toll on Gustave Weigel. During the last few weeks of the session, his friends in Rome had noticed that he was becoming increasingly tired. His long-time Chilean friend, Juan Ochagavia, was with him in Rome and he found his former mentor more quiet and tired than usual, yet he felt "that his Christian vision of things had become deeper and wider."[1] Warren Quanbeck recalled that Weigel was taking on a rather gray color and seemed lonely.[2] Albert Outler remembered a dinner in Bishop Thomas Gorman's apartment in Rome on the eve of the end of the session.

> The company, the food and the talk were all superb; but Father Gus was subdued, as I had not seen him before—listening but not talking much, slumped in one of the deep-cushioned chairs in the salotto. But he was back in St. Peter's the next morning for the closing session, chipper and witty as ever in his comments on the fuss and feathers of the great spectacle, fluent as ever in his translations and commentary.

Outler said Weigel's final aphorism to describe Session II to the observers was: "Not good enough, but far better than we deserved!"[3]

It was at another dinner party, two nights before leaving Rome, that Weigel let his hair down, showing both his tiredness and his discouragement with the council. That night his host, George Lindbeck, felt that he came to know Gustave Weigel, the man, better than ever before. For three hours they discussed the council in the light of St. Thomas' notion of Providence. In his discouragement, Weigel wondered if the Church would really be any better off because of the things that had happened in Rome the past two years, things which he felt were basically good. Would it really make any difference? Somehow he felt it wouldn't effect much, either good or bad. No matter what happened, though, he had faith that God could straighten out any mess people could make of things. Lindbeck stated that this was typical of Weigelian piety. It was deep without the slightest trace of piousness.

Father Weigel did feel that the Church was in for much trouble in the years ahead, as his last book, *The Modern God,* had explained. But the trouble, as he saw it, would not come from the council but from a godless world whose societal, intellectual and religious leaders were incapable of leading to "The Real." Yet, what happened would be what God wanted to happen.

Lindbeck remembered Weigel that night as a man whose spirit reflected pessimism combined with tiredness and yet a deep confidence that came from his faith and his sense of Christian brotherhood. In retrospect Gustave Weigel seemed like a man whose perspectives were changing; a man whose eyes were looking beyond terrestrial horizons to "The Real" beyond; a man who was preparing for death. He told Lindbeck that night that he felt about his work as St. Thomas did toward his writings at the end of his life. It all seemed like straw. Yet he felt he had had a good life, one that was worthwhile. And this was because he believed that God could make the works of humans to praise Him, even when they were rather stupid and silly.[4]

Robert McAfee Brown wrote: "Those who saw [Weigel] at the Council commented on how tired he appeared to be. In retrospect, we can see that he gave himself so unstintingly to the task of interpreting the Council to the non-Catholic observers and the press that he quite literally wore himself out."[5]

It was this tired and rather discouraged Gustave Weigel who landed at Friendship Airport in Baltimore at the end of the week in which the council closed.[6] All who saw him in the next few days recalled how wretched and tired he looked.[7] He told many that he would not return to the next session.[8] He had quipped to Outler at the close of the session "something about going back to his work at Woodstock and watching the next session from a more tranquil station." The Methodist felt moved to call after his friend: "Go with God." Weigel smiled and said simply and humbly, "But He always goes with me!"[9]

Father Weigel spent an evening with a former student shortly after his return from the council, John Giles Milhaven. Being a believer had never been an easy thing for Weigel. He had many questions and a proud mind. In some ways he was drawn to rationalism, as his private retreat notes in 1934 had indicated. He had to resist that drive to be the master of "The Real," of "The Truth." That night with Milhaven he made it clear that his whole life had been based on the risk that his intuition of "The Real" in faith was true. He was quite aware that he was standing over the abyss of doubt and might be wrong, yet he had gambled his life on the truth of his insight. His intellect took the gamble and all his intellectual life was intertwined with the risk of faith. Milhaven remembered him as very tired that night, perhaps with a sense of his coming death. He was quite pessimistic about returning to regular teaching.[10]

A few days after returning from Rome, Gustave Weigel addressed the faculty and students at Woodstock about the council proceedings. One of the students described the evening:

"A fascinating hour. When he prepares a talk or a press interview, he is smashing. 'The Christian unity movement is warming up but nobody should take off his coat yet.' 'Give man time and strength and wisdom and let him go ahead and work and everything will turn out . . . terrible.' Gus is wonderful: Christian pessimism!"

Weigel told a limerick that had been making the rounds among the council Fathers during the last session:

Gus Weigel, John Murray, Hans Küng
Today are on everyone's tongue,
   But Ottaviani
   Will get off his fanni
And see they're all properly hung.[11]

During the days before Christmas, Weigel met with his old friends in Baltimore: Mildred Otenasek and Dr. and Mrs. Richard Ferguson. He spoke several times about eschatology and death, something he did not customarily do. He claimed he was ready to die, though his friends said they were not. He said:

If I should live to 90, Thanks be to God.
If I should die tomorrow, Thanks be to God.[12]

Weigel predicted his coming death even more specifically to his fellow Jesuits at Woodstock after returning from the council. Two friends felt that he had always had, throughout his life, some sort of strange death wish.[13] He told someone at Woodstock that he was going to die soon. When he last addressed the community, he concluded with the statement that the council may or may not reconvene, may or may not handle certain problems. Then he said: "That, however, is your worry; for me, it is getting late, very late."[14] The council had made Weigel realize that both his ecclesiology and his approach to ecumenism were out-dated. They were no longer adequate and would have to be redone and he felt he just couldn't do it.[15] Physical exhaustion again brought out his tendency toward pessimism.

Father Weigel spent his traditional Christmas at home with his sister and her family in Buffalo. Mrs. Daigler remembered how tired he looked and acted. She thought he had aged, but once the old banter resumed, she was comforted, thinking he was really all right. However, when he flopped into a chair and refused the bourbon she usually had for him, Louise again felt deep concern about her brother's health. The day after Christmas, Mrs. Daigler and her son, Earl, drove Weigel to the airport for the return trip to Baltimore. His sister recalled those minutes at the airport vividly.

"He was unusually quiet. He told us to go, he would wait for the plane by himself. We stayed. I was saying something and I noticed he was dozing. I said to him: 'You are tired.' He raised his hands as if in despair. It came time to leave. We hardly ever kissed. I grabbed his hand and said: 'Thanks for everything.' He raised his forefinger in mock salute and walked away."[16]

Back in Baltimore that evening, he dined with Mrs. Otenasek and the Fergusons. Dr. and Mrs. Russell Morgan were also present. Dr. Morgan, a physician at Johns Hopkins Hospital, asked Weigel to come to his office the following Monday, December 28, for some x-rays since it was obvious to all that he was not well.[17] The results of the x-rays on Monday showed that Weigel was suffering from a tortuous aorta which sometimes develops into a dissecting aneurysm. Dr. Morgan explained that this is not uncommon in people between fifty-five and sixty years of age but few of them dissect. Should dissection occur, it would mean instantaneous death. Weigel was not told of the nature of his problem at the time. Morgan felt there was no need to alarm him and, besides, he seemed already depressed over the council.[18] Mrs. Ferguson and her son, Ricky, drove Weigel from Johns Hopkins. She remembered he was serious and quiet.[19] That evening, back at Woodstock, Weigel saw John Murray. Weigel told him that the results of the tests were good. But in the off-hand way the two affected between themselves, Murray warned: "Please don't think you are out of the woods." He answered: "I never was in the woods."[20]

On January 2, 1964, Weigel caught the train for New York where he was to go to participate in a taped ecumenical dialogue for television on January 3.[21] He went directly to America House, 329 West 108th Street, coming in shortly after lunch. Donald Campion met him and was shocked at his tired appearance. Weigel told him about Morgan's examination. He said the doctor had asked him if he had been meeting any unusual frustrations recently. Weigel laughed and said, "That's exactly it. The council!"[22]

That evening Father Weigel spent about three hours in the study of Rabbi Abraham Heschel at Jewish Theological Seminary. Heschel's deep spirituality had long commanded Weigel's respect. After a previous joint radio program with Heschel and a prominent Protestant clergyman, Weigel had told Heschel that he had felt closer to him as a person of faith than to the Protestant. That night they talked of prayer and death. They opened their hearts to one another in prayer and contrition and spoke of their own deficiencies, failures, and hopes. Heschel, noticing how tired Weigel was, chastised him for working too hard, for accepting too many speaking engagements. Weigel simply shrugged and said he could not help it. He was a "man driven," according to Heschel. Weigel left to return to America House at about eleven o'clock that night.[23]

At breakfast the next morning, Weigel asked for aspirin, saying he had a headache. Then he walked twelve blocks to the Interchurch Center at 475 Riverside Drive for the television taping with Heschel and Dr. Eugene Carson Blake.[24] He was scheduled to tape in Blake's office at about ten o'clock but became ill shortly before he was to go on. When Heschel arrived at eleven o'clock for his portion of the program, he was told that Weigel became ill and had returned to America House without doing the program.[25]

Father Weigel walked back to America House just before lunch. As he went up to his fifth-floor room, he asked the receptionist not to call him. He was going to lie down. No one else knew that he had returned. A few minutes after one o'clock a cleaning man mistakenly opened the door to a common bathroom near Weigel's room and found Gustave Weigel dead in the bathtub. He had been dead less than an hour.[26] He had had a problem with kidney stones and, often when they were bothering him, he would sit in a tub of hot water to relieve the pain. John Murray suggested that might have been what Weigel was doing when he died.[27] Interestingly, according to Ochagavia, Weigel had always been impressed by the fact that St. Ignatius of Loyola had died alone in his room in Rome.[28] Edwin Quain, S.J., remembered remarking that day how ironical it was that his old friend would have died in a bathtub since life so seldom found him there. Weigel felt all this bathing business was a bad American custom. The cause of death was an acute coronary thrombosis,[29] just what Dr. Morgan had feared might happen as a result of the tortuous aorta. Later that afternoon, about four o'clock, Erwin Geismann arrived at America House to take Weigel to his home for the weekend as they had done so many times since their meeting in 1950. He was shocked to learn that his best friend was dead.[30]

The next afternoon, January 4, Gustave Weigel's body lay in state in a second floor chapel at the Frank E. Campbell Funeral Home for two hours. Many New York Jesuits came to pay their respects.[31] Late that afternoon Weigel's simple black cloth coffin with silver handles was taken from the funeral home to be transferred to Woodstock College. Sunday, January 5, throngs came to Woodstock to pay their last respects to the man who had been both a close friend and an international personality.[32]

On the Feast of the Epiphany, January 6, a Low Pontifical Requiem Mass was celebrated by Archbishop Laurence Shehan of Baltimore.[33] In line with some of the liturgical reforms of Vatican II, but prior to their allowed usage, the Mass was celebrated facing the people and the large congregation of more than four hundred in the Woodstock College Chapel joined in the responses and some Gelineau psalms were sung. Walter Burghardt read the epistle and gospel in the vernacular and John Gallen, S.J., a seminarian, read a commentary. The archbishop gave a homily in contrast to the Jesuit tradition of no funeral sermons. In the final moment of his remarks, Shehan uttered the words that may best eulogize Weigel:

> Although we admire Father Weigel for the work that he accomplished and the books that he has written, yet we shall remember him for the man that he was—for his broad, deep, quick mind,

for his ready and pleasing wit, for his all-encompassing heart, for his unfailing kindness and generosity. What made him particularly effective in the work of Ecumenism was not only his great charity but also his sincerity and his utter frankness.

As seminarians bore their teacher's body to his grave at the edge of the small, wooded cemetery at Woodstock, a hymn was sung, "O Mighty God," written by William J. O'Malley, S.J., to the tune of Martin Luther's "A Mighty Fortress Is Our God,"[34] a fitting tribute to Gustave Weigel, America's pioneering Catholic ecumenist. A simple white stone marks his resting place. A few feet away rests Weigel's friend and colleague, John Courtney Murray, who died suddenly in 1967.

Robert McNally was charged with taking care of Father Weigel's effects in his room after his death. All of his papers were saved. McNally said that Weigel had practically nothing in the way of clothes. There were two suits which were unsuitable for a "scarecrow." Weigel had been a man vowed to poverty, even to death. Curiously, a book, opened to two of Shakespeare's sonnets, was found beside Weigel's Woodstock bed. They were about death.[35]

> No longer mourn for me, when I am dead,
> Then you shall hear the surly sullen bell
> Give warning to the world that I am fled
> From this vile world, with vilest worms to dwell;
> Nay, if you read this line, remember not
> The hand that writ it, for I love you so
> That I in your sweet thoughts would be forgot,
> Oh, if I say, you look upon this verse
> When I perhaps compounded am with clay,
> Do not so much as my poor name rehearse,
> But let your love even with my life decay;
>   Lest the wise world should look into your moan,
>   And mock you with me after I am gone.
>
> That time of year thou may'st in me behold
> When yellow leaves, or none, or few, do hang

Upon those boughs which shake against the cold,
Bare ruined choirs, where late the sweet birds sang.
In me thou see'st the twilight of such day
As after sunset fadeth in the west;
Which by and by black night doth take away,
Death's second self, that seals up all the rest.
In me thou see'st the glowing of such fire,
That on the ashes of his youth doth lie,
As the death-bed whereon it must expire,
Consumed with that which it was nourished by.
   This thou perceiv'st which makes thy love more strong,
   To love that well which thou must leave ere long.[36]

Weigel's tertianship retreat diary had contained a personal reflection on death:

Death I can only see as a passing through heavy, high, dark, thick, silent hangings. I would not care to go through them, not for fear of the other side, but because I feel that there are some things still to be done on this side. I don't know—there is something soothing, alluring, quieting about heavy, high, dark, thick, silent hangings.[37]

As his own words testify, during the last weeks of his life, Gustave Weigel felt his work on this side was finished. The soothing, alluring, quiet hangings beckoned to him. Behind them he deeply believed that he would discover what he had gambled his whole life on: "The True," "The Real."

One wonders how Gus Weigel would have adjusted to the post-Vatican II Church and world. Some of his friends speculated that he would be at home; others that he would have been at sea and disgruntled; still others felt he would have become critically accepting of where we are headed since much of what happened is not far out of tune with his own deep intuitions of "The True" and "The Real." If one were to judge from Weigel's pessimism at the close of Session II, it might appear that he could not have adjusted readily to changed realities. Yet his disappointments with Session

II were primarily with the slow pace and lack of change. However, since his health was poor in those last weeks of his life, that would not be a fair way to assess where Weigel might "be" today.

I prefer to take my clue from a talk entitled, "Brave New World," given probably during the middle of 1963, possibly at a graduation. In it, Father Weigel looked to the future, not so much for himself but for his listeners. His prophetic words, though they may not truly tell us where he would "be" today, are a beautiful legacy to those who do live in the post-conciliar era:

In the brave new world, how will man act . . .? His vision will be broader and narrower. It will be broader because he will, through science, know more and more about the manipulation of energy. He will see the possibility of human satisfaction in tree, stone and waterfall where our ancestors could only see God. He will rely more on organization to make men act reasonably than on conscience and faith. Greater control of material energy will satisfy more instinctive impulses. The notion of God will lose its nearness and religion, though not abolished or even persecuted, will have less and less to say about communal living. Private charity will become less. Public welfare on a humanitarian basis will become more. Philosophy will be more descriptive and less normative. Decisions will be more managerial rather than one person's responsible commitment. Where possible an electronic computer will make them.

But there is the double field of art and religion. Organized civil society will try to control them but there will be the prophetic souls who will express their ideas in material form. It will be new forms, different from my generation. The ideas will not be clear or precise but they will express rebellion, hatred for the suppression of the individual, a longing for something beyond the goods at hand. It will be vague and bizarre. But it will be there. In religious reflection man will exercise his freedom so restricted elsewhere. Rare religious ideas will develop with no guidance other than nausea and frustration. The upholders of traditional Christianity will have little influence on the vision of the land. Yours will be the Post-Christian world, the world of neo-paganism. It has already been born. You will see it grow.

What should you do in the Brave, New World? Live in it. You can't get out of it. Adjust to it; it will not be morally worse than my world. It will be farther from God. But God will not be farther from it. He will be as close as ever, and he who sees him can clutch him with no more difficulty than today.

The new world with less disease, greater creativity, greater material possibilities will be an uneasy world. It will not be at peace even should the threat of cataclysmic wars be abolished. In that uneasy world you must establish your own inner freedom which will mean a profound awareness of God and his action.

You must do more. You must be prophetic. The prophet speaks in the name of God and *protests* against its dereliction. His voice may make no impact on the society; it may win him the martyr's death or ostracism; most probably it will reduce him to social isolation. But the prophetic word is a seed. In a faithful remnant it will bring increased faith. In the good soil of your future's future, it may be a light for change.

It may be that your time's increased control of energy will destroy the teeming earth to a seared globe where thousands rather than billions will survive. If so that remnant must be told the saving truth. You will have to give witness no matter what happens. Let not what you have seen and heard pass into death with you. Transmit from old life to new. Your fate will be no different from ours. Only the stage will be different.[38]

The faith-inspired insight of these words are only one reason why coming to know Gustave Weigel through his writings and friends has been a personal inspiration to the author of this volume, indeed, a leit-motif for my own life.

He was indeed "One of a Kind." Robert McAfee Brown wrote "In Memoriam": "The ways of providence are mysterious, but both Catholics and Protestants, confronted with the completely unexpected death of the great-hearted man whom many called

'Gus,' can agree that there was probably no man on either side of the divide we could less afford to spare."[39] Abraham Heschel was perhaps correct when he told me that Weigel's greatness was not as an original thinker but as a unique, full human being. Heschel continued, "That is what we need today and this is why his passing was so sad. For we have not yet found his like among us. No one has taken his place."[40]

Endnotes

1. Juan Ochagavia, S.J., to James Malley, S.J., February 1, 1964 (Neft files).
2. Interview with Warren Quanbeck. The same impression was obtained from interviews with George Lindbeck, Daniel O'Hanlon, S.J., Robert McAfee Brown, Vincent Arthur Yzermans, Francis McCool, S.J., John B. Sheerin, C.S.P., and Donald Campion, S.J.
3. *One of a Kind*, p. 47.
4. Interview with George Lindbeck.
5. Robert McAfee Brown, *Observer in Rome* (New York: Doubleday, 1964), p. 267.
6. Gustave Weigel to Dr. and Mrs. Richard Ferguson, December 3, 1963 (Ferguson files).
7. Interviews with Walter Burghardt, S.J., and Sister Cleophas Costello, R.S.M.; L'Heureux, *op. cit.*, pp. 30–31.
8. *One of a Kind*, p. 21; Interviews with Walter Burghardt, S.J., and Sister Cleophas Costello, R.S.M.; Daigler reflections.
9. *One of a Kind*, pp. 47–48.
10. Interview with John Giles Milhaven.
11. L'Heureux, *op. cit.*, pp. 30–32.
Thurston Davis, writing in *America*, January 18, 1964, p. 58, commented upon Weigel's remark about things turning out badly if they continued long enough:
"That remark reveals the hard-core of Father Weigel's greatness. While a crusader, he was also a hard-as-nails realist. In that tough and rare amalgam of qualities we find the genuine Gustave Weigel—a man of the widest vision, yet one who knew how indispensable are long, grimy hours of lonely study and equally long hours of patient and seemingly fruitless dialogue. If finally, things turn out less badly than they might have, it will be because Father Weigel gave so unstintingly of himself to inch them on to fruition."
12. Interviews with Mrs. Mildred Otenasek, Dr. and Mrs. Richard Ferguson, and Mr. Raymond A. Kirby. Francis and Mildred Otenasek had divorced, with Weigel's sharp disapproval. Frank re-married.
13. Donald Hinfey, S.J., to Patrick W. Collins, Syracuse, New York, January 8, 1972; George Higgins in an interview with Vincent Arthur Yzermans.
14. L'Heureux, *op. cit.*, p. 34.

15. Donald Hinfey, S.J., to Patrick W. Collins, Syracuse, New York, January 8, 1972; Interviews with David L. McManus and Walter Burghardt, S.J.

16. Daigler reflections.

17. Interviews with Dr. Russell Morgan and Mrs. Frank Otenasek.

18. Interview with Dr. Russell Morgan.

19. Interview with Mrs. Richard Ferguson and Mrs. Frank Otenasek.

20. *One of a Kind*, p. 21.

21. Interview with Mrs. Frank Otenasek.

22. Interview with Donald Campion, S.J.

23. Interview with Rabbi Abraham Heschel. Cf. Heschel, "No Religion Is an Island," *Union Seminary Quarterly Review*, January, 1966, p. 129; Heschel to John Courtney Murray, S.J., January 10, 1964 (Neft files).

24. Interview with Donald Campion, S.J.

25. Interview with Rabbi Abraham Heschel; Eugene Carson Blake to Sister Olga Neft, Geneva, Switzerland, July 7, 1966 (Neft files); Eugene Carson Blake to Patrick W. Collins, Geneva, Switzerland, October 22, 1971.

26. Interview with Donald Campion, S.J. John Sheerin, C.S.P., on the contrary, said a visiting Lithuanian priest found Weigel dead. (*One of a Kind,* p. 73).

27. Interview with John Murray, S.J.

28. Ochagavia, *op. cit.,* p. 29.

29. Interview with Dr. John F. Maloney, Certificate of Death, 156- 64-100151, City of New York, Department of Health, Bureau of Vital Statistics.

30. Interview with Erwin Geismann.

31. Interview with John B. Rooney. Cf. also files of the Frank E. Campbell Funeral Home, 1072 Madison Ave., New York, New York.

32. L'Heureux, *op. cit.,* p. 34. The author remarked that "Gus" would have been amused by all the chaos at Woodstock at the time of the wake and funeral.

33. Other dignitaries attending the funeral were: Patrick A. O'Boyle, Archbishop of Washington; Ernest J. Primeau, Bishop of Manchester, New Hampshire; Philip M. Hannon, Auxiliary Bishop of Washington; John J. McGinty, S.J., New York provincial; John M. Daley, S.J., Maryland provincial; and James J. Shanahan, S.J., Buffalo provincial.

Other well-known persons in religious circles included Monsignor George Higgins; Francis J. Connell, C.SS.R.; Thomas A. Walsh, M.M.; Monsignor Joseph B. McAllister, vice-rector of the Catholic University of America; Vincent T. O'Keefe, S.J., president of Fordham University; Laurence J. McGinley, S.J., former president of Fordham University; Edward B. Bunn, S.J., president of Georgetown University; William F. Troy, S.J., president of Wheeling College; Edward J. Sponga, S.J., president of Scranton University; William F. Maloney, S.J., president of St. Joseph's College, Philadelphia; Vincent F. Beatty, S.J., president of Loyola College, Baltimore; Rev. Mother Mary Stella Maris, R.S.M., superior general of the Sisters of Mercy; Martin Luther King, Jr.; John B. Sheerin, C.S.P.; Roland Murphy, O.Carm.; Raymond Brown, S.S.; Rev. John Quasten; several representatives of Protestant, Orthodox and Jewish organizations. Also in attendance were the wife of the Ambassador to Chile, Mrs. Margot de Gutierrez, and Mr. and Mrs. Hugo Vigorena of the Chilean Embassy. (WCA II F 303, unfiled.)

34. *Catholic Review* (Baltimore) January 10, 1964; Data on Weigel's funeral in WCA, undated and unfiled.

35. Interview with Robert McNally, S.J.

36. The Pocket Book of Verse (New York: Pocket Books, Inc., 1940), p. 18.

37. WCA II F 303.22g.

38. WCA II F 303.20d, undated, handwritten lecture entitled, "Brave New World."

39. Robert McAfee Brown, *Observer in Rome* (N.Y.: Doubleday, 1964), p. 266.

40. Interview with Abraham Heschel.